A NEAR-RANDOM,

DOUBTLESSLY INCOMPLETE,

AND POTENTIALLY INACCURATE

COLLECTION OF

LIFE'S FABLES AND FOIBLES

BY WILLIAM D. TURNER

"There's a Pony in Here...

Somewhere."

William D. Turner

SNOWMASS VILLAGE, COLORADO

"There's a Pony in Here...Somewhere!."

BY WILLIAM DOW TURNER

Copyright © 2021 by William D. Turner

NOTICE OF RIGHTS
All rights reserved. No part of this book may be reproduced or transmitted in any form or by any means, electronic or mechanical, including photocopying, recording, or by any information storage and retrieval system, without permission in writing from the publisher.

ISBN 978-0-9964454-9-8

DESIGN | Curt Carpenter © 2021
Printed in the United States

Box 6065 · Snowmass Village, Colorado 81615

CONTENTS

PREFACE	xiii
INTRODUCTION | A Vagabond Life	1
PART ONE | Family, Friends, and Personal	7
Accidental Durability (70 years)	8
Accidental Durability (63 years)	11
My Sister Was an Only Child	15
Sporting for Life	18
Time Flies	20
An Inexplicable Ending	21
Ode to Mom	31
Politics at 14	34
Civil Wrongs	34
Fred from Akron	37
Two Times Darkness	39
Economic Challenges to Learning	40
Not Far from the Tree	42
The Champ was No Chump	42
Draft Averse	45
Blind Faith is Redundant	50
A Simple Sense of Risk	52
Mass Joy Admiration	53
I Remained Calm, Cool...and Collected	56

Travel and Traveling ... 65
   College Trips ... 66
   Germination of Wanderlust ... 70
   Settling Into New York ... 73
   Travel to the 'Country' ... 75
   Where in the World is Amelia Earhart? ... 76
   24-Hour Vacation ... 77
   Commuting to Milan? ... 79
   Down East ... 80
   A Six-Year Trip to London ... 81
   A British/English Rosetta Stone ... 82
   Failed Genealogy ... 83
   TV for the Blind ... 84
   Petra ... 85
   Growing Up in City Life ... 88

Another Stint Abroad ... 91
   London Redux ... 92
   It Was, and Then It Wasn't ... 93
   Surprising Korea ... 94
   Fragrant Harbour ... 95
   A Stop Down Under ... 96
   What's the Chance ... 98
   A Herd, An Aerial View, and A Close Call ... 99
   The Spice and Spite of Life ... 102
   Seward Was Right ... 104
   Airport Revenge ... 106

Driving and Cars ... 109
   Driving Around ... 110
   Trouble Over Bridged Water ... 115
   Running with the Tide ... 116
   RHD ... 118

PART TWO
Business & Career | Serendipity by Design — 121

- Growing Into Work — 122
- Taking a Job — 122
- Working in Chicago — 124

Falling Toward New York and Banking — 128
- Credit Where Credit is Due — 131
- Peak or Nadir of the Wall Street Man-Cave? — 133

The On-Ramp and Runway — 135
- Riding an Era of Change, 1967-2007 — 136
- Partial List of Changes Affecting Financial Institutions in the 1960s and Subsequent Decades — 138
- Jumbo's New Paradigm — 141
- Dead Letter File — 143
- Debuts from Hell — 143
- Lending Money — 145
- Accreditation of Threads — 146
- A Banker in the Twin Cities — 149
- Thief River Falls — 151
- Humbled — 152

Serving Bankers as Clients — 155
- A Consulting Career as Markets and Banking Evolved — 156
- An Alcoholic Career? — 160
- 'Balance' in the Eyes of the Beholder — 161
- Homeless at McKinsey — 162
- Watch or Walk Over You — 163
- Publish or Perish — 166
- Value Pricing — 167

Management Structure	169
10 Ways to Kill an Idea	170
Cubicalism	170
Consulting in a War Zone	171
Cambodian Window	172
De-Bugging, Really?	173

Moving Abroad   174
- A Random Meeting — 176
- Convergence of Interests — 177
- A Steel Trap — 180
- A Feisty Mentor — 182
- Winning Can Be Depressing — 184
- The Rodney — 185
- A Difference of Night and Day — 186
- Airport Security? — 187
- Trees and Fjords — 189
- The Platters Said It — 190
- Four Downs to a Touchdown — 191
- Mortification — 192
- A World Apart — 194
- Subtle Charisma — 199
- Eerie Èire—To Err is Human — 201

New Old Geography and Breadth   202
- Duluth — 204
- Manager's Remorse — 205
- Double Entendre — 207
- A.T. Kearney — 207
- Lucky to Go First — 208
- It's New York, Already — 210
- A Crystal Ball? — 211

Touring Asia   213
    Consulting Denouement   215
    Five Stages of a Consultant's Career   216
    Not Everyone Loves a Consultant   216
    Whither the Briefcase   217

PART THREE | **Retreating to the Mountains**   221

    New Math in Snowmass Village, Colorado   222
    A Customer Focus in Aspen   223
    Global Touches   224
    Veni, Vidi, Exii   224
    Cash Flows   227
    Markets in the Mountains   227
    Epitaphs   228

PART FOUR | **Appendices**   231

APPENDIX 1 | **Religion** | *Blind Faith is Redundant, but I'm Agnostic*   231

APPENDIX 2 | **Collections** | *I Remained Calm, Cool... and Collected*   250

APPENDIX 3 | **Cars** | *27 Keys to Transport and Freedom*   254

APPENDIX 4 | **Korea** | *Surprising Korea*   260

APPENDIX 5 | **Hong Kong** | *Whiffs of 'Fragrant Harbour'*   271

APPENDIX 6 | **Australia** | *The Largest Island*   275

ILLUSTRATION SOURCES   278

INDEX   281

DEDICATION

*For all the family members, friends,
business colleagues, and clients
who provided incalculable value, enjoyment,
and friendship in my eras of work and play,
but who are no longer with us.*

*This long list includes Bailey, Bales, Cahouet, Geldens,
Griffiths, Heestand, Hoogendijk, Kidder, Kline, Manley,
Marsh, O'Neal, Parker, Sella, Spieth, Stalzer, Thompson,
Tyler, Uphouse, van Westreenan, Vander Weyden,
among many others.*

"Finish it? Why would I want to finish it?"

Preface

IT HAS BEEN A DOZEN YEARS since ceasing full-time work, a period marked by adequate—read lucky—financial management, two 'uniquely intelligent and well-adjusted' new grandsons, nearly continuous travel with wife and friends for pleasure and hassle, and publication of biographies of two interesting but under-known ancestors.

This latter research and writing was prompted by the confluence of four conditions: (1) serious time on my hands for the first time since childhood, (2) a maternal great grandfather who was a sea captain around the turn of the 20th century, and a fraternal grandfather whom I knew as a Marine Corps 'hero' in World War I, (3) precious little documentation or family lore about either of them, and (4) a strong curiosity on my part to find out about them.

Being spoiled by these two efforts, I was thirsting for a next project, but struck out trying to identify something of sufficient interest and relevance to me, and potentially to others.

As my search for a new subject was producing serial dry wells, several friends suggested that I document particularly funny, consequential, and interesting experiences from my own life. To call their hand and punish them for those suggestions, I have done so, and this volume is the result.

This is not a biography or a chronology of events or activities in my life to date. It is more a memoir—a collection of experiences that stand out, or at least remain, in my mind as funny, consequential or interesting to me. It is far from comprehensive. And it need not—and may well not—be read with interest by anyone else.

The process of remembering, selecting, and writing has tended to array my subjects willy nilly across the eight decades of my existence. My assessments and reflections are somewhat random and might be best grouped around life-long or decade-skipping themes. This book is organized—or disorganized—that way. It is a compendium of mini memoirs.

Although this 'story' runs only up to 2020, I plan to draft an anecdotal summary of my life's second seventy-five years in 2095.

—WDT | January 1, 2021

NOTE: The title of this volume is appropriated from the following story.

A FATHER HAD TWIN BOYS and was concerned that one was a strong optimist, but the other a constant pessimist.

With Christmas coming up, he thought he would try to dampen their extreme behaviors. For the pessimist, the father filled a big box with toys of all sorts—electronic games, model airplanes, even an iphone. He filled the optimist's box with horse manure.

On Christmas morning, the boys came down to open their presents. The pessimist opened his box, took out all the toys, but then quickly and carefully put them back in the box and closed it up. When asked what was wrong, he told his father "I'll end up breaking or losing them all in a few days."

Meanwhile, the optimist, having opened his box, was scooping out the horse manure, slinging it all around the room and all over his pajamas. "What are you doing?" the father asked, and the son responded, "This is the best Christmas ever—there's a pony in here somewhere!"

INTRODUCTION

A Vagabond Life

My first 75 years exude two dimensions that are too pronounced to be by chance, but also were not by design.

The first is a propensity to see, try, and do many things, but never become the master or the very best at any of them—a mile wide and a foot deep, if you will.

The second characteristic—a geographic manifestation of the first—is an almost nomadic approach to life.

Neither of these life themes was chosen or carefully engineered by me, nor was I pushed by anything or anyone to be that way.

Yet, it is hard to believe that they could be the outcomes from purely random events.

Maximum Breadth, but Limited Depth

SINCE I WAS A KID, I participated in a lot of different things—which is good, I guess—but I also jumped from one to another either frequently or eventually. I've dabbled in many sports, including baseball, basketball, football, bowling, golf, Scuba diving, pool, hunting and riflery, skiing, fishing, cross country running, tennis, and sailing. Although I did well at some of them, I never really excelled in any, and my active participation in most fell away over the years. These constant shifts were not due to a loss of interest or a total lack of success, nor—thank goodness—to physical calamities. Rather, it was an implicit desire to do new and different things.

I have studied or dabbled in three languages but am still sort of fluent only in English. I love music and played the clarinet in grade school and the piano and harmonica goofing around on my own, but never got good at them. As for hobbies, I've collected everything from coins to vintage briefcases, and although I still enjoy doing it and the collections themselves, my focus and interest in the 'categories' ebb and flow over the years. Even in terms of jobs, I made management consulting my career partially because it was a never-ending string of interesting and challenging problems and issues to be solved with and for different clients, in different environments, over the years.

This fickleness, then, has not directly reflected likes and dislikes, or success or failure. It could be an inherent fear of failure or inferiority, lessened by moving on to something else, but I don't believe so. I am very happy doing something I enjoy or achieve, even if many other people do it better, and even if my skill or improvement plateaued quickly.

I attribute this trait to a nagging curiosity for what I don't know or do, combined with a near thrill of learning something new that I find interesting, important, or useful. This means, of course, that candidates for attention, participation, and chasing knowledge are unlimited. As a result, my flightiness, while not to the point of Attention Deficiency Disorder, is in the general direction of ADD, only slower and I like to think with more reason.

The fact of not mastering much—or even not being world-class good at anything—is a disappointment, but not devastating, and it never seemed to be worth putting all else aside to achieve—even if my smarts, skills, and talents might have enabled me to go farther.

Lack of sufficient skills and talent, whether natural or acquired, did indeed limit my achievements in many arenas. For example, I never considered being a Sumo wrestler or professional golfer—the first due to my survival instinct and lack of mass, and the latter due to plateauing soundly in amateur scores.

And, I have not considered an inability to master the many things I like to do as a failure. I did them and continue to do them because I enjoy it and enjoy doing better.

The results of all this is that I don't have a lot of trophies or world championships. But I remain with lots of—maybe too many—interests, and I'm still adamant about learning more and understanding more. But spreading myself thinly, I continue to be frustrated or disappointed at not doing more of what I don't do.

The Geography of Life

MONGOLIA is three times the size of France, with one-twentieth the population. 40% of Mongolians are nomads who move their households around the vast country at least four times a year. Private property does not apply to land, and fences are virtually prohibited.

This is a partial paradigm for movement in my life. I don't know if I was wired to travel and bounce around, but it was never a conscious desire or objective.

Growing up in a new Chicago suburb in the 1950s seemed fun

and nearly sublime at the time, and still appears so looking back. The semi-rural setting, good public schools, sports of all sorts, close friends all along, bikes and cars, summer jobs, and an easy commute to the big city, combined to make it a bubble in which to grow up. And, the booming post-war economy employed my father as an aspiring corporate manager downtown and provided my family with the necessities and relative comforts of an aspiring, middle-class life.

Family vacations came annually, in the summer for a week or two, and included, among others, a train trip to the new Disneyland in California, a week in Cape Cod with an uncle's family, another in Brooklyn with my grandparents, two consecutive summers at a 'country club' resort in southern Michigan, and some sightseeing via train to Washington, D.C. These were memorable and fun 'destinations' and experiences, but I didn't itch to do more, as there were plenty of adventures and distractions in my home territory, and that is where my friends were.

My dad traveled a bit on business and also conveyed many agreeable stories from his stint in the Air Force in the Middle East and Africa during WW II. My mother was always talking of her childhood trips to the Adirondacks and lobbying to travel more. It was more of a constant complaint than any realistic plan, but probably prompted the trips we did take over the years.

When it was time for college, at age 18, I had been out of the country only two or three times, driving between Detroit and Buffalo, to and from visits with my grandparents near Buffalo. I ended up at Brown University in Providence, Rhode Island. My high school counselor had responded to my applying to Brown with "Why would you want to go that far away?" (I didn't tell him I had also applied to Stanford.) But it was not distance or geography that got me to Providence.

Leaving the Chicago suburbs—where I had lived from age five to 18—for college marked the starter's gun for a life of moving around under the guise of work and career, as well as vacationing and 'touring.' Except for the initial three college-year summers that I lived 'at home' for summer jobs, I remained elsewhere.

* * *

Many of these vignette write-ups concern facets of my working career, travel, interests, and experiences. But, from a geographic perspective, the journey has been a smorgasbord or Whitman Sampler, and just as tasty. As a key dimension of my life, I would not have traveled less or lived in or visited fewer places.

The primary downside—though on balance not tragic—is giving up a sense of geographic family roots. The distances of far flung living and traveling clearly reduced contact with parents and other relatives, and during much of my life there were no internet, Skype, or Zoom, and long-distance phone calls were very expensive. As a result, for lack of proximity and contact, my relationships with parents, my (much younger) sister, and other relatives, while not strained, just did not develop as much as I would have hoped.

It was not so much the moving from place to place as it was that no classical family home was an anchor for those relationships. And, the moving around—not necessarily excessively, but rather constantly over decades—had the effect of stunting or truncating friendships that were strong and offered potential for life-long contact but were bound by our or their 'moving away.' We have friends acquired in myriad circumstances and places around the world—whom we would not have met without being there. But the depths of relationships and activities with those folks have been limited by rarely being in the same place at the same time.

Despite the richness, fascinations, and endless learnings that my geographic reaches have provided, there are of course 'tweaks' that I would have made, were I to do it over. Taking more and more-exotic vacation trips with our boys—especially when they were younger adults—is an example. Living and doing business in a non-English language is another. And, living for more years in some places may be another.

Kit Dietrich and Bill Turner, c. 1952

PART ONE

Family, Friends, and Personal

Along the course of my childhood, schools, consulting career, and incessant traveling, I have met too many fascinating people to remember, let alone to record all anecdotes that are important or might be interesting to others.

Many acquaintances were impressive in one manner or another, and many were not that impressive but were of consequence to me in some way.

In addition to a sample of those people and how they relate to my life—and vice versa— there are some aspects and events that transcend the decades and remain important ingredients to my story.

These are diverse and include family stories, race and civil rights, the military, religion, and embedded hobbies.

Accidental Durability (70 years)

When I was 5, in 1950, we moved into a 'starter' rental townhouse in Park Forest, a new Chicago suburb about a 30-mile commuter train ride from the Loop. Carved mostly out of farmland, the town was developed for post-WWII veterans and their young families as they began new careers. The central shopping center, theater, and churches were all new, as was the public-school system. My father was a commuter, and my mother a 'homemaker,' involved in the newly-formed Woman's Club, the new interdenominational protestant church, and 'pot-luck' dinners with friends. I was starting kindergarten.

Through these groups—and probably the PTA, if there was one—my mother made an assortment of friends, one of her first and closest being Dee (short for Adelia) Dietrich, the mother of a 5-year-old girl, Christine—called then and now 'Kit.' The Dietrichs lived several blocks away. Kit and I were in the same class through fourth grade, and her mother was an energetic organizer of kids' activities, including sort of acting and other playgroups. We often ended up at each other's house to play. In at least one instance, the two of us played grown-up by donning our parents' clothes—she in a likely mom's Jantzan bathing suit, and I in a huge pair of dad's bathing trunks. The photo on page 6 memorializes this.

And photos of our third and fourth grade classes capture our school outfits, which included plaid and checkered puffy-sleeved dresses and Cub Scout and cowboy-style shirts and pants.

Kit's father was a physicist and a lead designer of the first nuclear submarine, the *Nautilus*. He was called Joe or Bob, depending on who you were. In 1954 or 1955, he took a new job, and the family moved away. My mother and Dee, however, continued to correspond throughout their long lives.

* * *

A decade later, as freshmen at Brown University in Rhode Island, my roommate Fred and I decided to hitchhike to Palm Beach, Florida, for our spring break. An aunt of mine had invited us to her house there. No doubt at my mother's or Dee's suggestion, we arranged to stop for a night at the Dietrich house in Clearwater, on the way to Palm Beach.

Fred and I headed out from Providence, had good weather and good luck with rides, made good time, and crossed the causeway into Clearwater the next morning. We chatted and slept all day, and Kit's parents were gracious and welcoming. She took us to a Roy Orbison concert that evening, and she and I talked well into the night, having had no contact for ten years. She was a freshman at Stevens College for women in Columbia, Missouri and was home for spring break. All in all, a nice time. Fred and I moved on the next day, hitching the remaining 225 miles to my aunt's home, where we had a full week on the beach and at debutante parties, before returning to Providence for the spring semester.

The next three years saw me return to the haven of Palm Beach each spring, but never again did my route go through Clearwater, as the Dietrichs had relocated to West Hartford, Connecticut.

* * *

Graduating from Brown in May of 1967, I moved immediately to Manhattan and graduate business school. Shortly after arriving in New York, and again no doubt as a result of my mother's continuing correspondence with Dee, I learned that Kit had graduated from Stevens and was pursuing her long-sought career as a flight attendant (then called 'stewardess'), stationed in New York. In 1968 and 1969, we met up several times, maybe more than several, over about a year, primarily going to East Side pubs and mingling with her roommates and other acquaintances. Kit shared a one-bedroom apartment with at least two other stewardesses, which made it a busy place, all the time. Her modern apartment building, Envoy Towers, in the United Nations neighborhood was 'protected' by an Irish doorman named Tommy. She was flying routes to the West Coast a lot, and then some Las Vegas charters, which were raucous but lucrative. Our meetings up were sporadic and irregular, due to her schedule and my schoolwork combined with my 4-hour, 5-days-a-week job at Lever Brothers, to make ends meet.

At least once, I visited her and her family in West Hartford, which was good fun. Her father, a smart, but reserved, quiet, and polite scientist, was also a champion punster, which had double the effect because it was so unexpected. He was one of my heroes. Kit had two younger brothers, who also were good fun and poked fun at their sister endlessly, addressing her as 'Kitso.'

* * *

Late in 1969 at my first real job at Chemical Bank, I met Suzanne who also worked there, and we married in August 1970. Hard at work climbing corporate ladders, we had two sons in 1977 and 1980, and then moved to England for six years. After returning to New York in 1986, we divorced in 1993. I married Paula, whom I had dated in college but had lost touch with until 1990, after 22 years. The boys went off to college between 1995 and 1998, and Paula and I moved to London, Seoul, and Hong Kong for a six-year tour of duty. I retired from consulting in 2007, and we began splitting our time between New York and a mountain house in Snowmass Village, Colorado.

* * *

My mother died in 2015 at the age of 95. She had been a pack rat, and I spent many hours and days sorting through and doing away with piles of papers, pictures, and letters. Although Dee had passed away in 2001, at age 85, I found a batch of her old letters in my mother's files. One even talked about Fred and my visit to Clearwater 51 years before. Rather than throw them all away, and recalling Kit's somewhat uncommon married name of Challoner, I googled away, found that they lived in Newport News, Virginia, and mailed off the bunch of letters to her in the fall of 2017.

She responded, and Paula and I visited Kit and husband Mike at their home on the James River in Newport News in the fall of 2007. Kit and Mike both have family roots there and have been married since 1971. Mike has run his successful ship servicing company since its beginnings. Kit flew as a United flight attendant for 24 years (and was named Flight Attendant of the Year in 1975, although she has never mentioned that). During and after those years, she also founded, owned, and ran the successful Junior Cotillion in town. They have a son and daughter.

We have visited the Challoners three years running and are hoping and planning for them to visit us in Colorado as soon as the COVID-19 virus allows. Geography and some health issues will require a sustained effort, in order to spend more time enjoying each other's company and 'exceptional' senses of humor, but we're intent on it.

* * *

Kit is my longest-standing friend. Despite gaps of 9, 4, and 48 years between knowing what the other person was doing, or even where they were, some connections are just pre-destined. This one's 70 years and counting.

Accidental Durability (63 Years)

WHEN I WAS 12 in the summer of 1957, we moved into a house in a new neighborhood and town—Chicago

Bill Turner & Pat Morrissy • 1959

Heights—about 25 miles south of Chicago. The house next door was about 60 feet away, across the two driveways and a small strip of grass. Patrick Morrissy, also 12, and his family had moved there from Detroit before us. My dad commuted to offices in downtown Chicago; Pat's dad was a manager at the Ford stamping plant, only a few miles from home.

Pat and I grew a friendship early on, despite going to different schools—he in the large area Catholic school system, and I in the nearby Flossmoor public school district. Weekends, summers and many days after school provided time for joint ventures, and the neighborhood served as a kind of melting pot for us and others of different ages, and who attended various schools. Pat came to know many of my school friends, and I his. In high school, we dated best friend girls for a while—one double date involving a drive to the new restaurant 'oasis' on the Tri-State Tollway near O'Hare airport. We were also on the same Pony League baseball team one or two summers, went water skiing on Indiana lakes together, collected coins together, and at one point planned to apply for summer jobs at a National Park in Florida.

We befriended other adults together, including one named Ziggy, a middle-aged local builder, and another we called 'the coot,' who was a retired skilled woodworker with an elaborate lathe set-up in his garage.

I had other good friends, one perhaps my best friend in high school, but Pat was in a special category, one that came to create implicit trust—for instance borrowing and lending things like cars, showing up at long-agreed places and times, sharing sports and other interests and priorities, and being impressed and upset—and humored—by the same things. Other than school, there wasn't much we didn't do together.

* * *

When we graduated from high school—he from Mendel in Chicago, me from Homewood-Flossmoor—we went our different ways—he to the University of Detroit, I to Brown University in Providence. Pat worked college summers in Detroit, and his family moved back there. As a result, and with disparate locations, college programs and job interests, we moved in our separate directions and eventually lost touch.

Early on though, I found myself in Cleveland for a weekend in 1968 at a party with a group of his Detroit friends and his fiancé named Scoobie. They soon married, and he disappeared, spending a stint in San Francisco and taking a job in the Detroit area. Meanwhile, I was permanently on the East Coast, graduating from college, moving to New York City to go to graduate school, and then working in banking and management consulting there—where I have had an apartment since 1967.

* * *

In 1980, after five years at Chemical Bank (now part of JPMorgan Chase), and seven years as a consultant at McKinsey—

living all the while in Manhattan—my wife Suzanne and our two sons, aged two years and five weeks, moved to London, England, for what turned out to be a six-year stint. Besides interesting work there and around Europe, it was exciting to treat London as a hub for touring all over the British Isles and the Continent on weekends and vacation breaks.

In 1984, my wife's sister and brother in law visited us, and we left the kids in London and went to Paris for a long weekend. Suzanne, who worked for Mobil Oil and had business colleagues in Paris, got a recommendation for a good neighborhood restaurant in a suburb east of central Paris. Although it was a twenty-minute drive from our hotel, we decided to suffer the taxi ride and have dinner there.

The four of us enjoyed the typically excellent and lengthy meal, pretty informal without the dressy bustle of Paris. When we were finished and got up to leave, I heard a voice behind me say, in English, "I think that is Bill Turner." I turned to see Pat Morrissy and a lady sitting at a table, finishing their dinner.

After 16 years of no contact or knowledge of where the other was, we had bumped into each other in this remote restaurant, 4,000 miles from where we grew up. Pat was there with Jean Campbell, his girlfriend and future wife and an attorney with a practice in New Jersey, having grown up in Denver. Pat had spent a decade leading tenant, housing, and neighborhood initiatives in two northern New Jersey towns, aimed at rehabilitating and growing downtrodden neighborhoods, which would become his life's work.

At the time, they lived on the Upper West Side of Manhattan, about three blocks from where we too had lived for seven years. It turns out that we had overlapped living there, shopping at the same stores and even buying Christmas trees from the same vacant lot vendor. After we saw them in Paris, Pat and Jean married and bought a home in New Jersey, and subsequently bought a weekend house in Columbia County, about 120 miles up the Hudson from New York and their NJ home. We also had a weekend house 50 miles south of theirs, in Dutchess County.

After we moved back to NYC from London in 1986, we stayed in touch with the Morrissys over the years, as they had a son, spent a year in Rome, had twins, and pursued careers as a family legal practice, and a successful housing and neighborhood development organization.

* * *

In 1998, my wife Paula and I bought a house in the ski town of Snowmass Village, Colorado. We and our two sons liked to ski in the west, and that location was not only beautiful, but also closer to the boys' homes on the West Coast. Since I stopped full-time work in 2007, we have shifted home life mostly to the mountains.

In 2015, no doubt largely due to Jeannie's upbringing in and love for Colorado—and all three of their kids living in the state at the time—the Morrissys decided to build a retirement house in Carbondale, just 30 miles down the road from us.

Our friendship and time and trips together have continued. Both couples like to bounce around the world, and we sometimes go along together. In 2018, we toured World War I battlefields in France.

Some friendships and trusting relationships just don't wane, even with different, divergent lives and lengthy gaps. In this case, over 63 years since seventh grade, and counting.

My Sister Was an Only Child

...AND SO WAS I.

IN 1957, I was 12 when my mother, father, and I moved into the three-bedroom split-level 'colonial' house in Chicago

Heights. Our subdivision had the good fortune to be just within the school district of the adjoining town of Flossmoor. Entering seventh grade, I was a new boy in the midst of kids who had been at school together for years. But they too were new to the building, and it was the first year that all of us had a homeroom, and then rotated through different classrooms and teachers for the various subjects. The regimen was new for everyone, as were the sports and dance class. All in all, I made new friends fairly easily and quickly.

My first junior high sport was basketball, under the direction and encouragement of an excellent gym teacher who led the team in daily practices and weekly games against other schools.

That fall, it became evident that my mother was pregnant and that our family would soon expand by one-third. On January 22nd, 1958, when I called home to have my mother pick me up from basketball practice, I was told that she had just delivered a baby sister, and I'd have to find an alternative ride home. Which I did.

The change in venue, having to build peer relationships from scratch, and heading into the years of hormonal change and challenge, consumed me as a self-absorbed and hyperactive teenager for the next five years (some would say the next 65).

My schoolwork, sports at school and in the summers, summer jobs, the transportation progression from bicycles to motor scooters to cars—along with the discovery of girls my age—all took more than 100% of my time and attention during those years. I was generally uninterested in the baby and budding little girl, Cindi, who lived in my house and drew a great deal of attention from my parents. Net, net, that was a plus.

I now feel that I should be embarrassed not recalling a single event, discussion, activity, or situation that occupied my sister Cindi all those years. I was busy with all the other things in my life, and she was, frankly, irrelevant. I had my own bedroom and

Cindi
Mystic, CT 1963

was out of the house as much as possible. At the same time, I don't recall any interference, inconvenience, or other grievance that she caused me. She didn't compete with me, and, in fact, may have run interference for me, absorbing my parents' oversight and attention.

* * *

In the summer of 1963, I had just graduated from Homewood-Flossmoor High School and had spent the summer making contact lenses in Chicago. Around Labor Day, all of us piled into my dad's 1962 Pontiac Grand Prix (2 doors, 5 seats, 4 people) to drive east and drop me off at college at Brown University, in Providence, Rhode Island. Nearly there, we stopped at Mystic Seaport in Connecticut, and a nice photo of my sister on the old whaling ship Charles W. Morgan anchored there reminds me that she was along and a nice little girl.

Looking back, that trip marked the end of my really living with them at what from then on was *their* home. I was 18 years old; my sister was 5. The 13-year difference was a light year.

I returned to the house and earned spending money during the subsequent three college summers, but my sister became no more relevant, as I worked, played and traveled away from my 'bunk' at home. And, following the summer of 1966, when she was nine, we were never to live under the same roof.

* * *

So, the two of us grew up and out of the nest basically as two only children. I lived on the East Coast and overseas; she stayed in the mid-West for college, work, and her own family.

Many years later, we became much closer—including her daughter Tracy—and we remain so. My visits to see my parents evolved over the years to seeing Cindi and Tracy. And, after my father died and my mother moved to an elderly-care home, my sister and I coordinated closely, sharing the oversight—although she bore the brunt.

Geography continues to keep us mostly apart, but not like two only children, as in the first 40 years.

Sporting for Life

I GOT INTERESTED IN and followed most major U.S. sports as a kid and kept up the interest to this day, although in recent years I have tended to pay attention mostly toward the playoff and championship ends of the schedules.

As far as participating myself, baseball was a favorite early on—'pick-up,' school, little league and pony league, and even as a college freshman. As a pitcher I became fair but far from great. My high point was probably in the summer of 1962, pitching in a pony league tournament game. I was put in late in the game with a one-run lead. After giving up a single and a walk in the last inning, we were still leading with two outs and the batter was their best hitter who had hit a three-run homer in an early inning. I struck him out. From our team's reaction, I realized that the last pitch and the win wasn't for me but for the team.

Starting in seventh grade, basketball assumed the spotlight—I was new at it, I was not short, and I loved it. Touching the rim to my second knuckle once in a while, and with a fairly decent jump shot, I was solidly on the second team in high school, but that was it. A high point before that was tying for the school free-throw championship in eighth grade, making 14 out of 15 in the 'finals.'

I also liked to bowl as a kid, and for at least two years at age twelve and thirteen, I was on a team in a Saturday league. The last bowling day of the last year (1958), the whole team was at their best performance and luck, resulting in an award for the highest team score all year of any American Junior Bowling Congress team in the country. Other activities and living for many years in New York City largely curtailed bowling beyond high school.

I played golf as a teenager and liked it, and then, much later, played as a member at the Quaker Hill Country Club just outside New York City. At a local tournament when I was 17, I placed second in a driving contest with a 310-yard shot. My best ever was a score of 80, and, again, a busy life and city living pretty much edged out golf for decades.

Skiing first appeared on a church youth trip to northern Michigan, followed by maybe 10 or 12 trips during college to Vermont, and continued commutes from New York City. Only this century have I gained confidence on expert runs and now visit the Colorado slopes 50 or 60 times a season.

We learned to SCUBA dive with the boys in 1993 and became seriously certified in Korea in 2002, making a couple dozen dives since then in some pretty interesting places, including the pitons in St. Lucia, JeJu-do Island in Korea, Australia's Great

Barrier Reef, Langkawi Island in the Philippines, and off Nha Trang in Viet Nam. Living far from the combination of good water and good weather, it did not become a regular pastime, despite the potential.

Time Flies

One of Chicago's best hotels has for decades been The Drake on north Michigan Avenue. Its Cape Cod Room flourished as one of the city's finest fish restaurants, and Queen Elizabeth visited the hotel on her first visit to America in 1959.

In the 1950s and early 1960s, my father was in the advertising business and was the account director for the Drake. In 1961, the hotel decided to open an extension hotel, named the Drake Oak Brook, in the vicinity of six-year-old O'Hare Airport, 18 miles west of Chicago. Drake executives and the ad agency came up with the slogan 'Where Time Stands Still', and they wanted to integrate it into their crest, in Latin. My father offered to find the appropriate Latin equivalent, and, knowing that my high school basketball coach was a Latin teacher, asked me if I could get a translation.

Which I did, and the hotel's inscription became *Ubi Tempus Quietus*. The phrase came to be quoted in English as 'where time rests.' Since 2009, the hotel has been refurbished and managed by different owners, unrelated to the downtown Drake. But the phrase remains alive today with the current owners and is still prominent on the building's facade.

An Inexplicable Ending

ONE SUNDAY EVENING in February 1997, my wife, younger son, and I were hanging around our house in Dutchess County New York, when the phone rang. It was my father at home in the Chicago suburbs, wanting to chat. During the conversation, he mentioned that he was going to clean his various guns—a shotgun, two 22 caliber rifles, and a couple pistols and an army carbine from WWII—which he kept in the attic but got down to clean every year or two. He asked me if I wanted any of them, and I said not really, as we had a couple target rifles at the house, and it would be awkward getting his from Chicago to New York.

* * *

Two days later, I was back in the City at work when my mother called in the late afternoon, frantic with the news that my dad had shot himself and was about to have surgery at the local hospital.

It seems that when she returned to the house from the store that day, he came down the stairs bleeding heavily from the neck and nose, telling her to call an ambulance, which she did. It was his 45 automatic from the Air Force, and he claimed he must have mistakenly left a bullet in the gun's chamber. While standing in the upstairs bedroom, the pistol had fired up from underneath his chin, with the bullet going through the roof of his mouth and exiting out through his nose. It had then gone through the ceiling and through the attic roof, the path attesting to where he had been standing and the direction of the shot. Besides the immediate and heavy bleeding, it had broken a bunch of jaw and nose bones.

I flew out to see him in intensive care, where over the next day or two they reconstructed the jaw and other bones. He was conscious and awake most of those days, but could not really talk, even when not sedated, due to all the wiring. During his hospital recovery over the next week or 10 days, he contracted MRSA (the hospital environment infection), then pneumonia, then suffered a heart attack, which killed him on February 26. He was 76.

* * *

When I called his twin brother the day after it happened, his reaction was, "He tried to kill himself and botched it." I believed then, and still do, that this was the case. My father was an engineer, meticulous and precise with all things mechanical, especially guns, and would never have accidently had a bullet in the chamber or pulled the trigger while pointing it upward under his chin. It is not credible that he fired a bullet that he hadn't intended to, or that he aimed and shot at anything unintended. And he was an accurate shot. The reason it did not kill him outright was that the barrel was pointed from beneath his chin at an angle forward, rather than toward the center or back of his head.

Because a firearm was involved, the police had come too and took and kept the gun. We did not ask for an autopsy, since the heart attack in the hospital was clearly the cause of death.

Afterwards, I learned from my mother that a recent PSA test showed a very high count and that he had been scheduled for a prostate biopsy the very next week, which he probably feared greatly. He did not like doctors or medical procedures and tended to be squeamish about things like blood tests and vaccinations—not to the point of complaining or talking about it, but avoidance was his approach. Although we'll never know for sure, he may have psyched himself into believing he had prostate cancer, would have a slow or non-recovery from any related operation, so the hell with it.

Because of his critical condition and difficulty communicating, I never had the opportunity to ask him exactly why and what happened, let alone confront or challenge him with it all.

It is terribly ironic that if he meant to take his own life in order to end it without suffering whatever would be forthcoming from prostate surgery, in the event he spent the last two weeks of his life in hell—bedridden with a wired jaw, tubes for inflows and outflows, and virtually unable to talk.

Afterwards, I found his home file drawer of financial records impeccable and up to date with well-tabbed folders for insurance, bank account, will, and all other important records. Although admirable, this hinted at getting ready.

And, the call a day or two before had let the world know that he was cleaning his guns, conveying that any shooting would be accidental. Suicide might have voided his modest life insurance policy.

* * *

As a son growing up in the post-WWII suburbs in a reasonably close-knit middle-class family, I viewed my dad as a smart, engaging, successful businessman, who was not forceful in his opinions or dictatorial in his fathering. He valued his military ancestry and his prep school, college, and Air Force experiences, emphasized academic achievement, and had enduring interests in stamp and coin collecting, duck hunting, listening to classical music (he played the violin as a young man), and found

Egyptology fascinating. And, although he wasn't very interested in sports, and was indifferent to vacation travel and touring, he encouraged me in most things I liked to do and was generally upbeat. Criticism was rare and often in the form of a question. He had a sense of humor throughout his life that never waned, something that I inherited either by osmosis or in DNA.

On the one hand, he rarely if ever said he loved me, but, on the other hand, he never said or did anything to raise the notion that he didn't. And, although he never openly addressed whether he was happy, thankful, successful, or content, he also never complained about his plight, or expressed displeasure with his own life.

However, there are important aspects of Don Turner's life that may well have contributed to his probable conclusion that he would rather not live any longer. These factors included finances, job ambition, drinking, his and mom's relationship, and depression—all, no doubt, intertwined. Although their relative importance is only conjecture on my part, these factors certainly did not heighten his verve for life.

FINANCES | I never felt disadvantaged by our family's levels of income, spending and assets, despite seeing that many of my high school and college friends and classmates belonged to country clubs, took exotic vacations, and drove newer cars—things we didn't do or have. My work during the summers—which included cutting lawns, caddying at the nearby country club, being a dentist's grounds keeper, making contact lenses, painting houses—were positive experiences, enjoyable, educational, profitable, and generally fun. And, it was all I knew and needed, in terms of earning money to supplement a small allowance.

However, and mostly only with hindsight, my dad was not very successful over time in terms of income and assets, relative to the pay and pay trajectory of his business executive peers. He and the family always watched our spending, never had much savings, were forever frugal and cut cost corners, and were never 'independent.' Although 'hardship' was never the case and money was rarely discussed specifically, family life was always budget-bound. My dad never complained about money or lack of it and kept any financial worries or disappointments to himself. He didn't act or pretend to be poor but clearly was never independent in terms of doing whatever it was that he wanted to do. This was similar to his father, a career Marine Corps officer and pensioner, who retained his government job during the Depression, but fell further and further behind in terms of monetary and material wealth over the decades, without striving to do better financially.

This lack of wealth had no erosive or corrosive effect on my upbringing and, in fact, may have subconsciously raised my financial sensitivity and/or ambition. However, it may well have eaten at dad's ego and sense of self-worth relative to other family and friends. Not being able to afford a more active, broader, independent life may have put a lid on his optimism or satisfaction.

JOB AMBITION | It was never clear how ambitious he was, which, in itself probably means he wasn't very. He conveyed to me—or I gleaned from him—a sense of success and implicit ambition in his engineering and psychology college programs, his active and far-reaching Air Force service, and his first two jobs. Even after that, he followed his interest in psychology and personnel management, and went with companies that were private, decent organizations in interesting, growing businesses. But he never seemed to strive for or seriously seek positions with greater challenges, responsibility, pay, or trappings. I believe his first job move, from Glenn L. Martin company to Grant Advertising in Chicago, resulted from his search for a new position, as the aircraft manufacturing industry was about to consolidate. However, his three further job changes—accompanied by jobless periods of varying lengths—were not voluntary and may have had the effect of further dampening his ambitions. In terms of job satisfaction and security, he may have treaded water for 25 years.

DRINKING | Ever since I knew him from about age five, he liked his wines and martinis. Throughout the 1950s, he was a 30-year-old player in the MAD MEN era of advertising, drinking often at lunch and after work, and at dinners and social gatherings around home. After 12 years, his advertising position evaporated in 1962 due to the agency's fatal loss of its largest client, from which it never recovered. He was among a group of executives that were let go.

His business work ethic, habits, and behavior had been formed. From then on, I surmise—in retrospect and without empirical data—that he drank at lunch virtually every day at all his companies.

It took him nearly nine months to find work after leaving the advertising agency. Then, seemingly well-positioned as Director of Personnel at a leading contact lens company, he suddenly was gone after only two years. I once called him at work there from college, and the company operator said he was no longer at the company. This was a double-barreled shock I've never forgotten: one, that he had lost his job, and two, that he had not told me. I'm sure he didn't quit, and I've always assumed he was bounced and that drinking probably caused it.

After more months between jobs, he found a seemingly good match as Manager of Personnel Services at a quality management consulting firm, Lester B. Knight & Associates. He remained there about seven years. The company was run by its namesake, a tough, no-bullshit executive, and I would not be surprised if even a hint of a drinking problem would be terminable.

His next and last job was to head the personnel division of a well-established and successful engineering consulting firm, Sargent & Lundy, which he joined in 1970 and where he spent the last 15 years of his career. This position, like at the other firms, was a good fit—that is, a professional service-based company, with a good business that needed an experienced head of personnel and its associated functions. And, he knew what he was doing and had the skills and knowledge from the several previous corporate environments. But, at S&L, after eight years as personnel head, he was demoted to Assistant to the Head, and then, two years later, assigned to be the company's EEO Supervisor. Over the 15 years, and in the various positions, the company did keep his compensation edging higher, and he retired with his small and only pension. His annual salary moved from $17,500 to $39,000 between 1970 and 1985.

I pieced all this together not too long ago, as he virtually never discussed his career or any job issues or problems with me, and few with his wife, my mother. As my college and business careers progressed, I considered dad's career moves a combination of there not being any or many serious issues—i.e., that things were fine—and of his keeping anything that was bothering him to himself, without bothering others with negative karma. And if, as I suspect, his drinking and its consequences were a major force in his job plateauing in his early 40s, he may well have been in denial and/or embarrassed to talk about any of it.

DON AND MARY'S RELATIONSHIP | My mother was an incessant talker, loved and wanted to travel, played the piano, ate endless salads and vegetables, and cooked such dishes as calf liver, fried green tomatoes, and even creamed kidneys on toast.

Don & Mary Turner
c. 1990

Early on, she was active at Women's Clubs, participated with friends and neighbors who held pot-luck dinners, volunteered for many things, and had a pet cat (before we had a rabbit and turtles). Although she had worked in a lens factory near Buffalo during WWII, she was the epitome of the post-War housewife and mother during my lifetime. The common word used more and more by her friends as she aged, was that she was a "real sweetie," which was accurate.

But she was also, and increasingly with age, a complainer, avoiding confrontation but finding fault with much, which often turned into nagging and carping. And, my dad was the target for much of it, and the audience for the rest.

Their relationship appeared stable enough, and my sister was born in 1958, which provided them a virtual second generation of child focus and upbringing. Don and Mary went to church regularly, partly out of a sense of duty, partly as a social gathering that they enjoyed, and partly with real faith, at least on my mother's part. Since the 1950s, they and the family took some notable vacation trips, including around the U.S. that, while prompted perhaps by a desire to see and show the kids the country, they seemed to enjoy. In the 1980s, they enjoyed a trip to London and Paris, and also made some trips to our 'country house' outside New York City to be with us and their two grandsons.

He was away a lot at the ad agency but less thereafter, and they developed separate interests including at home, where both spent most of their time when he wasn't at work. During his layoff times and after he retired, he would sporadically commute into Chicago and walk around for hours, largely out of habit.

This cohabitation with separateness must have become more extreme after my sister moved out around 1980. Mom cooked; he ate. He read books; she read the newspapers. They both watched TV, but different programs on different sets. They didn't share a bedroom since about 1963. She played the piano; he listened to classical music and collected stamps.

Both tended to be a bit sullen and negative, and they did less and less together, got along less and less, had their own lives, and his was particularly sedate. She got a small inheritance in the early 1960s when her father died. It was not much, but enough so she could do and buy this or that in subsequent years without having to take the family's money from the family's bank account.

Lack of expanded or new horizons was driven by a continuous lack of discretionary money, but I am not sure what they would have done with two or three times as much.

DEPRESSION | In any case, dad never complained about his jobs, or how he was being treated by employers. But he also never expressed any desire to do something different, or more or better, including financially. I had no reason to believe, at any age looking back, that he was not happy on the job, with his companies, with his marriage, and with life in general. Subjects like that never came up.

At odds with his earlier myriad interests in engineering, big-band dancing, hunting and fishing, and even golf for a few years, he had become a non-self-starter with few interests and not much visible energy. For a long string of years, he continued to collect wine labels (with his own ratings) and stamps, and to go duck hunting. All seemed to wane with age, as did the friendships that were plentiful in his 30s and 40s but that fell away as mutual interests and money were limited.

Although I don't recall any behavior on his part that would trigger an outward sign of clinical depression, keeping most feelings and concerns inward was his mode and no doubt an indication in itself. He could be a 'hot head' occasionally, with a burst of anger about some pent-up subject or something mom did, but his normal demeanor was on the docile side. And all the observations recited here—even if only one or two of them are accurate—might be revealing to a professional and consistent with depression.

Whatever the forces acting on my father, it was as if he 'peaked' and became increasingly stunted following the War years. In his youth, he was a curious engineer, an avid hunter and fisherman, a competent swimmer, and an accomplished and enthusiastic ballroom dancer who loved the 'big bands.' Then, he loved the travel, sights, and people he met flying all over the world as an Air Force Navigator. He married his sweetheart, had a son and eventually a daughter, both of whom he loved and became fairly engaged with. But, like his father before him (the Marine Corps career officer), he couldn't seem to define, seek, or find a career path that would provide the stimulation or financial footing to do more of what he wanted to do or try.

* * *

As I have written already, I consider my childhood, upbringing, and family life to have been very positive, with encouragement and support from my mother and father throughout. My sister—13 years younger than I—may have seen and felt more negativism and may have been more bothered by it. And, as a family, we were not open about problems and, especially, feelings. Both my parents allowed and implicitly encouraged me to be independent and go my own way, for which I have been grateful—and have tried to encourage with my sons. But, that independence, from high school age onward, served to keep sensitive but important subjects unspoken, to reduce the possibility of a close-knit family atmosphere, and to limit even further the emotional understanding among us.

It is sad to consider that my dad may have been unhappy to the point of taking his own life, but there you are. It's difficult to argue that happiness, a feeling of success, comfort, or the beneficence of others entered into it.

Ode to Mom

MY MOTHER—Mary Dow Turner—was never sure what she wanted out of life, and she achieved it. Born in 1920, she shrewdly outlived virtually all her friends and all her contemporary family members, who generally knew her as sweet, kind, and generous. She outlived her husband by 19 years.

The youngest of four children, she lived in Hamburg, New York, a suburb of Buffalo, from age 7 to 18, when she went off to Russell Sage College in Troy, New York. She met my dad Donald—completing his sophomore year at nearby Rensselaer Polytechnic Institute—and they were married during Don's leave from Air Force duty in Coral Gables, Florida, in 1943. She preferred and was dealt the role of housewife and mother, which she played her entire adult life.

In 1945, nine months following another home leave in Florida, I was born, and the small new family lived in Ann Arbor, Michigan, while my dad finished his bachelor's degree. Then, following a three-year stint in Baltimore, the family moved to Chicagoland, where mom and dad lived for the last half-century of their lives. My sister was born a dozen years later, in 1958, so we were basically two only children.

My mom's dad Richard—my grandfather—was a pal to me, although I only saw him on sporadic visits to Hamburg and the house my mother grew up in. I recall the cribbage board, pipe cabinet, cuspidor, and ostrich eggs in the house, all handed down from his father—my great grandfather—a career and somewhat famous sea captain. Richard was the first of 11 generations in America to live south or west of Boston. Also vivid in my memory were two oddities he kept in his bedroom: an unloaded Derringer pistol resting on a small set of antlers on the wall above the bed, and his pickled appendix in a jar on a dresser.

My mother hardly ever mentioned or referred to her grandfather sea captain, and it wasn't until I was in college and became interested that I realized the rich history and began to search for detail. The captain—George W. Dow—died the year before my mother was born, so she never knew him. She seemed proud of the captain as her grandfather and was pleased that I was interested and researching him and his ancestors in the years before she died.

Over the years, Mary's interests and activities included playing the piano, which she had learned in her youth, and she particularly liked to play pieces that were a bit more difficult than she could handle. She was active in several women's clubs in the area, enjoyed automobile trips to almost anywhere, and attempted to photograph every person, animal, or inanimate object she encountered.

She did all the cooking—mostly the meat and potatoes kind—and she was partial to salads and vegetables, which I resisted. She had a pronounced sweet tooth, which I inherited, and I also became quite keen on some of her weird dishes, including creamed kidneys on toast and fried calf's liver.

All during my childhood, she shuttled me around to the myriad activities and events related to school, sports, and friends, and I believe she did this for my sister as well, after I had moved away.

Following the Watergate scandals of the early 1970's, Mary corresponded for about five years with fellow Hamburg High School graduate, spy, and Watergate break-in mastermind E. Howard Hunt, as he went through his prosecution, prison in Florida, and living in Mexico. She bought one of the 40+ paintings he completed while in Federal prison.

She loved to bowl, which she kept at for forty years. Beginning in the mid-1960's, Mary was a regular team member in the Powder Puff and United Women's Church leagues, winning a Perfect Attendance Award many times. And, while never taking the sport too seriously, she was pretty good at it. In 1965, she received the Most Improvement award, and two years later rolled her best score ever, a 262 game. She exceeded 200 many times, and, into her 80's, her league season averages were 140 - 150.

She (and my dad, Don) were founding members of the United Faith Protestant Church of Park Forest in the early 1950s, and Mary retained close ties with that Church for more than six decades, although infirmities kept her from attending services in later years.

Mary was predeceased by husband Don in 1997, after 54 years of marriage. She remained in the house in Chicago

Heights for another few years, finally moving into two successive nearby elder living quarters for her final 15 years. She was beset with 'mild' dementia for some years, but the last 'memory care' unit was very agreeable, and she passed away comfortably in her sleep from a general body shutdown at age 95.

Politics at 14

EARLY ON IN MY FIRST YEAR of high school in a brand-new school, a classmate pushed me to run for the 'office' of Freshman Class President. I agreed on the condition that she would be my campaign manager. We made a 30-foot long banner out of shelf paper and convinced the farmhouse owner across the street to let us nail it to their fence on election day. The huge sign with red letters said simply, "BILL TURNER FOR PRESIDENT" and every school bus slowed down right there to turn and drop off the students. I won, wholly unexpectedly—amazing, since more than half the class had come from a different town and hadn't a clue who I was. Maybe that swung it.

Civil Wrongs

GROWING UP in two new suburban developments outside Chicago in the 1950s and 1960s, I rarely saw black folks or foreigners—in my neighborhoods or in my schools. My elementary, junior high, and high schools had nary a one. Even my liberal Ivy League college, Brown University, could count only eight African American students in my entering class of about 1,100 in 1963, and I can't recall any non-Americans. My MBA class at Columbia in 1967 had many foreign students, but no people of color that I remember, and only two women.

Yet these were the germinating years of the civil rights movement, full of protests, riots, killings, marches, and legislation by which the country was pivoting toward major advances in 'equal opportunity' and a much more integrated citizenry and world.

My parents weren't racists—at least they certainly did not practice or teach it. They were republicans of the law-and-order and fiscal-responsibility type. But they were pretty interested in everyone they met and never in my memory denigrated or rebuked personally anyone or particular groups. My father was a WWII veteran, and an aspiring businessman, climbing the corporate ladder in the post-war corporate world. But he never drew the distinctions of class, race, religion, or other prejudices that were there for the taking. In fact, he reveled in the other peoples and cultures he had been exposed to in the Middle East, Africa, and Asia during the war. Yes, the family's chosen home neighborhoods were white and relatively homogeneous, but that wasn't a conscious criterion for living there. Price, suburban green, and good schools guided my parents to where they landed. They also preached and enforced good manners and admonished me to be polite and have respect for everyone I met. Some of it stuck.

* * *

It was eerie, especially at Brown, joining and becoming a part of liberal causes as the civil rights movement grew (complemented by strong anti-Viet Nam War sentiment), while at the same time never growing up or living in a racially integrated 'community' of any kind. And having so few people who were not pretty much like me where I lived and went to school, including at Brown. While I came to understand the shortcomings and wrongness in that, and as JFK, Lyndon Johnson and other leaders led or backed the many initiatives to combat the injustices, my academic and other time and activities kept me from being very active in protests and rallies.

As it all unfolded and consumed the news and on-campus

life, the civil rights events and movement took on a somewhat academic and detached nature. Guest lecturers on campus, national news coverage on all the media, and topical books incorporated into course syllabuses, had the strange effect of reinforcing distance from the problems. I hadn't grown up involved in the issues, and my new, increasing, and serious interest was gleaned at school and from the media.

* * *

In the spring of my freshman year, my roommate and I set out to spend our spring break in Palm Beach Florida. Early one April morning, after turning in our registration cards for the fraternity where we would live for the rest of our time at Brown, we walked to Angell Street in Providence with suitcases in hand and stuck out our thumbs at the curb, to hitchhike to the sun. We had "FLA" in large, white adhesive tape letters on one of the suitcases.

In those days, hitchhiking was common, being quite safe and a virtual social network for connecting those cars (and trucks) traveling point to point, with those car-less folks wanting to go the same route. To better sell ourselves, we wore blazers, white shirts, and ties.

We had good weather and good luck, and later that day, after only three rides, found ourselves near the Washington D.C. bus station. We decided to take a bus to Richmond, which would put us on a direct line south, to continue our hitching. The next ride took us from Richmond down highway 301 to just outside Florence, South Carolina.

It was still the middle of the night when we were dropped off on the highway next to a gas station. It was an old station—not clean but not dirty—in the middle of nowhere, with a single attendant to pump gas and no traffic or even other buildings in sight. We walked around to the back of the station to use the bathroom and wash up a bit.

There were three doors, each with a black and white metal sign overhead: "MEN", "WOMEN", and "COLORED". I had never seen that before, and it jarred me with the physical reality of the impact of race in the country. I had read and studied about slavery, racism, and social injustice. And I was steeped in the issues of the day and their constant news coverage. And, I backed and participated in campus events and causes aimed at making changes. But that scene—in the dead of night at a rural gas station—etched in my brain forever the cultural reality in major swaths of the country, and in the minds of swaths of Americans far beyond the South.

That image has not faded over more than half a century, and, unfortunately, it's still not irrelevant.

Fred from Akron

SOUND STUDIO. My college roommate, Fred, and I shared a 15' x 15' double bedroom on the ground floor of the fraternity house, across the hall from the pay phone booth and men's room. For three years. In that space, Fred taught himself how to play the electric guitar—mostly from records of current rock hits—and he organized a band that practiced there at least once a week. As a result, I never considered studying in the room and for three years did all my reading and other schoolwork in the library.

During our sophomore year, Eddie, a senior who lived in the room next door, did study in his room and virtually all the time. When Fred started up the music, Eddie would come around and swing open our door, demanding that the noise end. And, although Fred generally ignored the pleas, Eddie's interruptions got on his nerves.

So, Fred hooked up a car ignition coil to the inside brass doorknob. The coil could deliver a powerful punch, and when turned on it made a loud buzzing noise. Fred called Eddie over, and with the coil turned on, Fred touched a normal light bulb to the *outside* knob, and the bulb lit up quite brightly from the current. The point was to demonstrate to Eddie that if he comes around and tries to open the door, he's likely to get a shock. Eddie, who had a heart murmur, understood immediately and stomped away.

For a few days, Fred kept the coil plugged in while he or the band played, and Eddie could hear the buzzing and didn't dare come around. Then, Fred realized that the noise was the key, not the actual coil. So, he recorded the buzzing on his tape recorder and merely turned that on each time he knew Eddie was in his room, while Fred was making music.

* * *

50-LB. CURLS | Fred had been an Ohio state wrestling champion in high school and was aggressively recruited by Brown's wrestling coach. But Fred had no intention of wrestling at Brown, did not accept any scholarship, and concentrated on his studies and music. However, each year, he worked out briefly and entered Brown's intramural wrestling tournament, winning every match, some in less than a minute. Fred noticed that the wrestling coach stood largely out of sight and watched each of Fred's matches, no doubt lamenting his intercollegiate absence.

* * *

POST-GRAD | Majoring in aerospace engineering and economics, Fred applied to several business schools. To meet the personal essay requirement of the Harvard Business School application, he described how he had seduced the daughter of a minister in New Hampshire. He refused to let me read it but received an acceptance by HBS. It was a 'deferred admission,' and rather than wait the necessary year, he started that September at New York University's Stern School instead.

* * *

AN INVOLUNTARY BUT CALM REACTION | Over the years, Fred would invite one or two local girls (referred to as 'townies') to our room in the afternoon or evening to chat and listen to music—usually on Friday or the weekend.

Once, a friend of ours went away for the weekend and asked us to keep his 15-inch long iguana lizard. We had done this before and readily agreed. It was silent, stayed under the bed or in the closets, made no mess, and didn't try to run away.

That Friday evening, one of the girls had come to listen to records and was sitting on the small couch against the wall, listening and talking. Unbeknownst to any of us, the iguana crawled up the side of the couch and onto the three-inch ledge atop the back and along the wall, stopping just behind the girl's head. Not noticing it—and with it lying there perfectly still—she slowly turned her head until she saw its full length and the ugly, threatening face about six inches from her face.

Without moving a muscle or uttering a sound, she fell forward onto the floor, fainting, out cold. Although revived quickly and unhurt, she was not happy and left.

Two Times Darkness

ON TUESDAY, NOVEMBER 9, 1965, I was reading as usual in the Brown University library at about 5:30 in the evening in a leather chair looking west out the window wall over the city of Providence. The sun was just down, and it was getting quite dark, with all the lights of downtown standing out against the nearly black sky.

All of a sudden, about a third of the city on the right side—the north—went totally dark. Then, over the course of a minute or two, all the rest went out, including in the library and other campus buildings. Emergency lights came on, so we started leaving.

This turned out to be the great northeast blackout, affecting 30 million people in 8 states for about 12 hours. We partied late.

* * *

On Saturday, July 13, 1977, my wife Suzanne and I had dinner at a business colleague's house in Greenwich Village. It was brutally hot that summer, with temperatures in the 100s earlier that week. Suzanne was 6 months pregnant with our first son.

About 9:30, the lights went out and looking out onto the street, there were no lights visible in any direction except headlights in the streets. Lightning had started a chain reaction of substation outages, and the city's lights weren't restored for a full 24 hours.

A few limousine and taxies were available at $1 per block, so we had a leisurely 70-block walk up Eighth Avenue home.

Economic Challenges of Learning

MY FAMILY AND I lived a comfortable, post-war middle-class life, and I attended a new suburban public high school. For college, I went to Brown, the seventh-oldest college in the U.S., with a proud Ivy League history and a ratio of applicants to acceptances among the highest in the country. I was lucky to get in—and probably would not today—and I graduated in 1967.

I received a financial aid package at Brown consisting of a student loan of $700 per year, and a campus job working in the dining hall 2 hours each morning of the school year, for something like $1.50 or $2 an hour.

In addition to this assistance from Brown, a great aunt of mine chipped in each year, and I worked summer jobs to build up pocket money. My father paid the rest. In my senior year, I also ran a youth group program in Providence for two hours each Sunday, which earned me $15 a week more. Although these amounts sound puny today, each source made a difference, and I never felt financial vulnerability or questioned if I could afford what I was doing or wanted to do.

From the spring of my freshman year onward, I had a motorcycle and eventually a used compact car that cost me $600. A gallon of gas cost about 32 cents ($2.45 in today's dollars). I hitchhiked a fair amount, including to Florida and home to Chicago at various times. There were half-price student discount deals on the major airlines.

The biggest cost of college by far—and the predominant cost in my life for those years—was tuition and room and board. In my senior year, tuition rose by more than 10% to $2,000 ($15,340 in today's dollars) for the year. (I have a full-page letter from Brown President Keeney announcing and virtually apologizing for the increase.) Room and board never reached $1,000 during those years ($7,670 in today's money). So, my senior year's total cost was less than $3,000, or $23,900 in today's dollars.

Brown's tuition today stands at $60,696, and room and board is $15,908, for a total of $77,604 per year, nearly 26 times my senior year's level, and more than three times the rate of inflation since 1967! Regular gasoline hovers north of $2.50/gallon. Summer jobs are not plentiful. Hitchhiking is out of fashion, perceived as dangerous or otherwise to be avoided by travelers and drivers alike. And, to unburden students, Brown has done away with student loans, converting them to grants.

This comparison is meant to be neither nostalgic, nor melancholy. Rather, it is to characterize a change over the half century that I do lament. The financial hill that was there for me to climb 50 years ago appears to be a cliff today—for comfortably well-off high school graduates, let alone for those with less. In terms of the financial resources and opportunity, I was privileged, lucky, and one of the 'haves' being able to strive to learn, progress, and succeed in starting and creating the life I wanted to live.

The current severity of financial challenges facing potential college entrants, make the combination of education, opportunity, and success (via hard work) less attainable today. The gulf between the 'haves' and the 'have nots' is ever wider.

Not Far from the Tree

AN INVESTIGATIVE NEWS STORY on TV about a decade ago focused on the degradation and insufficiency of the U.S. education system.

The program included an interview of a mother of a teenager, asking how she felt about her son's long record of poor grades in high school. The reporter asked the mother if she was surprised by her son's latest weak showing.

The mother responded: "I knew that Justin was not in the top half of his class, but I had no idea he was in the bottom half!"

The Champ was No Chump

IT WAS IMPOSSIBLE not to notice and take account of Muhammad Ali (1942-2016). Looking back, he stands out in so many ways beyond being a loud-mouthed boxer. He overcame a lot by working hard and making good choices, excelled in world-class terms at his chosen profession, molded his beliefs and stood his ground on them, and became a hero and role model to millions of young people around the world because of what he achieved and his persona.

As young bankers in Manhattan, a friend and I bought bad, but expensive, tickets to Ali's fight with Joe Frazier at Madison Square Garden in 1971, known as the 'Fight of the Century.' We sat in the top, last row, with our backs to the cinder blocks, seemingly about a mile from the ring. But it was spell binding, with entourages from the boxing world and Harlem, mayor John Lindsay and City bigwigs, and sports and Hollywood figures all making their entrances, in respective costumes, to ringside seats. Whether you were a boxing fan or not, it was a spectacle, led by the 29-year-old kid from Kentucky. Ali lost in a unanimous decision for Frazier, but the spectacle really won that night. That fight remains the only boxing match I have attended. (Ali came back and beat Frazier again three years later, and then regained his world title from George Foreman in Zaire, at the 'Rumble in the Jungle.')

* * *

I ran into Ali twice after that, both times by accident, and each lasting less than two minutes. Sometime in the late 1970s, as a striped-suit-wearing and briefcase-toting management consultant, I was walking up Park Avenue, when I spotted him walking the other way, alone, across the street. I crossed over at the corner and met him head-on, pausing on the sidewalk. Congratulating him on his title, I asked him if he would autograph my quadrille note pad, which was my only half-decent piece of paper. He obliged, shook my hand, and thanked me for recognizing him and being a fan. There were people of three generations, in cities, deserts, and jungles all over the world that would recognize him. In those years, Ali was believed to be the most famous and recognized person in the world.

The second time I (virtually) bumped into him was about a decade later in London. I was living there and was off to a meeting with a client at the Les Ambassadeurs Club just off Hyde Park Corner. As I walked from the front door down a hall from the lobby toward the dining room, there he was, sitting on a small couch waiting for someone. There was nobody else in sight. I stopped briefly, said hello, and shook his hand. Suffering from Parkinson's Disease for years by then, he wasn't very responsive, but his eyes sparkled and communicated, and he smiled, patted my arm and wished me well, as off I went.

But, running into the famous person a couple times isn't why I respect and admire his contributions. He was smart as a whip, worked hard, and took advantage of the opportunity that his sport offered to pull himself up from an urban poor upbringing and make a positive difference. As Cassius Clay and then Muhammad Ali, he excelled, gaining success, fame, riches, and especially freedom and independence to think, do, and talk as he pleased. Whether you like or abhor boxing, it was his ticket and he was the best at it for a good while.

His banter with Howard Cosell and many others—publicly, like a megaphone—was usually witty, often insightful, and always intended to serve a purpose. Whether you think his "I am the greatest!" was pure self-aggrandizing ego, mere showmanship, or psychological positioning, he was pumping up himself and his image. And, after all, for some years he was the greatest.

When he refused to be inducted into the Army on religious grounds in 1966 during the Viet Nam war, he stuck to his opposition, which cost him three years of boxing at the peak of his career. It also cost him dearly in terms of money and image in some quarters. In time, though, even detractors came to respect his bravery and honesty. Whether you believe the validity of his religious and anti-war protestations or not, he defended his position and acted upon it, despite the consequences. One of his most poignant quotes was in response to being classified 1A for the draft in 1966: "I ain't got nothing against them Viet Cong…none of them ever called me 'nigger'!"

* * *

Statements quoted and attributed to Ali were original and concise, even when sometimes childish and blusterous. He never lost his humor or playful approach, even when touching on serious subjects, including lost fights or his severely declining health. His thoughts and words were his own, and he delivered them in character, effectively, and often memorably.

A few of my favorites:

"Get up and fight, sucker!"
(While staring down at first round knockout victim Sonny Liston in 1965.)

*"If you ever dream of beating me,
you'd better wake up and apologize."*

"I'm so fast that last night I turned off the light switch in my hotel room and was in bed before the room was dark."

"The man who views the world at 50 the same as he did at age 20 has wasted 30 years of his life."

"Live every day as if it were your last, because some day you're going to be right."

Draft Averse

MY UPBRINGING always had a strong dose of military history and lore. My father and his twin brother had been officers in WW II (Air Force and Navy, respectively), and they had serious but positive recollections and stories to tell about their service. My uncle had been called up again for a year in Korea. And their father—my grandfather—had been a career Marine Corps officer, losing a leg playing a key role in a pivotal battle in France in World War I, for which he had been put forth for the Medal of Honor. I knew him fairly well from childhood until his death in 1972. So, I was inculcated with notions of duty, service, and the necessity and fog of war.

In March of 1963, upon turning 18, I registered for the Selective Service—the 'draft'—which was a legal requirement. I still have my draft card, which was required to be carried by all males 18 and over.

It was only about a dozen years since the Korean War had ended, Viet Nam loomed as a growing deployment of young American men, and Russia had just attempted to plant missiles in Cuba, 100 miles from Florida. So, the draft was visible and newsworthy at the time, and affected all my friends. However, although they were drafting some boys, the total demand was relatively low, and the target age was something like 22 to 24.

My local draft board was headquartered in the working-class town of Harvey, about 15 miles south of Chicago. Harvey was much larger than the town I lived in, and most of the boys and young men growing up there stayed around. As a result,

that draft board had little trouble meeting its quotas of draftees over the relatively calm years of the late 1950s into the 1960s. And you stayed assigned to your local board for life, no matter where you went.

*　*　*

Off to college I went in the fall of 1963. My roommate and I signed up for Air Force ROTC on campus, but with all the other academic, sports, and social stuff going on and competing for time and attention, we both dropped out the next spring. Although the Viet Nam conflict was escalating and thought to be unjustified or worse by most people on most campuses, we left ROTC primarily out of boredom and lack of relevance, rather than as a protest of any kind.

JFK was assassinated in November of 1963, and Viet Nam continued to escalate during the ensuing years, requiring deeper and deeper dips into the national draft pool. For the first three years, draft-aged boys were exempted if they were in a full-time college or graduate school program. Then, however, when the supply began running short, a nationwide test was devised and given to all registrants who were in school. Those scoring 80 or above remained off the eligible draft rolls during graduate school, while those scoring 79 or less were defined as nonexempt. In the spring of 1966, I took the test with a large room full of other Brown boys in the psychology building on campus, scored an 83, and breathed easier again.

Only two weeks after graduating in June of 1967, I began an MBA course at Columbia Business School in New York City. They had a trimester schedule, with a full semester during the summer. As a result, I could remain a full-time student through that summer—and continue to duck the draft. I attended three semesters of the program's four back-to-back in the summer and fall of 1967 and the spring of 1968, and then spent the summer of

'68 working at a New York bank to make some money and take a break prior to my last semester that fall. This plan worked well, as LBJ abolished deferments for graduate studies late that year.

* * *

Although my draft board back in Harvey would contact me once or twice a year to reconfirm my status, I remained immune as I graduated with my MBA and started at my first real job at Chemical Bank in January 1969. They left me pretty much alone, evidently with enough others in their pool to meet their quota.

However, the Nixon administration decided that school status and test results were criteria tainted with elitism and replaced the prior system with a lottery, that would determine the sequence for drafting individuals from the pool. It went according to your birth date in whatever year you were born, and March 17 was drawn 33rd. This was not good for me, being in the first 10%, even though they aimed at 19-year-olds first. So, early in 1970, I received a notice to take my qualifying physical examination.

Each time I received a notice from the draft board, I would delay in responding as long as I could, then protest or ask a question back, which would keep the correspondence going for weeks and months. So, I was able to delay the physical for a while.

Many of my friends from high school and college had had some affliction or other which exempted them from the draft—that is, deemed them 4-F, which meant they were released forever. The most prevalent reason was having asthma as a child. If you took adrenaline or similar medication for the asthma, that did it, you were out. But, fortunately in all other ways, but unfortunately from a draft eligibility point of view, I knew I was fit. And, I had never been arrested.

My examination was eventually scheduled early in 1970, at Whitehall Street, a government building in lower Manhattan captured accurately and forever in Arlo Guthrie's song *Alice's Restaurant*. I 'spread them' and passed the physical, and, for the first time, foresaw getting a formal draft notice—famously starting with the salutation "Greetings."

* * *

I attempted to join both the New York National Guard, and also an Officers Candidate School, but was unable to gain quick admission, although I can't recall the timing and specific reasons.

In the fall of 1970, the Nixon Administration added a regulation prohibiting draft boards from drafting any man who had reached his 26th birthday. But I had months to go.

A colleague at Chemical Bank suggested I contact Jeremiah Gutman, a civil rights lawyer who at the time was specializing in dealing with draft boards, among his many other anti-war activities. Although he charged $1,000 (my salary was then $13,000 a year), I agreed to have him help me, and we added to the stalling tactic by appealing for a deferment on some conscientious objector grounds. (Having seen combat and received a Purple Heart in WWII, Gutman was a founder of the New York Civil Liberties Union, and his clients over the years included Abbie Hoffman, Jerry Rubin, the Hare Krishnas, and the Rev. Sun Myung Moon.) Jerry drafted appeal letters for me, and as long as they did not say anything with which I didn't agree, I signed and sent them to my draft board. It took only two of those letters to extend the back and forth process into 1971.

Although the draft board rejected whatever I was arguing by a 3—0 vote, they could not send me an order to report for induction until March 22nd, at the earliest. Because I turned 26 five days before that, I never heard from them again. I had run out of process and deferments, but the Nixon Administration's new regulation had saved me.

* * *

Despite nearly four years of worry, I was fortunate to be able to get my MBA, start my career, and get married during that time, and then to be freed from serving in a war that was probably a mistake and heading for a bad ending. My father was OK with it all, encouraging me to follow my conscience and the law. Although pangs of guilt have come and gone sporadically over the decades since, I would do it again in those circumstances in those times. Whenever I visit the Viet Nam War Memorial in Washington, the travesty of all those names slaps me around a bit and makes me angry again.

Blind Faith is Redundant

MY PARENTS were church regulars, Sunday school was interesting, and I have marveled at some fabulous religious edifices and sanctuaries around the world, but I've never gone for the faith part.

With religion such a visible and prevalent part of human history and today's world, but with it not playing a central role in my life, I feel guilty that I don't feel guilty about it. As Ron Reagan declares in a TV ad for an atheist society, "I'm not afraid of burning in hell"—but maybe I should be.

I'm not anti-church, anti-god, or anti-faith. In fact, 'some of my best friends are religious,' which I respect and, in a way, admire. And, I see great value for individuals able to rely on and be guided by faith in a god, the Bible, Torah, or Quran, and church preachings. They can be a source of hope, a perceptibly impartial or divine authority, and a source of perspective and guidance. I just do not understand how folks attain faith in a divine creator, supreme being, redeemer, an afterlife, and the like.

Appendix 1 lays out my thinking, notions, and rationale about religion and supernatural powers. Subjects discussed include religion's role in society, the central question "is there a god?", the conundrum that "faith is at the core," the issue of predestination versus free will, and the struggle of faith versus science, hope, and luck. To summarize my conclusions:

Although I—and everyone—cannot factually answer the question "Who or what created the universe?" or "Who created Nature?", I believe there is not a god as many religions define it. However, I fully subscribe to many of the teachings and norms of behavior held by many religions and their scriptures, and I try to live by them. I am unhappy and feel guilty when I don't abide by or follow through on those tenets and am dedicated to doing better. More specifically:

- The adoption of faith and practice of religion have proven valuable to society to assuage individual insecurities, fears, and other psychological needs that affect most of the world's population in one way or another.

- The advent and development of faith-based religion—"the church"—has emanated partially as a means and institution for building and exerting power and governance over peoples and their societies.

- Perhaps the cumulative value of faith at the individual level over the centuries, is greater than the wars, suffering, and lives lost in the name of god; perhaps not.

- To the extent that church teachings have reinforced constructive and non-selfish morals, ethics, and behavior, religion has been positive and helpful in that way too.

- Non-scientific and physically unprovable faith is required to believe in god and his/her divine powers, in predestination, or in an afterlife or reincarnation. It is an interesting issue as to whether such faith can be taught, and how it is otherwise acquired.

• From a risk management perspective, I try to act non-selfishly, morally, and ethically, but with a presumption that there is no god or, if there is, that the outcomes of my life are not in god's hands, but my own. After all, it's not the "fear of god," but actually the fear of bad outcomes.

A Simple Sense of Risk

IN 1982, the World War II aircraft carrier *Intrepid* was established as a museum at a pier on New York City's Hudson River at 46th Street. The museum has grown to include dozens of military planes on *Intrepid*'s 800-foot-long flight deck, along with other explorable ships including a Concorde, submarine, and Space Shuttle.

When I first visited the ship with my 10-year old son in the late 1980s, the flight deck was unobstructed, but there were a variety of WWII bombers and fighters on the hanger deck below. Walking around them and reading the good signage, the refurbished bombers (especially a B-25, a SB2C Helldiver, and some others, if I recall), were noteworthy with their images of bombs on the front fuselage. Each painted bomb signifies a bombing mission flown by that plane, and some had more than two dozen.

The 1995-6 Chicago Bulls had the best season record in NBA history, with 72 wins and only 10 losses—an 87.8 winning percentage. And the Chicago Bears in 1985 won all but one game out of 16, for a 93.8 winning percentage. In baseball, the best season winning percentage in the last 100 years was 72.1% by the Cleveland Indians in 1954.

I keep reflecting on such win-loss ratios, the real probabilities involved in a succession of events or attempts, and the risk of bombing missions losing their planes and entire flight crews on any given sortie.

Every plane that I saw on the *Intrepid*'s hanger deck—and all the planes that now crowd the flight deck—has a win record of 100%. If they were shot down or otherwise destroyed, even once, they are not there. An image of 27 bombs on a fuselage means a record of 27-0 for that plane and crew.

Mass Joy—Admiration, Just Short of Envy

THERE ARE MANY QUALITIES and abilities I see in others that I respect and admire, some of which are relevant to me, and that I try to emulate and build on in my own life. I am impressed and happy to see people who do something nearly unimaginably well. This can be almost anything—for example, accomplishing a great deal despite physical or personal tragedies, making the perfect ice cream or lobster bisque, designing the perfect house, or continually breaking par at golf.

The ability to bring joy and happiness to others weighs heavily in building my admiration. As a result, popular musicians are hard to beat in terms of their impact and 'conveyance of joy' to millions of fans, especially at live concerts.

Although personalities, cool behavior, and marketing and promotion play their roles, basically it's the music. And no matter how many records, tapes, disks, or streams an artist or group has or has not sold, most fans continue to seek to attend live performances. The electricity and unbridled anticipation, and then the real-time enthusiasm, is palpable at venues ranging from a small club with a hundred chairs, to a 100,000-person crowd on a park lawn.

A few first-hand examples for me:

- At the first Eagles concert I attended—in a sold-out Earl's Court in London in 2000, even the 60-year-old maroon-uniformed British ushers knew every word of every song. (The Eagles billed it as their 'First Farewell Tour', and Joe Walsh said he couldn't really remember the 1980s.) My most recent Eagles concert was in 2019, with 16,000 people of all ages at the MGM Grand Garden Arena in Las Vegas. The seat price was in the neighborhood of $150, and most of the crowd had flown in for the three-hour-plus non-stop concert. I saw them at Madison Square Garden in between.

- The Rolling Stones have also popped into my life several times: the first in an old movie theatre in Providence, Rhode Island, in 1965, where my seventh-row seat was $4, and Brian Jones was very much alive. Further exposure and mirth occurred at a filled New Jersey football stadium, and then especially at a small outdoor park in Hong Kong overlooking Hong Kong harbor.

• I never did see Elvis live, and I only saw the Beatles live once, on one of their early trips to the U.S., at the Comiskey Park ballpark, probably in 1964. (A mother and young daughter had the seats directly in front of me and had brought a pair of binoculars to inspect the band that was on a stage over the pitcher's mound. The mother became enthralled and never stopped peering through the binoculars over the hour and a half concert, despite the daughter constantly tugging at her and begging for a turn at the close-up view.)

There are many other artists that only their touring schedules and my proximity have kept me from repeat visits, including John Fogarty, Elton John, Levon Helm, Darlene Love, Van Morrison, Rod Stewart, Roy Orbison, and Bob Dylan. Many others are gone or nearly gone, but there are younger, newer riveting artists who will be performing for years to come, for the enjoyment of millions.

Although the legendary 1969 Woodstock concert gets the most press, the original Live Aid concert in July 1969 at Wembley Stadium is, to me, the pinnacle or apex of genuine happiness generated for each person in a crowd of 72,000 live, and 1.5 billion simultaneously around the world.

A slew of recent documentaries portrays the origins of some of these long-playing artists, as well as that spontaneous, over-the-top appreciation of live audiences. Hopefully, these will keep coming as the generations of top artists get longer in the tooth and disappear.

My point here is admiration for the impact and value of these performers and their music in making literally millions of people happy by doing what they do. For the musicians, the crowd reaction and feedback is real time and in person, which has to be satisfying, no matter how repetitive the tour and how many times they must sing the falsetto ending to *Take it To the Limit*.

The performed music continues to enhance so many people's lives. The same might be said for star athletes and their teams, but that is a competitive world, and in music there are no losers.

Especially in the current era of streamed, pirated, and low- or no-cost music available to everyone 24/7, live concert gigs are unlikely to diminish. For many artists, concerts will remain the norm.

If there were reincarnation, and I could come back as a rock star, I'd take it.

I Remained Calm and Cool…and Collected

I DON'T KNOW WHY I started collecting things I liked but didn't need. Practical value never entered into it, and I like a great many more things in this world beyond what I've chosen to collect.

By 'collecting,' I mean seeking, acquiring, and nearly coveting items I find. They tend to be attractive; of wide variation but individually unique; meticulously made; often of multiple materials, colors and textures; and usually of daily use by some people. I like to think of them as 'decorative,' but that is in the eyes of the beholder. Artistic interest of some sort plays a role in deciding what to collect, which individual items I value the most, and perhaps when to move on and begin collecting something else.

Although I have progressed from one collection to starting a new one many times over the decades, I don't seem to lose interest in or devalue the older ones, even long after the acquisitive verve has subsided. Walking in on, or looking over, a decades-old collection at any time is still a bit of a thrill, and I find myself loving the items and glad to have them.

NOT NOSTALGIA | Nostalgia has not been the point of my collecting, since some objects were never used prominently in my lifetime or around me (e.g., oil lamps and snuff bottles), and others that were all around me were not considered interesting until they struck my fancy (e.g., ice cream scoops and cocktail shakers).

But 'vintage' has been a central theme, as the passage of time has created wide varieties of items, often with superb designs and craftsmanship of past decades and centuries. Vintage, to me, is the notion of "they don't make them like that anymore," rather than connoting old, or used, or memories.

NOT FINANCIAL INVESTMENTS | Price and monetary (or 'investment') value has never been an objective or important criterion for selecting what to collect, or which items to go for or pass up. In fact, as I've gone from no bank account as a boy, to comfortable living in recent decades, what to collect and my 'standards' for selecting individual items have been little affected by item prices.

I have only collected things that are generally inexpensive. With that said, the number of items among the various collections may have been influenced more by affordability. In almost all my collections, some of the most iconic, rarest, and highest-priced items are absent. So, I guess price has indeed limited the extent and comprehensiveness of the collections to some degree.

IDEALLY DISPLAYED | Display has always been a conundrum. On the one hand, I want to be awash in my attractive, interesting, and comforting collections, as I move around my home. But, on the other hand, there is only so much shelf and table space, and some of the collections have more pieces than could ever reasonably be displayed. As wall space is the limiting factor for a serious art collector, so shelf space is mine. Despite hundreds of linear feet of shelf and display case space in two homes, we are more than full, and several of the collections are crammed tightly together, reducing ideal spacing in favor of having more of them to see. In the last few years, I got rid of about 400 books in both homes, to free up space for 'other things.'

My desire for displaying is so that I can see them, and not so that others will. I am indifferent if nobody else sees or likes them.

Only a few collections—stamps and coins, for instance—do not lend themselves to open display and are unavoidably relegated to drawers. The small batch of guns is kept locked up and out of sight, for obvious reasons. And, a recent trove of vintage ice cream scoops will require some creativity to devise a way to display them well, as will a growing inventory of vintage soft-sided leather briefcases.

BEYOND UTILITY | Very few fit the bill for usefulness. I don't paint, I don't use snuff, and I don't need oil lamps. I don't recall ever using a piggy bank as a kid, and I make coffee in a modern maker. I don't shake mixed drinks, and I haven't had a model railroad layout since high school. I prefer beer in glasses or bottles, and always default to a single favorite modern ice cream scoop. I use a briefcase or satchel only when travelling, after carrying one every day and everywhere for nearly 40 years 'for business,' before retiring a dozen years ago.

I do use a handy opera glass occasionally to gaze at nearby Colorado mountains but tend to use the same one each time. And, I use a single, proper pickle fork (that is, 19th Century silver and bone-handled) to retrieve cornichons from their acidic jar. But, all in all, I have not collected anything with using it in mind.

That said, I am not averse to using anything in my collections. Just as I would never own a car that I would not be willing to drive, I would drink beer from any of my vintage steins if I wanted a lidded, quarter-liter vessel to do so.

WHAT BRINGS IT ON? | But, then, why do I collect? We lived in a fairly rural suburban development from the time I was five years old, and I could catch turtles from swampy areas nearby. I kept them a while, fed them, then let them go. There once were 11 of them living in a couple of home-made cages in the basement. They varied in size from about two to 10 inches and included painted, blanding, box, and an occasional (small) snapping species. I never considered this 'collecting,' but maybe it's a tip that I liked to have more—and a variety—of things I enjoyed.

Starting in the 1950s, family vacation trips often produced felt pennants from the places we visited (e.g., Knott's Berry Farm, Niagara Falls, Washington, D.C., Navy Pier). By high school, I had maybe 10 or 15, and I once helped decorate a school dance room with them. Afterwards, I waited so long to take them back, that a janitor threw them all away. It is only in retrospect that I consider that a collection, and probably only because I lost them all at once.

My father and his twin brother collected stamps and coins since they were boys, from around 1930. And, dad hunted and had a few relic guns from World War II, so those collections were a part of him as I grew up.

In high school, a close friend and I began to collect coins on our own, when you could still find old Lincoln and zinc pennies and other old coins in your change. We bought blue Whitman paper folders and tried to fill them with the coins from each year. Looking for missing coins, trading them, finding some at dealers and an occasional trade show, kept us interested. We eventually had all the Lincoln cent issues to date—each year, and from each of the Philadelphia, Denver, and San Francisco mints—except for the '5 keys' which were extremely rare stampings and way too expensive to buy.

This was my first episode of collecting, and my friend and neighbor and I were pretty active at it for several years. To scale up our mining for missing and valuable pennies from dribbling pocket change, we would scrape together $50 and buy a bag of pennies at the teller window of the local bank. The 'bag' consisted of 100 roles of 50 pennies each and was quite heavy—about 30 pounds. At home with the bag, we dumped the contents on a bed and split the roles between us. We would carefully unfold the end of each roll, slide its contents out onto the bed, flip through each penny seeking our targeted rarities. If we found none of interest—which was usual—we slid the 50 coins back into the paper roll, twisted shut the end, and put it back in the bag. When we found a keeper, we would remove it from the others, replace it with another penny, and refill the role. As a hand-eye coordination activity, we got pretty good at this process, and could go through a bag in an afternoon. I recall some quizzical glances from the bank tellers, as we returned the bag, intact, the following day. We could only use the bag approach for pennies, since bags of nickels, dimes, and quarters required fronting hundreds of dollars—out of the question.

The coins remain a fascination since I ceased adding to them half a century ago, and they are stored in drawers and a safe deposit box. Although I inherited and integrated my father's coin collection when he passed on, mine was better!

I never really collected stamps, but my dad kept that up his whole life, and I have his quite extensive, and in parts beautiful, store of sheets, first day covers, etc.—but, again, in drawers. Same with a few rifles, shotguns, and pistols that he had, and with which we hunted and target shot long ago. My sons and I did the same when they were young, in upstate New York and Texas.

COMMON THREADS | My collections are pretty narrowly defined, and the objects of interest are mostly intricate and small. Part of the narrowness is an effort—subconscious at first, but explicit as time went by—to limit the flood of purchases that could result from an unbridled search. A few of the subjects are narrow by nature. For example, the advent of porcelain electric coffee pots in the early 20th Century had a variety of manufacturers, shapes, and designs. Yet that universe was actually quite limited, as porcelain quickly gave way to metals and plastics that were much less breakable. As a result, limiting my focus to the more interesting porcelain lines—and ignoring porcelain waffle irons and toasters—greatly reduced my targets and accumulation. I have 11, and they are wonderful.

The emphasis on smallness may have been accentuated by an admiration for fine, detailed things. Living and travelling around England for eight years in the 1980s and late 1990s lured me to myriad Victorian artisan items, artfully designed and meticulously made. Examples ranged from apple peelers, to fish and pickle forks, to toast racks, to gold coin scales and chimney sweep brushes—most of which I resisted collecting. The materials, time, and effort that French and British craftsmen put into small opera glasses was incredible, producing fine pieces of both beauty and practical use.

SEARCHING AND LEARNING | Essential to the dedication and excitement of collecting is the search and chase, once a new interest or an initial item raises my eyebrow. Not only does the ensuing chase allow me to find and accumulate the items themselves, but the process reveals the history and nuanced variety in the particular category. Invariably, I acquire an initial 'specimen' at a store, market, or somewhere else, and notice if there are others like it that are as interesting and fine—perhaps even more so than the one in hand. The pursuit includes canvassing thrift and consignment shops, antique stores, and flea markets.

In recent years, eBay and other online markets have, of course, transformed the chase. The instantly available breadth and depth of vintage things now lets me search for and examine anything I want and allows me to compare the attractiveness and price of what I have in mind or want to learn about. It's as if walking through a vast museum or souk, as I see the range and variety of what's available, and refine my 'taste' for which versions, designs, colors, and conditions I want to add to a collection.

BEYOND COLLECTIONS | There are many things that I own and relish for many of the same reasons, but which I do not want to collect. For example, again citing super-crafted items of past decades and centuries, English silver utensils, Italian (Deruta and other) porcelain vessels, Chinese bamboo headrests/pillows, unique silver napkin rings, novel pepper mills, and many other things are attractive and interesting to me but have not sparked a drive to collect them. And, there are motorcycles, cars, aircraft, boats, jewelry, artwork and other fascinating but larger and more expensive categories, that are excluded by virtue of price or impracticality. I love my 150-year-old silver pickle fork, a superb English set of fish knives and forks, and my 23-year-old German sports car, but have no particular desire to have more of them.

The line between collecting and not collecting is difficult to draw, and the rationale for wanting to amass more of one item, and none or one of most others, is even more elusive. Money and space are two powerful limits, but that still leaves thousands of other, eligible items as collectible candidates. Thank goodness.

DISPOSITION? | I have never gotten rid of a collection but am reaching the point with a few of them that I would be happy to have someone else enjoy them, rather than continue to keep them and hope that my two sons will be interested. Perhaps from laziness and partially due to digital-selling ineptitude, I will probably leave them to my sons, with the suggestion that they—not I—post them on eBay or otherwise find relatively scarce aficionados on whom to unload the many items. That assumes, of course, that neither son becomes sufficiently interested in the stuff to hold onto and enjoy it.

Appendix 2 contains a list of my main collections, which the medical profession would no doubt call 'symptoms.'

"I should have bought more crap."

"Travel is the sherbet between courses of reality."

Travel & Traveling

The place and role of traveling in one's life—at least for me—go far beyond the list of places encountered and visited.

Travel usually starts with some knowledge, preconceptions, and/or expectations about places and their peoples before visiting them in person. So much is written and available on-line about most everywhere, including extensive guided-tour videos.

But first-hand visits can't be beat for employing all the senses, absorbing it all, and experiencing the unexpected. Taking a wrong turn, or even getting lost, in places as far flung as Dublin, Diriyah, Anchorage, or Luang Prabang, often proves better than not taking that wrong turn.

And then there is the process of traveling: Deciding where, when, and how to go; taking the trip; and dealing with the people from start to finish. All of that—and the inevitable changes, problems, and inconveniences that pop up—adds to the mosaic that life-long travel creates for each of us.

This section comprises a small portfolio of experiences, touching not only on some of the places visited, but also on aspects of traveling, including a missed flight, airplanes and boats, visas, airports, and high latitudes.

College Trips

THE PRINCE | As in all four of my college years, I spent 1966's spring vacation in Palm Beach, flying down and driving my aunt's car back to the northeast a week later. Toward the end of my stay in that, my junior year, I bought a foot-long caiman (read 'alligator') as a gift for my girlfriend Paula who had gone somewhere else for that spring break. The animal fit perfectly in a shoebox, and although it had little appetite, I got a glass rod and appropriate dry food to keep it nourished, even if by gentle force. And, there was no problem keeping it warm.

The drive north to Pennsylvania was uneventful—I merely had an extra shoebox. And, the same on the bus back to Brown in Providence. Upon my return, I presented the living present to Paula, who named it Machiavelli, reflecting her current semester's studies.

With less than six weeks to go before the summer, however, the issue soon arose as to how she would get the creature home to Dayton, Ohio. It turned out not to be a problem, and she took it on the plane with her. The gate baggage check was not rigorous, and the necessary air holes in the box were cut on the sides up under the top so as not to be noticeable.

They both made it to the Dayton house, and on a visit that summer, I noted it was still alive and at home in an old bathtub in a basement room.

A RAY AWRY | Before its 'Renaissance' beginning in the 1960s, Providence, Rhode Island, was sometimes called the 'armpit of the country.' Although that name was applied to other old and unattractive cities as well, the label had special relevance to Providence, because the outstretched arm of Cape Cod from the south shore of Massachusetts and Buzzards Bay does, indeed, place Providence at its armpit.

Proximity to the Cape was an important attraction for us at Brown, especially during the school year, which for the most part found the Cape a long, desolate and deserted series of sand bars and summer villages. It was refreshing and actually seemed wild during the winter, and we explored it all we could.

One weekend, Paula and I drove fairly far out past Chatham and the 'elbow' to Nauset Beach to see remnants of one of the early transatlantic cables that exited the shore on its way to Europe. We stayed the night at one of the few small motels that were open out there, that time of year.

On Sunday morning, walking along the empty beach, we came upon a stingray that had washed up out of the water. It was approximately round—about three feet in diameter. With the tide now far below it and receding, it was immobile, but appeared slightly alive. We decided to take it with us, of course, and using some small boards and maybe a tarp of some kind dragged it to the car and lifted it into the trunk.

When we arrived back on campus late in the day, and adopting the myth that with any kind of water, it might live a bit longer, I put it on the floor of the tiled double shower stall in the men's bathroom, right across the hall from my room in the fraternity house. Covering the drain, it sat in about four inches of water. Although it probably was dead already, it remained there a couple days, until I boxed it up and disposed of it. I was the only one to use the shower those few days—everyone else went to the floor above and used those showers.

THE GLOVE'S LITTLE FINGER | In 1966, I visited girlfriend Paula's home that her family rented on the shore of Glen Lake in northern Michigan in the town of Glen Arbor. They rented the house each summer, and it was a delightfully low-key resort area, with swimming, dune climbing, and boating of all kinds. Glen Lake had been named one of America's most beautiful lakes by *National Geographic* or a similar 'authority.' Lake Michigan was less than a mile away, as was the Sleeping Bear Dunes National Park. The cottages and houses in the surrounding small towns were filled with summer residents from Chicago, Detroit, and other parts of Michigan and northern Ohio.

In later years, Paula's dad purchased a house nearby—also on Glen Lake. And, in 1998, Paula and her siblings inherited it. It was unheated and not insulated, but had its own beach, dock, bevy of boats, guest house, and garage. It could sleep upwards of a dozen people. The four siblings divvied up the summer into two-week slots, and each family agreeably used the house at the appointed times for about 15 years. Our slot was the week before and the week after Labor Day, which was ideal in that many folks had departed as the school year began prior to Labor Day, and the weather and water were still relatively warm as the summer was starting to wind down.

Leelanau County and northern Michigan is a sandy, hilly landscape, with many small lakes and adjoining Lake Michigan, with small villages and old farms scattered throughout. Vineyards now cover significant acreage. It is also not easy or convenient to get to, being, for example, 280 miles from Detroit. This remoteness, of course, has been essential to preserving the rural and non-citification of the area. Although our set up there was superb and we made some close, lasting friends over more than a decade, we were unsuccessful in convincing our sons or any of our close friends from elsewhere to visit the house. "Why don't you come visit us this summer—it's so delightful and there's so much to do?" drew blank stares at the mention of "northern Michigan." Their loss.

Although a very different setting, with different people, activities, and pastimes than other northern latitudes in the world, our time in northern Michigan was a five-star taste of the North Country.

NEAR MISS | In early August 1967, I was off to my last final exam of my first term at the Columbia Business School in New York. I was preparing to hitchhike to visit my girlfriend Paula in Dayton, Ohio, to begin the few weeks of summer downtime.

To save time and get on the road immediately after the exam, I planned to hit the road directly by taking the subway north and then begin my journey on the interstate highways to western Ohio. In my apartment on West 120th Street, I packed a small bag and took it with me to the mid-day test in a building on campus adjacent to the subway entrance at 116th Street and Broadway.

Finishing the exam, I took the Number 1 train up to the George Washington Bridge stop and stuck my thumb out on the approach to Interstate 95 and the bridge. The weather was fine, and despite the somewhat complicated route and rides to reach the Pennsylvania Turnpike, I was on my way for the long ride through New Jersey, Pennsylvania, and Ohio.

The Turnpike and I-70 took me most of the night—with two rides and a lengthy wait in between. Not long after dawn, I got a ride from the exit at Vandalia, Ohio, straight south to Dayton. I took a still-early-morning bus just a few miles down Far Hills Avenue, shared with a half dozen domestic workers heading to their jobs at homes in the leafy, upmarket neighborhood of Oakwood.

Walking the last bit to the house on Oakwood Avenue, I let myself in the front door and curled up on the couch in the comfortable wood-paneled 'library' to grab a little sleep and wait for the family to wake up.

Paula's father was the first up and greeted me pleasantly. He was glad that I had had a successful and uneventful trip. Then he mentioned that he too had been in New York the day before on company business and had called me a couple times at my apartment to see if I wanted to ride back to Dayton with him on the company jet. The flight took a little over two hours.

After more than half a century, I still wish he hadn't told me.

Germination of Wanderlust

PAULA, my college girlfriend, went to Italy late in 1967 to work at a paper company in the Lombardy region not far from Milan. I was hard at work at Columbia Business School in New York, having started there two weeks after graduating from college that June. She invited me over for a visit between semesters in late January 1968. Unlike many of my college mates, I had not been out of the US, beyond travelling through Ontario, Canada, so I was quite game to go.

I borrowed money from my hometown bank for the next semester's tuition and the plane fare and flew out from JFK on Alitalia. The round trip ticket was $379, and the DC-8 was nearly empty, allowing me to spread out across three outside seats and get a semblance of sleep on the overnight flight. I had done no preparation for the trip, other than look at an Italian language primer a few times.

After a few hours of sleep, I woke up, pushed up the plastic window shade and looked out, as it was morning wherever we were. All I could see below was bright green. Digging out a route map from the seat pocket in front of me, my suspicion proved correct—it was Ireland through a clear sky and solid green from tip to tip. Crossing the Irish Sea, we 'entered' England, still very rural, but not as green or distinct. Passing north and out of sight of London, we approached the east coast and there appeared a stark white strip right along the waterline. Again, feeling ignorant about the specific topography, it was evident even to me that those were indeed the Dover Cliffs.

We crossed the English Channel, but despite only a 70-mile crossing over the water, no land was visible on the other side, because we flew above a giant cloud bank covering the entire Continent. A while later, we passed slightly to the south of a handful of snow-covered mountain peaks poking out from the cloud cover, and I was able to locate a few of them on the crude map I had. The closest was Mont Blanc. We were descending then, and eventually emerged below the clouds not far above the Milan runway where we landed, pretty much on time. We evidently were lucky to be able to land in the early winter morning fog.

Paula and her boss's chauffeur, Romano, picked me up in his Lancia and drove the hour or so, beyond the small city of Bergamo to the much smaller town of Alzano Lombardo. The town is in the foothills of the Alps—the land was flat looking south but rose steeply up looking north. Paula was staying with an Italian family—the paper plant's chief engineer—and I was put up in a room above a bar and restaurant nearby. The first night, the non-English-speaking folks from the bar came up to my room late, knocking hard at the door. They seemingly were asking me what was wrong, and I discovered that I was sleeping on top of a button that called them with an alarm buzzer down at the bar.

"Here's your salad, sir, with a little Italian dressing on the side."

FAMILY, FRIENDS, AND PERSONAL | 71

I ate a bunch of dinners at Paula's 'family' home, where the older teenage son was the only English speaker in the family. My first night there I had seconds of the excellent creamy pasta dish, only to find out that it was only the first course, with two more coming up. After dinner, we watched TV, which included a long siege of consecutive commercials all bunched together for the evening. I had my introduction to grappa (Italian for kerosene) there.

In almost three weeks with Alzano as the base, Paula and I drove her Volkswagen Variant on trips exploring Bergamo, Milan, Florence, Venice, Rome, and Lugano, Switzerland. Even now, I am speechless to describe the eye-openings, discoveries, people, places, and things I encountered and absorbed on that trip.

Some 10 months later, Paula stopped briefly in New York on her way to visit her parents in Ohio for Christmas, and we had dinner. I was about to finish graduate school and begin my banking career, and she was about to stay in Italy. After that, we didn't see each other—or know where the other was—for 22 years. (She had gone back to Italy for another six years, then settled in Chicago.)

But that trip hooked me into a life—professional and personal—of virtually constant travel and a search for new things and people. Professionally, travel and location were not specific objectives, but, looking back, a lack of travel and new places would have been a lifelong detriment.

* * *

In the 1990s, Paula—now my wife—and I dropped by Alzano and had dinner at the restaurant where I had stayed upstairs some 30 years before. After explaining our earlier history to our waiter, he said that Paula's former boss and his wife were eating in a private dining room on the floor above, and we spent an extremely coincidental visit with them.

SETTLING INTO NEW YORK

GRADUATING FROM COLUMBIA and starting my full-time job at Chemical Bank in January of 1969, I moved from the Upper West Side to a second-floor studio apartment at 25 West 13th Street, in Greenwich Village. It was my first home alone and cost $280 per month. With my first paycheck, I bought a hide-a-bed couch and a Sony color TV. The West Village in the 1960s and 70s was a great place, and over the decades since, I have had feelings of regret about leaving it. Washington Square was completely open and much less formal and manicured than today. Small clubs and bars were everywhere and affordable. And the real population of the Village—once the cruising suburban visitors had gone home—was relatively limited, because there were so few buildings more than five stories tall.

In late 1969, Suzanne Keys Thompson, a young journalist from Amarillo, Texas, and via SMU, who had joined Chemical Bank's public relations department, interviewed a few of the new MBA's for an article in the bank's house newspaper, me included. We were married in August of 1970, and Suzanne

Suzanne Keys Thompson

eventually moved on to serious public relations jobs at Mutual Insurance Company of New York, and then at Mobil Oil.

We moved into a third-floor walk-up one-bedroom apartment on East 29th Street, just west of Park Avenue. The building was owned by a mature, large Italian lady who ran the restaurant on the ground floor. Her husband had died prior to our moving in, and she had gone back to Italy and imported another—Gaetano Fede, I believe.

For several years, Suzanne and I developed a close-knit group of city friends; explored all aspects of New York; went to beaches, mountains, and other cities on many weekend jaunts; and began taking two- or even three-week vacations overseas, largely to western Europe but also to Yugoslavia and other places further afield.

Each year, we would visit my in-laws in Amarillo, a highlight of which was quail hunting with Suzanne's father and usually a dog or two. Having grown up in the Midwest, I was used to flat terrain, but nothing like around Amarillo. The tallest building in town—I believe it was twelve stories—could be seen from more than ten miles out of town. Nearby Palo Duro Canyon was a special place and introduced me to Audad Sheep, which were weirdly named and tough to spot. Prairie dog towns were also a phenomenon I had only known about in cartoons.

In the spring of 1973, I changed jobs, moving from Chemical Bank in the Wall Street area of lower Manhattan, to McKinsey & Company with offices at 46th Street and Park Avenue.

So, I had the luxury of walking to work from our apartment at 29th and Park, 17 blocks straight north. This commute lasted only a few months, as we purchased our first house, the top two floors of a brownstone on West 93rd Street, a few doors from Central Park. It was a recent renovation of nine contiguous brownstone buildings that were gutted and combined into thirty-two unique apartments. Ours had four bedrooms, two bathrooms, two powder rooms, and an open living/dining room with a small terrace and roof skylights.

We got to know well many of our neighbors in the building. Betty Friedan (to some the mother of 'women's lib') and Michael Crichton (author of *Andromeda Strain*), had had apartments there but had moved out before we moved in. Later on, the journalist Molly Ivins stayed for a couple years, and Dede Allen was a long-time resident and an award-winning film editor (e.g., *The Hustler, Bonnie and Clyde, Reds,* and *Slap Shot*). She parked a Jeep in the garage across the street with the New York license plate 'SLAPSHOT.'

It was a small, low-key building and atmosphere on a reasonably quiet side street with an entrance to Central Park half a block away.

Travel to the 'Country'

IT SEEMED that all our peers at work and socially had escapes not far from the City—some near the coast, from Massachusetts through Connecticut, Long Island, and New Jersey, and others in the 'country' inland in Connecticut, New York State, New Jersey, and even northeastern Pennsylvania. Many of the escapes were with relatives, but a growing number were second homes. We had no such escape.

But in 1975, we found and bought an 1850 home on twenty-two acres in Dutchess County, New York, about 70 miles due north of the City and about half a mile west of the Connecticut border. Being on a knoll in the woods at the dead end of a one-lane dirt road, it was a respite for 35 years. The first year we had the house, we spent 50 out of the 52 weekends there.

Especially with our sons when they were young, it was a venue for everything from cross country skiing, to ballgames and target shooting, to wood chopping, and there were wild

54 Askins Road, Wingdale, Dutchess County, New York

turkeys, deer, snapping turtles, and bull frogs.

Over the years, the property also provided me a venue for keeping fit, including mowing a big field with a 1952 International Harvester Farmall Cub tractor, taking down extensive fencing the former owner had used to corral his two horses and four goats, and forever chain-sawing trees across the land.

In October of 1977, our son Nicholas was born, and we began the more complicated but attractive life of a real family, two jobs, and a nanny when in the City. Travel in those years became primarily to the country house and surrounding areas, with annual trips to family in Amarillo and Chicago.

Where in the World is Amelia Earhart?

I BECAME MILDLY INTERESTED in Amelia Earhart when I learned that a great aunt of mine had earned a pilot's license in 1931, being one of a very few women flyers of that era.

My first father in law's best friend and long-time business associate, Paul Allingham and his wife, Winney, lived in Atchison, Kansas, in an 1861 Gothic house at the corner of North Terrace and Santa Fe streets, overlooking the Missouri River. The Earhart family had owned the house before Paul and Winney, and Amelia was born and raised in it.

As a young New York banker, covering corporate business in the Midwest in the early 1970s, I found myself in Omaha one week, and arranged to drive down to Atchison and visit the Allinghams for dinner and a sleep over on my way back to New York. It was a pleasant stay, with engaging folks, whom I had not seen for a while.

At least two decades later, as I moved down a crowded airplane aisle after flying to Chicago, a couple in front of me was talking about the endless search for Amelia's aircraft—lost over the Pacific in 1937—and referred to her Midwest roots in Wichita. Interrupting a conversation that I wasn't a part of (as often happens), I said that she actually was from Atchison, not Wichita. "Oh, that's right," they responded agreeably. I couldn't help myself and added: "Yes, I slept in her bedroom, but she wasn't there either."

24-Hour Vacation

IN JUNE OF 1971, I found myself working in London for two weeks on bank business, with a free weekend coming up. Seeing a newspaper ad for a package trip to the upcoming French racing Grand Prix, I decided to go. It was exceedingly cheap and included round-trip flights, 'accommodations' on a luxury motor coach, and general admission to the racetrack grounds.

Since 1928, the race—24 Heures du Mans—was one of the original courses on the international grand prix circuit. The race begins on a Saturday at 3:00 PM, and goes for 24 straight hours, with the winner being the car that goes the farthest in that time, usually about 3,000 miles. Each car has two drivers, who alternate, allowing for some rest, but little sleep.

Leaving Gatwick airport on Saturday morning, I took the one-hour flight to Beauvais, just outside Paris, where the large coach with very cushy reclining seats picked us up and drove the three hours to the track in the small town of Le Mans. Parking in a large lot next to the racecourse, we were able to come and go for the next 24 hours.

Although we general admission fans were some distance from the prime viewing grandstands—and could never even lay eyes on the pits—the eight-and-a-half-mile track provided a great many viewing spots along the straightaways and around the many turns. Food stands provided decent meals whenever you felt like it, and people-watching was the main diversion from the cars rocketing by at up to 210 mph. Zillions of portable toilet stalls, spread around the countryside, were a 'luxury' unexpected in France.

The roar of the cars, spread out into clumps as the hours went by, never seemed to get boring. Perhaps the most thrilling vison I recall was standing and sitting near a sharp curve in the middle of the night, with the oncoming cars careening around the bend with their headlight beams streaming across the fields and directly onto us spectators, as they at first slowed for the turn and then quickly accelerated again near the apex. That combination of sounds and headlights in the dark night was unique.

The team of German Helmut Marko and Dutchman Gijs Van Lennep won the race in a Porsche 917, with an average speed of 132 mph.

Despite the limited sleep in a reclined bus seat, the weekend proved to be unexpectedly exciting and refreshing.

Commuting to Milan?

IN MAY OF 1972, wife Suzanne and I arranged a three-week vacation to Italy and flew over on a special Icelandic Airlines deal. To avoid the prevailing European airfare cartel (called IATA), the destination had to be Luxembourg, and the flight had to stop briefly in the airline's home city of Reykjavik, Iceland. No problem, since we had not been to Luxembourg, and we booked rail tickets from Luxembourg to Milan.

* * *

The overnight flight from JFK was uneventful, and the stop in Reykjavik was about a half hour, with no need to leave the plane. Our early morning arrival in Luxembourg gave us much of the day to wile around the city, as our train was to leave in the late afternoon. After walking around a bit, we ate lunch in a local restaurant, noteworthy for not only having oxtail soup on the menu, but also offering a choice of thin or thick versions. The thick was excellent. Tired of lugging our luggage around, we watched some local movie and dozed a bit.

We punctually made our way to the train station and by the time the train arrived we were on the correct platform and at the spot designated for our car that contained our reserved seats. We were not alone. The platform was so full of people with suitcases, you couldn't see the pavement for the entire length of the station. Most of them seemed to be Italian.

* * *

When the largely empty train pulled in and ground noisily and slowly to a stop, it was bedlam. There was a mob at each door at the end of each car, but most noticeable were the dozens of folks—young and old—throwing their suitcases and other bags and packages through the open windows into the train compartments, before rushing to join the press of people at the doors. A scene not anticipated or seen before or since.

Surprisingly quickly, but after jostling and 'moshing' exceeded only by our trepidation, we boarded, found our cabin with four seats on each side facing the other, stowed our bags in overhead racks or in the already-narrow corridor, and took our seats for the 12-hour plus ride to Milan. The trip was long but uneventful and reasonably on time. But, why was half the population of Luxembourg taking a Friday night train to Milan?

* * *

Unbeknownst to us, it was the time of government elections in Italy. All Italians living abroad were required to return to their home country to vote, and the transportation to do so was paid for them. No wonder virtually everyone on the platform—and everyone we saw on the train—were Italians. Following this unexpected start to our vacation, everywhere we went for the next three weeks seemed uncrowded.

Down East

I FIRST SET FOOT in Maine in the early 1970's with my wife and friends who borrowed a house on an island in Penobscot Bay next to a local lobsterman. There for three or four days, we went out with the neighbor to tend his traps at daybreak, marveled at the ten-foot tides, and chased the lobsters as they jumped loose from the pots of boiling water on the stove. On the drive up, we took pictures of each other in the field that Andrew Wyeth painted as *Christina's World*, and ate at handy restaurants in Camden and Rockland. A quick, memorable first dose of the Maine coast.

When I was growing up, my mother had mentioned that her grandfather had been a sea captain from Maine, but it was not hyped, and there was nothing written about it. I'm not sure my mother had even been to Maine.

* * *

In the years around 1990, and living in New York, our two sons went to summer camps in western Maine—around Sweden, Harrison and Bridgton—and we drove them up and back, usually via Conway, New Hampshire. It was truly north country (at 45° north latitude), what with the plethora of lakes and woods, and the absence of people and even roads.

* * *

As I checked my email in my office in Hong Kong in 2004, a note from what turned out to be my third cousin, introduced me to the world of genealogy regarding the sea captain and his ancestors, all of which centered on central Maine around Bar Harbor and the county of Hancock. This led to more than a decade of serious research on my part, including annual trips up the main coast, tracking down everything from ancestral homes on Deer Isle and Mount Desert Island, to the captain's first home in Ellsworth and all the associated family history. The trips were great, enjoying yet another unique local north country population along a sparsely settled seacoast of generally untouched natural beauty. Although the drive from New York City took me through the states of New York, Connecticut, Rhode Island, and Massachusetts, more than half the distance to Hancock is in Maine.

A Six-Year Trip to London

OUR SECOND SON, Andrew, was born in April 1980, and we moved five weeks later to a temporary apartment

CONTINUED PG. 83

A British/English Rosetta Stone

What the British Say	What the British Mean	What Foreigners Understand
I hear what you say	I disagree and do not want to discuss it further	He accepts my point of view
With the greatest respect	You are an idiot	He is listening to me
That's not bad	That's good	That's poor
That is a very brave proposal	You are insane	He thinks I have courage
Quite good	A bit disappointing	Quite good
I would suggest	Do it or be prepared to justify yourself	Think about the idea, but do what you like
Oh, incidentally/by the way	The primary purpose of our discussion is	That is not very important
I was a bit disappointed that	I am annoyed that	It doesn't really matter
Very interesting	That is clearly nonsense	They are impressed
I'll bear it in mind	I've forgotten it already	They will probably do it
I'm sure it's my fault	It's your fault	Why do they think it was their fault?
You must come for dinner	It's not an invitation, I'm just being polite.	I will get an invitation soon
I almost agree	I don't agree at all.	He's not far from agreeing
I only have a few minor comments	Please rewrite completely	He has found a few typos
Could we consider some other options	I don't like your idea	They have not yet decided

near Wimbledon, and then into a five-story town home at 32 Walpole Street in the Chelsea neighborhood of central London. We rented out both the New York City and Dutchess County homes while we were in England. The London house was ideally located for work, play, and shopping, and having signed on for two years, we lived there for six. Suzanne had secured a transfer to Mobil's European regional public relations office in London.

The boys began attending British schools in London, and with their English schoolmates and local nannies, acquired marked British accents. Late in our stay, when checking out of a Safeway store with the boys talking between themselves, the check-out lady was surprised to hear Suzanne and me with American accents after hearing the boys—British with American parents?

London was ideally located as a hub for travel all over the UK, Europe and beyond. So, as a family, we travelled around the British Isles and most of Europe, including starting off the boys skiing at Meribel in France, sitting at the end of the runways at annual air shows, visiting castles in the Black Forest, climbing up the side of Mount Vesuvius, and many other ventures.

Failed Genealogy

LIVING IN LONDON and travelling at least once a week to cities all over Europe made me understand the utility and efficiency of having universal European Community (EC) passport entrances at airports, where holders were not stopped upon arrival. I, of course, had an American passport. Even after receiving a resident status visa in the U.K. (after one year with a work visa), I had to go through the 'Other Countries' lines at all the airports I visited, jealously watching the vast majority of arriving passengers walking through the 'EC Passports' portal without missing a stride.

TV for the Blind

> This is an annual television license application in the United Kingdom in 1985. The annual fee was 58 British pounds (for Monochrome and Colour), but note that "registered blind persons pay 1.25 pounds less"!

84 | THERE'S A PONY IN HERE SOMEWHERE!

Then I saw an article mentioning a long-standing British law that allowed a U.K. resident to qualify for an EC-wide visa if his father or grandfather had been born in Britain. Yes, only males were eligible, and only if father or grandfather—not mother or grandmother—were British-born. And with that visa, I would get a passport cover that would allow me to walk through the EC door.

Wow, I knew my great-grandfather had indeed been born and lived in Yorkshire before emigrating to the U.S., but I was not sure in which country his son, my grandfather, had been born. So, I hurriedly tapped all the family's sources to find out, since it meant tens of minutes each time I came or went through an airport.

Alas, no dice. My grandfather was in fact born in Wilkes-Barre, Pennsylvania, about nine years after his father came to America. Just in case, I made sure great-grandfathers were not sufficient, and the denial held.

Thereafter, naturally, the longer the lines for me, the more I suffered the one extra generation.

Petra

IN THE 1980S, while living in London, I made 35 business trips to Saudi Arabia, plus quite a few more to Bahrain, Kuwait, and Cyprus. It was a 4,000-mile six-hour flight to Jeddah, usually on British Airways but sometimes on Saudia Airlines. (Unfortunately, frequent flier mileage programs did not yet exist, but Saudia had uncensored Rambo movies.) They were easy, comfortable flights in Business Class, and the mid-afternoon flight from London got me into Jeddah about midnight. The Sheraton where I stayed had a 24-hour cafeteria-style dining room, where I learned to feast on moutabal (baba ghanoush, but without the tomato, pomegranate and herbs), humus, and fried kibbeh. The grand buffet also had an unattended ice cream bar with a hot fudge dispenser. I and an occasional flight crew were usually the only ones there that time of night.

The return flights left Jeddah well after midnight and got me into Heathrow in the early morning. As a result of these efficient schedules, and in order to be away from home the least, only once did I take advantage of these business trips to see something special from the ground, rather than only from the air.

*　*　*

In December of 1985, I arranged to make a stop in Amman, Jordan, on my flight back, in order to see the fabled city of Petra. Renting a car at the Amman airport, I drove the 150 miles of two-lane desert highway south to the small new motel that had just opened in the tiny village of Wadi Musa. The road was good, the scenery mostly stark and empty, with some large transport trucks the only traffic. I was stopped and suspiciously nodded through at two heavily guarded check points on the highway and got in just before dark. Wadi Musa was immediately adjacent to the Siq, the ancient main 'entrance' to Petra.

*　*　*

Petra was built, settled, and occupied by the ancient Nabataean people, starting several centuries BC, and prospered for centuries as the trading junction of north-south and east-west trade routes. It is a bowl-shaped valley, isolated by surrounding steep hills of solid rock. The Siq is a ¾-mile long narrow and curving slot in the rock wall, ranging from 30 to only 10 feet wide, between two steep rock walls that extend straight upwards as high as 250 feet. All structures in Petra are relief carved into the rock, and include a Treasury, a Monastery, and many other 'buildings' and caves—all spectacular. Petra's population grew to about 20,000 in the first century AD. Abandoned as trade routes changed, and with earthquakes in the fourth and sixth centuries causing further disruption, Petra declined and virtually disappeared for some 700 years from the 12th century until re-discovered in 1812 by a German explorer. A 19th century Englishman characterized Petra as "The rose-red city, half as old as time."

* * *

In the morning, early, I walked through the Siq. Rounding the last turn with the impressive Treasury first visible through the slit ahead, then towering over a small square as I entered the valley utterly alone, I realized this was something extra special.

I spent most of the day walking the central path and branching out to see and partially climb into building after building, cave after cave. Three or four Bedouin families were living in caves scattered around, with a few goats roaming untethered. I climbed up to a sacrificial rock at the crest of a steep hill, where Aaron (brother of Moses) is supposedly entombed. Far along, I

Petra

found a man with two tables and a few chairs who was selling cokes and a few pastries—in middle of nowhere, with nobody in sight. On my six- or seven-hour walk through the ancient town, I saw perhaps half a dozen other tourists, the Bedouin families, the refreshment man, and the goats. In 2019, Petra had 1.1 million visitors.

Dusty and out of time, I walked back out to the motel, drove back to the Aman airport, and took the midnight flight back to London. I regret not having taken greater advantage of all those trips to the Middle East in the 1980s, to see more of the sites around the region.

Growing Up in City Life

AFTER SIX YEARS in the London office, by 1986, the McKinsey financial institutions practice had a solid group of young partners in London. Suzanne's successful stint at Mobil in London was not sustainable. Nick and Andrew were 8 and 6 and although their local British schools had been very good, we thought they should shift from British to American schools. And we had been away from our New York apartment and the country house for six years.

With extensive interviews at New York City private schools, both Andrew and (one year later) Nick ended up at Collegiate School, on the upper west side of Manhattan, where they stayed through high school, with pretty good results. The school was established in 1628, when the City's population was 200. Dutch was spoken at the school for about a century. The boys took the public bus (with a short walk) from age seven; sports were held in the gym, and field sports at various parks around the City.

Families led us regularly back to Texas and Illinois, with the boys dabbling in hunting and fishing. Weekends and some holidays took us to the country house, which began to include target shooting, golf and tennis, and exploring the surrounding counties and their movie theatres, country fairs, a serious aerodrome, and occasional sports in the field next to the house. We skied at two small ski areas near the upstate house but got more serious with regular winter jaunts to Vermont and northwestern Massachusetts. And my father's side of the family had aunts, uncles, and cousins in and around Wilkes-Barre, Pennsylvania, which was less than a three-hour drive from Manhattan, and provided a chance to make friends and mingle with contemporary family folks.

Farther destinations included annual ski trips to the west for Spring Vacations, moving around to include Colorado (Snowmass and Steamboat Springs), Wyoming (Jackson), New Mexico (Santa Fe), and Utah (Park City, Deer Valley, Alta, and Sundance).

During the dozen years after returning from London, I changed jobs twice, moving from McKinsey to Price Waterhouse in 1988, and then to A.T. Kearney in 1995, all the while based in New York City and with the preponderance of travel within the U.S.

In 1990, my wife Suzanne and I split up after 20 years, but living one block apart, we were able to minimize the disruption and disappointment with the two boys, who were 13 and 10 at the time.

In 1993, my former college sweetheart Paula and I were married in St. Lucia, during a week of scuba lessons and vacationing with the boys. We had not seen each other for more than 20 years, and have had virtually two lives together, one in the late 1960s and the current one since 1993.

We bought the apartment (that we still have) at the corner of West 92nd Street and Central Park West in Manhattan. Facing the park but only on the second floor, the view changes with the seasons: nice green leafy trees in the summer, and longer vistas

Nick, Bill, Paula, and Andrew, August 20, 1993, in St. Lucia

across Central Park in the winter. With Paula came the first of our three dogs, a Dalmatian named JB. (The second, a terrier mix named Scruffy, arrived from the humane society in 1995, and the recently-deceased Lola, a Havanese, was imported to Colorado in 2007.) Paula worked as a special-claims analyst at the Social Security Administration and after a few years commuting to their office in Jamaica Queens, retired in 1995.

In the late 1990s, the boys went off to college, Nick to Pitzer, one of the Clairmont colleges in the southern California desert, and Andrew to USC in Los Angeles. I have accused them of wanting to get as far away from us as they could without getting wet. As it turns out, both have stayed on the West Coast, Nick in Seattle and Andrew in Portland, Oregon.

Another Stint Abroad

With the boys away from the nest,
we agreed with glee to my firm's request
to move to London for two years,
which we did.

Paula and I knew Europe from somewhat different perspectives—
mine with a family based in London for six years,
and hers as a working single living in four Italian cities
for seven years—
and we were keen to explore the infinite number
of new places.

London Redux

WE LIVED IN A TWO-STORY mews house at 11A Ennismore Mews in Knightsbridge, halfway between Kensington Road (and Hyde Park) and Brompton Road (and Harrods). Combined with my office in Barclays Square, we were in the thick of London's West End. We parked on the street immediately in front of the house, and our dog Scruffy barked wildly each day as the mailman dropped the mail through the slot on the door. We took full advantage of London events and sights, and spent many weekends plying the countryside.

The boys visited us in London, and we all visited the Isles of Scilly, off the west coast of Cornwall. My great grandfather, a sea captain for 40 years, had shipwrecked there in 1907 aboard the only seven-masted ship, the *Thomas W. Lawson*, and it was great to be able to trace the events in this group of tiny islands.

After two years, and preparing to return to New York, a call from Kearney headquarters led us to Seoul, South Korea, instead. Knowing little about the country, we agreed to consider it and traveled there to meet the people, scope out the city

View of Ennismore Mews from the front door of 11A

of Seoul, and see where and how we might live—kick the tires, if you will.

It passed muster, so we signed on. Many of our 'friends and family' thought we were nuts, as nobody seemed to know much about the country, and they certainly hadn't been there.

It Was, and Then It Wasn't

AFTER TWO YEARS in London, Paula, our dog Scruffy, and I returned to New York on the Cunard Line's QE II. After six days of wiling away time reading, eating, and gazing over the open waters and the shallows of the Grand Banks, we approached New York in the early morning of Tuesday, September 4, 2001.

Passing into New York Harbor for the first time, it was clear-sky magic as the ship made its way under the Verrazano-Narrows Bridge between Brooklyn and Staten Island. Then, the Statue of Liberty off the ship's port side and facing us, with its majestic patina, torch, and message that had welcomed a century and generations of immigrants "yearning to be free."

Straight ahead, just up from the Battery Park of Manhattan Island, rose the 110-floor twin towers of the World Trade Center, majestic and reflective in many different ways, symbolizing modern prosperity and the heights of civil society. We bore left up the Hudson and soon disembarked on Pier 90.

It was a grand return to the States, on a grand ship, with grand views of the City and its up-stretched arms welcoming us back home.

* * *

A week later—to the hour—I was on an early morning conference call in my office on the 43rd floor of Citicorp Center, when my colleague in Washington said he'd heard that a plane had crashed into one of the Trade Center towers. On the phone, we recalled that a small plane had struck the Empire State Building in the 1940s.

I asked a secretary to check the news on a TV we had on a different floor. She returned a few minutes later, ashen-faced, and reported that the towers were burning and death was everywhere.

The story unfolded over the next hour, as the attack and resulting carnage encompassed the Wall Street area and the towers burned and collapsed. My window faced west, so I could not see the scene. But we quickly surmised that it wasn't safe to remain high up in a blatantly obvious, 59-story tower in mid-town—we could be next. Citicorp's largest shareholder was a Saudi prince who could well have been in Osama bin Laden's sights as a Royal Saud family 'infidel.' So, we cleared our company's three floors of offices, bidding all the employees to make their ways home.

As I left the building onto Lexington Avenue, the sky to the south was black with smoke high up and between the tall buildings, in stark contrast to the clear blue sky in mid-town and to the north. With the subways closed, I turned north and walked the two-and-a-half miles to my upper west side home.

So much can the exhilaration, civility, imagery, and history change in seven days' time.

Surprising Korea

SEOUL WAS OUR FIRST experience living in Asia and in a country where we could not speak the language proved interesting, rewarding, and fun.

We lived in a rented modern house with a fenced yard for the dog in the close-in neighborhood of Sungbokdong, which housed some diplomats and Korean corporate executives. It was set against the charming and stark range of low mountains around Seoul and a short drive past the President's house (the 'Blue House') and through a short tunnel to downtown and the office.

We were there nearly two years and enjoyed it immensely. Besides making a number of Korean and fellow-ex-pat friends, we took advantage of the location and visited Mongolia, Japan, Viet Nam, Cambodia, Thailand, Bali, Malaysia, and Indonesia.

Appendix 4 contains an extensive description of interesting aspects of Korea and the Koreans, most of which were new to us and made the stint rewarding.

Fragrant Harbour

IN 2003, the firm asked me to move to the Hong Kong office and lead and stabilize that practice. So, we moved from Seoul to Hong Kong over a protracted few months in the face of the SARS epidemic, which originated among an animal called the Civit Cat in the markets of mainland China and put a pall over life, and especially travel, across Asia.

View of Hong Kong Harbour from high mid-levels

We settled into a high-floor modern apartment at The Aigburth, on Tregunter Path, in 'mid-levels,' almost all the way up to Victoria Peak on Hong Kong Island. Our windows overlooked most of the city, the harbor, and across to the Kowloon side on the Mainland.

Hong Kong was fascinating in every way—local people, visitors from everywhere, food, transportation, and culture (including an outdoor Rolling Stones concert overlooking the Harbor). And besides being a great place in itself, its location in the world's fastest growing and developing region, and its excellent airport and flights to almost anywhere made it a unique hub.

Our stay of less than two years in Hong Kong gave us the sense that we were in the commercial and cultural center of North Asia, in the window or doorway to China, and in a mix of cultures unlike any other in the world. More aspects and impressions about Hong Kong are found in Appendix 5.

Combined with plenty of personal travel, my stay there represented a life of travel with work fitted in. Had I been 15 years younger, I would have considered staying in Hong Kong permanently.

A Stop Down Under

PLANNING TO RETURN to New York in the summer of 2004, we packed up the dog and a few pieces of furniture we had bought in Seoul and Hong Kong. But, again, not so fast. The firm needed a partner to lead a new project for the largest bank in Australia—would I consider leading that effort for four months in Sydney? We shipped the furniture and the dog to the States from Hong Kong and flew to Sydney.

During our brief and hectic stay, we got only a taste of the vast Australian island continent. (The distance from Sydney on the east coast to Perth on the west coast is the equivalent of

Sydney Harbour Bridge, with traffic and water below

from New York to Salt Lake City, but with close to nothing but desert outback in between.)

Similarly to our stay in Hong Kong, the time in Sydney, while instigated by the consulting assignment which was important and interesting, was marked by mind-blowing travel and exposure to new and very different peoples, history and culture markedly different from our own, and natural and man-made features and 'attractions' far beyond our expectations.

In Sydney, we lived in a hotel-like residence in 'The Rocks' neighborhood, adjacent to the Harbor Bridge and a short walk from the Kearney and Westpac offices. We climbed and walked across the top of the Bridge and beat around Bondi Beach and everything else we could find in town and around Circular Quay and Darling Harbor.

We also managed to travel out of town, down the east coast a ways, west to the Blue Mountains and the wine country, and farther away to Alice Springs and Uluru (or Ayers Rock) some 1,200 miles west, and to Cairns and the Great Barrier Reef 1,500 miles to the north, where we Scuba dived. We never got to Perth and the West Coast, or the north coast, but vowed to return to see and do more. Some additional impressions are described in Appendix 6.

The few months flew by, and we finally flew back to New York.

* * *

We had been living far away for nearly six years, but upon unlocking the door to our New York apartment and unloading the luggage, we were immediately comfortable back in our home there. And thanks to the internet and world-wide web, our communications and daily financial and other 'transactions' had not skipped a beat and had proven to be truly global. Our main address remained the e-mail one and forwarding of critical 'hard copy' mail or goods had been minimal.

Back in New York and working at Kearney only half-time before retiring in 2007, we continued to travel frequently from wherever we were—New York City or Snowmass Village.

What's the Chance?

MANY YEARS AGO, we visited Charleston, South Carolina, for the first time and also drove down to take a look at Savannah, Georgia. A local baseball team—the Savannah Sand Gnats—had a great logo, and I bought a baseball hat with the logo on it. We hadn't known what a sand gnat was, let alone heard of the local ball team.

A couple years later, we drove up to Yellowstone National Park with another couple from our home in Colorado. It was summer, and we wove our way through the main park

A Savannah Sand Gnat

road, stopping at the spectacular sights, vistas, hiking trails, and the occasional buffalo along the way. One parking lot was full, so I dropped the other three at the trail head and finally found a parking spot when another car pulled out at the far end of the lot.

As I was walking back to the trailhead to meet the others, a waiting SUV's window came down, and the driver said, "You know they won last night."

Startled, I asked, "Who won what?"

He responded, "the Sand Gnats, they beat Augusta 3 to 2."

I was wearing my hat in Wyoming, 2,100 miles from Savannah.

A Herd, An Aerial View, and A Close Call

IN 2011, we finally got to South Africa and spent two great weeks plying Cape Town, Livingstone, and Victoria Falls, and a large private game preserve in northwest South Africa on the Botswana border. So many things stand out as noteworthy, it is difficult to select a few, but here are three, all coincidentally in the vicinity of the Falls.

For our few nights near Livingstone, we stayed at a 'camp' resort—Tongabezi Lodge—on an island in the middle of the Zambezi River about a mile up-river from the falls. We were ferried back and forth to the south bank, which was Zambia, with the town of Livingstone and access to the falls. That shore was about a half mile from the island and filled with a dozen or so hippos, from which the ferryman kept a good distance. The other shore, to the north, was much closer to the island, with a hundred-foot wide channel of water. That was Zimbabwe.

PACHYDERM LUCK | On our first night on the island, the boat pilot who took us to the island said he had seen a herd of about 30 elephants just down the river and encouraged us to let

Close in at mealtime on the Zambezi   A lawn chair above Victoria Falls

him take us down to look for them, which we did.

There were only six of us in a small outboard boat, and after less than a ten-minute ride down the river, we pulled in next to the heard that was milling around the high reeds in the shallow water near the shore, eating the vegetation. There were every size and age, with the females the largest. The pilot turned off the motor as we slowed and stopped about 30 feet from the nearest ones. They all seemed wary but kept eating and moving slowly around among the grasses. The females were most attentive and over about ten minutes deliberately went through their threatening routine of showing their ears fully out directed toward us, then stomping their legs, and finally raising their trunks and making unfriendly noises. Although the pilot convinced us not to be worried, as some of them had moved closer, and we had a lot of photos taken, he started up the motor and we returned to our island at dusk.

ULTRA-GREAT | In signing up for adventuresome options long before our trip, we had checked the box for an ultra-lite plane ride above Victoria Falls. There was a sizable helicopter operation too, but the smaller planes sounded more interesting. We showed up at the appointed time at a field just outside Livingstone, signed our lives away, paid, and were each assigned to a tiny contraption, consisting of an aluminum frame with two seats, one behind the other. There was a lawn mower sized engine on the back with a propeller facing to the rear, and a giant thin cloth-covered wing high up. My pilot was a 20-something German guy who did this day-in, day-out and turned out to be wholly competent and interesting to boot.

Sitting behind the pilot, there was nothing to hold on to and just a normal seat belt across my lap. He revved up the motor, and we gained some speed on about a 100- or 120-foot run, and the lawn chair lifted off.

Within four or five minutes we were pretty high up and had headed out over the vast falls—the largest in the world, being 5,600 feet wide with spray and mist billowing up all along. We flew back and forth over the expanse, and he diverted toward another shallow pool after spotting some elephants in the water that we could buzz around. The 45-minute ride was unique and spectacular. I don't know why I wasn't petrified, without any control, out in the open like a motorcycle but hundreds of feet up in the air and being driven by a kid. Turns out the planes are outfitted with a camera at the wingtip facing back and down on the plane that snaps a picture every 20 seconds. So, we have photos of the flight showing not only us and the plane, but also views of the falls and ground.

THE LION DOESN'T SLEEP TONIGHT | The camp itself consisted of six or seven large tents spread apart and with canvas sides that could be raised up to provide air flow and cool things down. There were common bathrooms a little walk away and quite a nice large outdoor dining area for dinners that were luxuriously prepared and served to us.

On our last night there, about four in the morning and sound asleep, we were blasted awake by an incredible double or triple roar of a lion that was clearly in or just outside our tent. Ordinarily, I would have leaped out of bed, but I immediately nixed that response since I would die for sure. We sat staring at the perimeter of our tent walls as the hours went by until dawn, and we could at least see that there was no lion in the tent or immediately next to it.

Eventually, we found out that the lion—a "large male"—roared out of frustration from not getting anything to eat on his hunt that night, and that he had been on the Zimbabwe riverbank, about 100 feet from the island.

So, I said to the head guide, "I thought lions could swim."

He responded, "Oh, yes, they are excellent, strong swimmers."

I probed, "If he was hungry, and can swim across easily, why didn't he come and eat us?"

Answer: "They know there are crocodiles in the river, so they won't go in."

Luckily, our lion remembered that.

The Spice and Spite of Life

SEVERAL YEARS AGO, Paula and I were lucky to take a cruise on the four-masted sailing ship *Sea Cloud*. The eight-day route from Piraeus, near Athens, up along the Dalmatian Coast was delightful—the scenery, sailing, and visits to the various ancient ports along the way. And the crew knew and imparted tons of history both about that part of the world and about the ship itself. One of the stories is of family intrigue and

Sea Cloud

strong will, associated with the boat's original owners.

Sea Cloud was built by Marjorie Merriweather Post and her husband Edward Hutton in 1931. Ms. Post owned and ran the General Foods Company, while Mr. Hutton ran the large brokerage firm that he founded, E.F. Hutton. They virtually lived on board until they divorced in 1933, and after that Ms. Post continued to run her business from the ship as it sailed the seas.

Their daughter, Nedenia Hutton, born in 1923, had her own cabin and lived on board six months a year. Attractive, elegant, and having attended a series of elite private schools, the daughter became interested in acting and wanted to make a career of it. Her father Hutton, however, was against it, believing the life and persona of an actress to be beneath the family's place and a waste of the daughter's potential. Nevertheless, she was determined and in her early 20s took odd jobs to pay her own way and not be beholden to her father's wealth.

As she prepared to formally begin acting as her life's work, she decided to adopt a new name—Dina Merrill. Her acting debut in a 1945 Broadway play, *The Mermaid Singing*, began a very successful movie career, and she became a household name through several decades.

But, why the name Merrill? Determined to act against her father's wishes in following her heart, she chose as her permanent name, that of his primary brokerage competitor, Charlie Merrill of Merrill Lynch.

A spectacular spite, no?

Seward Was Right

IN 1955, for one Quaker Oats serial box top plus $1, my father and I each bought one square inch of land in the Yukon Territory of Canada, a few hundred miles straight east of the Alaskan border. I was 10; he was older. Two decades later, the discovery and production of oil from Alaska's north slope and Prudhoe Bay kept the top bankers in New York where I worked in a tizzy for years, financing the business and then dealing with the mid-1970's oil crisis. In the 1980s, we lived down the road from Lowell Thomas, who's son, Lowell Junior, had permanently (and prominently, as it turned out) emigrated to Anchorage in 1960. And Senator John McCain brought Alaska to the fore by choosing Sarah Palin as his Vice President running mate.

That had been my lifetime exposure to Alaska, until a new Colorado neighbor, who owns a fishing lodge there invited us up two summers ago. It's an exquisite rendition of 'north country' and, at 63° N latitude, it's the farthest north I've been.

What a place. The lodge is in Larsen's Bay on the west coast of Kodiak Island, accessible only by boat or small plane. The plane ride from Anchorage was a 40-minute leg to Kodiak City on the island's east shore, then another 40-minute leg to Larsen's Bay. I can recall seeing two roads along the entire way, and those disappeared eventually. Larsen's Bay itself is tiny—the home of a large but partially closed down fish cannery, and docks for fishing boat access. Between 2000 and 2010, the town's population declined from 115 to 87. The local school recently closed for lack of students (totaling in the single digits), requiring the few remaining school-age kids to commute weekly to Kodiak City or the mainland.

The lodge itself—Kodiak Legends—accommodates up to 20 guests and is considered large in the town. To add a new one-, or two-unit cabin requires persuasion and approval by the locals.

Fishing is the main activity. I don't list fishing as one of my sports or life's activities, not having done it for more than 60 years. It was spectacular. The lodge's two boats are guided by folks who know the area, the rules, and the fish. Going out each day for hours, we would see another boat or two somewhere in the distance .... probably. It was easy to stick to the size limitations for black bass, cod, and especially halibut, because it meant waiting only a few minutes for one big enough to keep. Besides the fish and the excellent meals prepared with them, there were crabs for the catching, bald eagles all around the harbor, otters swimming and 'fishing' in the bay, and a couple special little 'general stores' around the cannery.

Taking advantage of the trip to Kodiak, we explored Anchorage and travelled inland to Denali National Park. Anchorage is small enough to get your arms around and enjoy its restaurants, shops, antique dealers, and outfitters, but it is also a center of Alaskan life. Tides there can reach forty feet, the highest in the U.S. Denali provided a taste of the vast inland mountains, lakes, rivers, and fauna that fills the rest of the state —the largest in the U.S. and four times the size of California.

Alaska is a typical 'north country' place—that is, beautiful, mostly unspoiled and sparsely populated, with unique and idiosyncratic local people who are proud, protective, and provincial, and welcoming of visitors who like all that and enjoy trying to fit in.

Beyond that, however, Alaska is one of those rare places in America that is part of the United States but seems too different, special, and detached to not be a foreign country. (Hawaii is another, although the opposite of Alaska in climate and very different in some other respects.)

Airport Revenge

ONE OF MY OBJECTIVES on both the personal and business sides of life has been to spend as little time as possible in airports, and it's been a challenge. I have failed in this regard all my life, as a banker, management consultant, and someone who has always loved to travel and see new things. It would be too depressing to estimate how many hours and week- and month- equivalents my time in airports has totaled.

Once trapped there—often not knowing within hours how long it will be—one dozes, reads, eats, and shops, especially in the days before cell phones delivered movies and other potentially absorbing entertainment. That being said, as travel interruptions in airports accumulated over the years, there have been a few discoveries here and there that a traveler might seek out to partially offset this time in purgatory.

Here is a memory dump of items that proved to be handily available in various airports that, albeit not worth a special trip, would be happily at hand and not easy to find elsewhere.

• **Dark chocolate truffles**, by Vosages and Neuhaus, at Brussels Airport | Perfect taste, large and mouth-watering, and well-boxed. Buy twice as many to ensure a few make it to your next destination.

• **Dan Dan Noodles**, at the Cathay Pacific lounges—The Pier or The Wing—at Hong Kong's Kai Tac airport | Freshly made to order by experts, perfect for any time of day. Quick to buy, and gratis.

• **Weiss Wurst** at several restaurants/bars at the airport in Munich | Available through the day, but extra special for breakfast, with mustard and pretzel, of course.

• **Ties in Rome** | Although the best selections at a couple of large duty-free shops at Fiumicino Airport seem to come and go over the decades—as does the demand for silk ties—there are usually some spectacular colors to be found.

• **Live lobsters** at Logan Airport in Boston | On the way to the gate on the shuttle concourse, they used to put live ones in containers to carry with you.

• **Cuban cigars** in Geneva | Although the best cigars have migrated away from Cuba, and Cuban bans have loosened, the Geneva airport still has large selections.

• **Wild rice** in Minnesota | The Minneapolis-St. Paul airport has had 5-pound bags of nearly pure black rice—it's hard to find that purity anywhere anymore.

• **Sourdough bread** in San Francisco | After leaving your heart downtown, you can pick up big loaves of fresh sourdough bread at the airport on your way out, in red, white and blue rappers—good to go with the Sees or Ghirardelli's chocolates.

• **Smoked eel** in Amsterdam | Schiphol Airport has shrink-wrapped packs of smoked eel. Bring it back to the

States for yourself, buy gravlax for the others, and Droste orange and dark chocolate disks for everyone.

• **Feast** in Istanbul | The pickings are endless, delicious and convenient at the Turkish Airlines' vast Business Class Lounge; and the food stations are endless. Don't eat the day before, and you won't eat the day after.

• **Champagne truffles** in Zurich | It's a toss up between Brussels and Zurich and will require sustained sampling to pick a winner.

• **Maltesers** in Bangkok | Nearly gone from the U.S. and seemingly limited distribution elsewhere, ply the shops throughout the airport for different flavors and 'bulk' prices. ◆

Driving & Cars

Yes, cars and driving are merely a form of transportation
and an integral component of 'traveling.'

But as a teenage boy in the 1960s, and from then on,
cars and driving have taken on a life of their own
as a 'machine' of great interest, a source of independence,
and a way to reach and peruse many new
and foreign places.

Here are some notable aspects and events
along my sixty years of driving vehicles,
including some escapades, close calls,
and driving on the 'wrong' side.

Appendix 3 contains a list, descriptions,
and pictures of a few of my vehicles—the '27 keys to
transport and freedom.'

Driving Around

I LIKE TO THINK, and do believe, that I have always been a good driver. My motor skills (pun intended) are good; eyesight, depth perception, reflexes excellent; and I have enjoyed operating sensitive machines, including cars and motorcycles.

Passing my driving test and getting my first license 10 days after turning 16, I have driven on five continents, and have owned 24 cars and three motorcycles. They have ranged from a $75 1949 Oldsmobile, to owning three Porsches at the same time, garaged in upstate New York, Colorado, and Hong Kong.

Cars were the ticket to independence and transportation as a teenager in the Midwest, and they have been central to travelling and touring. My driving probably totals nearly a million miles over 50 years and has been full of pleasures, occasional mechanical and weather problems, and many unlikely anecdotes. A few events stand out with trepidation and demonstrate inexplicable good fortune.

KEYS ARE NO LICENSE | By the summer of 1960, I was ready to drive, although it would be another nine months until I turned 16 and could get a license. No worries. My dad drove his car to the commuter train station each morning, and it sat in the parking lot until he picked it up in the evening on his way home from the office in downtown Chicago. A friend and I had borrowed a yellow and black rubber traffic cone from a construction site and strategically kept it in the car's trunk. And, of course, we had made our own set of car keys.

On the appointed day, we biked to the parking lot and took the car, placing the cone in the parking place, so we could put the car back in the same spot when we returned. At least once, we drove to the Indiana Dunes State Park for a few hours on the beach. The light summer traffic on the divided U.S. highway begged us not to slow down, and it was on one of these outings that I passed 100 mph in a car for the first time. Speeding and carelessness were not the main point, however, and, for the most part, we were obsessed with obeying laws and not being stopped. In any case, the plan worked, and my dad was never the wiser.

Another time, when we hopped off our bikes at the parking lot to retrieve the car, a local policeman noticed us in the lot and spotted the keys in my hand. We said they were for our car which was at home, but the policeman was suspicious and tried the keys in the four or five nearest cars—including ours. But he must have turned it the wrong way or used the trunk key on the door, because it didn't work. So, after he left, we 'coned' the spot and drove off for the day.

GET WHAT YOU PAY FOR | A car I bought for $50, kept for a month, and then sold to a junk yard for $50, was a 1952 Chevrolet, painted in flat black primer. It ran ok but the hood latch didn't work. I found that out while accelerating to about 40 mph, when the hood flew up and plastered itself back over the entire windshield and part of the roof. After sticking my head out the side window to see around the hood, I pulled over and on to the shoulder. From then on, an old belt ensured that the hood would only open when desired.

ONLY TWO WHEELS | Despite not having a car my freshman year at college in Rhode Island, it was easy going places with others who had cars. (In fact, I met my future wife in a friend's car in which I was accompanying them to a hockey game in Boston.) Nevertheless, spring brought itchiness to be able to get wherever I wanted to go, 24/7. So, I bought a Yamaha motorcycle from a

Brown senior who was getting married and needed cash. I gave him $250, he gave me the title, and I spent the rest of the afternoon in a deserted parking lot learning how to balance around turns and how to work the foot clutch and the handle gearshift—all at once.

At the end of the semester, I rode the Yamaha home to Chicago for the summer. Trying to enter the New York State Thruway near Albany, the toll booth attendant wouldn't let me pass, indicating that although my bike had a 250cc engine, it was too light to be allowed on the toll road. So, I rode off to the next entrance 10 or 15 miles farther on, to try again. But the first toll booth lady had called ahead, and the second one denied me too. On the third try, however, nobody cared, and I started a free-spirited ride to Buffalo, over the Peace Bridge, and west on Canada's Kings Highway toward Detroit. It was fantastic, with nice weather and little traffic, heading toward a summer job and fun. Two other bikers joined for a couple hours before peeling off to wherever they were headed. About 80 or 100 miles from Detroit, a driving rain spoiled the trip for a bit, as I had no windshield or leathers, and there was no shelter on the highway. The water drops felt like machine gun bullets on my face.

That summer, I traded my Yamaha for a newer and slightly more powerful model, and drove it back to Providence in the fall, going across I-90 and stopping for a day at a college friend's house in Rocky River Ohio. That year, the bike was my transportation, and I even 'taught' my girlfriend how to drive it around local Roger Williams Park. She was short and preferred never to come to a full stop, as the bike would fall over and be too heavy to pull upright.

One late party night, after dropping her at her dorm, I drove through the College Green—in one gate and out the opposite one about 100 yards straight ahead. Since even bicycle traffic was not allowed there, no guards were prepared for a motorcycle cutting through, and I got away with it, without being chased.

Nearing graduation in the spring of 1967—and having traded the bike away for a car a year before—I borrowed a big Triumph 650 from a lower classman whom I knew from high school back in the Chicago suburbs. With the girl on the back and no helmets, we cruised from the campus south onto I-95 towards that park that we had ridden around on the first bike. On the way back, I proved that the Triumph can easily get past 100 in just a few seconds. Stupid.

ONE NEEDS ONE'S SLEEP | In the fall of 1965, my junior year in college, a classmate down the hall acquired a like-new Ford Mustang convertible, but it was in Miami and he wanted somebody to drive the car up to Providence. So, he enlisted— and paid for—another fraternity brother and me to fly down to Miami, pick up the car, stay the night at the Edan Rock hotel in Miami Beach, and then drive the car to Providence. Which we did. Driving north, Bob and I alternated driving, about 6 hours to a shift, in order to drive the 1,400 miles straight through. I was driving as we entered Rhode Island in the morning, and, all of a sudden, we were bouncing over the stone curb on the right edge of the road. I had fallen asleep, gradually pulled the car to the right, hit the curb, and had come to a quick stop on the grass just off the road. Two tires were blown, which required a short tow to replace one and repair the other. Bob and I had been jarred awake, but we and the car were otherwise unhurt.

27 years later, my wife and I, with our 14- and 11-year-old sons, set out after work one Friday in the winter for a week of skiing in Stowe, Vermont. Driving our maroon Toyota Previa van (which we called the Whale), we had picked up our ski equipment and were moving north on NY highway 22, probably in Rensselaer County. All of a sudden, we were careening down the steep shoulder of the road on the right at some speed.

I pulled the steering wheel to the left, kept the speed, and used the 50 or 60 yards of clear shoulder ahead to pull back up the hill to the highway. I had fallen asleep again. As we edged back onto the road, the right rear-view mirror clipped a mailbox on the roadside, and I stopped the car and retrieved the severed mirror casing. The boys had awakened, to say the least, but all was ok, and we went on to a successful vacation.

Six years after that, in the summer of 1998, Paula and I visited her sister in Pittsburgh, and were returning to New York City via I-76. We were in our Mercedes ML320, which I had bought six months earlier. (I had been impressed by the fact that Princess Diana, in a Mercedes, had crashed into a concrete pillar at 90 miles per hour, without a fastened seatbelt, and had lived for 45 minutes.) I was trying out the cruise control, which I really never liked or used, before or since. There was some traffic, but pretty light. All of a sudden, the car was bouncing off the left-hand steel guardrail, going hard right toward a similar guard rail on the other side. I turned the wheel hard to the left and tried to slow but still hit the right rail fairly hard, before coming to a stop on the right shoulder. I had fallen asleep yet again.

Although monotony and silence were present in all three cases, there really is nothing to excuse them. I know when I'm tired, and I have come to know when the possibility or probability of dozing off is present. And, in the 22 years since the Pennsylvania incident, I have prevented it from happening again. It is somehow ironic that I had to be in my 50's before figuring out how to stay awake in such situations.

These three occasions put all kinds of people and property in danger by unintentionally turning a car into a potential missile. Due solely to good fortune, no one was injured, property damage beyond the cars was unnoticeable, and none of the cars were mortally wounded.

Compounding that good fortune is the long odds that in the three instances—all on divided highways and at 50 mph plus—my car hit no other cars, buildings or people. What are those odds?

Even though these events were accidental and proved inconsequential, the humiliation of falling asleep at the wheel lingers forever.

I'm a good driver only when awake. I may have given up motorcycling too soon—it's nearly impossible to fall asleep on one.

Trouble Over Bridged Water

FOR THE 1965 college spring vacation, my classmate and friend, Gary Uphouse, joined me at my great aunt's house in Palm Beach, Florida. We had a great week there and, as was the case each of my four college years, I had agreed to drive my aunt's car back to her summer home outside Wilkes-Barre, Pennsylvania, on our way back to Brown in Providence.

Gary and I drove straight through to Pennsylvania—about 1,200 miles—alternating as driver every five or six hours. Crossing North Carolina into Virginia, we decided to take the Chesapeake Bay Bridge Tunnel up toward Delaware and New Jersey. The bridge opened in 1960, and stretched 23 miles high above, low above, and beneath the surface of the water. It is an eerie seascape for much of the way, with land nowhere to be seen and the roadway stretching boringly forever, just barely above the surface of the water.

We had driven a good 15 hours or more from Palm Beach. With dawn breaking in Virginia, it was my turn to drive from Virginia Beach, where the bridge starts. Gary curled up on the front passenger's seat, covering himself up with a trench coat to sleep. Some minutes later, I began snoring, louder and louder. All of a sudden, the trench coat flew off and into the back seat, and Gary jumped up and grabbed for the wheel. Seeing me laughing and clearly not asleep, he began shouting and cursing that my act was outrageous, mean-spirited, even cruel. I don't think he slept again on the trip.

Running with the Tide

A GREAT AUNT—actually my father's cousin—had the charity and lunacy of inviting me to spend each of my college Spring breaks at her home in Palm Beach, Florida. She lived most of the year on a wonderful 'farm' with a lake just outside Wilkes-Barre, Pennsylvania, but spent the winter social season in the warm weather of Palm Beach, just a little up the road from Mar-a-Lago. When I arrived each time, she would hand me the keys to one of their cars for my stay and also a sheaf of invitations to debutant parties and other events that I could attend, at the Bath & Tennis Club, Everglades Club, and a few of the grand homes on the island.

The end of spring break—around Easter each year—would also mark the end of the social season, and a return to Pennsylvania for my aunt and uncle. Rather than drive their main car—usually a Chrysler or Cadillac—back themselves, they asked if I would drive it north to their PA home, then make my way back to Providence. I thought the arrangement was great, paying only for gas, and I did it all four years.

* * *

Each year, I invited a college friend along—we hitchhiked the first time but flew to Florida the last three years. In my senior year, however, I went alone, knowing that my girlfriend Paula would be in nearby Lauderdale by the Sea with girlfriends from Pembroke and her Dayton hometown, and that we could spend time together in both Palm Beach and Ft. Lauderdale. Which we did. As the vacation ended, Paula and I set out to drive my aunt's car up the coast to the Pennsylvania house, stay with other relatives for a night, and then return to Brown.

The car that year was a 1967 Cadillac Eldorado Hardtop Coupe. It was a beautiful dark green color and only a couple months old, with few miles on the odometer. And that model was the first of the front-wheel drive cars.

* * *

We left in the morning and, a few hours up the coast, decided to take a brief detour at Daytona Beach and drive along its famous wide beach. Back then, there were two or three lanes of car traffic each way.

Neither the town nor the beach were crowded on that hot weekday, so we drove right onto the beach—it was free then—and slowly wound our way north. Before long, however, and swerving ever so slightly around a group of kids walking along, we sank about a foot down into a sand rut and stopped short. The sand was soft that day. And, unfortunately, the full weight of the engine bore down on the front drive wheels, pushing them ever deeper into the sand, as I spun both ways in an effort to extricate ourselves.

After some futile attempts at digging around the wheels, and every type and speed of rocking the car back and forth, it was clear that we were stuck. It was also clear the afternoon tide had been coming in steadily, to the point where there were only single lanes open. The shocking possibility loomed of having to call my aunt to report that the tide had swamped her new Cadillac under several feet of seawater, while driving on a Florida beach.

Fortunately, the sight of the car in obvious distress and

impending doom had attracted a small crowd of passersby. A dozen big guys volunteered to push the car out of its two front holes and up onto firmer sand. Once free of the sand holes, we made our way quickly to pavement and left Daytona towards Pedro's South of the Border and the trip back.

Even with this happy ending, there was never a need to bother my aunt with that tale of woe.

RHD

ON MY FIRST ever trip to London—in about 1970, on Chemical Bank business—I had a weekend off and decided to take the Friday night train to Edinburgh, and then drive down to visit a high-school friend living in Rutland, a county in the north of England about three quarters of the way back towards London.

After puttering around Edinburgh Castle on Saturday morning, I went to the Avis office in the city center to pick up my rental car. It was a red Vauxhall that they brought around to the garage exit. I finished the paperwork and opened the door, but there was no steering wheel there. Trying to be nonchalant, I went to the other side, got in, started the car and contemplated where the various gears were likely to be on the stick-shift console, and whether the clutch was still the left-most pedal. Finding first gear, I edged my way out to the sidewalk that was thick with weekend lunchtime pedestrians passing in both directions, and then through to the street, also teeming with traffic. Thank goodness it was one way to the left, so I didn't have to think about which lane to aim for.

The next 20 minutes were gut-wrenching, as I crept along—mumbling to myself "keep left but not too much" and "turn into the left lane,"—and watching for signs to get me out of town toward the south. Shifting with my left hand was new and constant. Luckily, traffic was crowded and slow, and one-way streets reduced somewhat the probability of driving head-on the wrong way. Once on the outskirts, the 'highways' opened up, the traffic dissipated, and I could practice driving on the left, and especially around the roundabouts ("look right, keep left").

By Monday morning, driving to and in central London was only slightly less terrifying, and I was glad to give it up and return to a taxi-enabled workweek.

Since then, living in right-hand-drive countries for a cumulative 10 years, and owning four RHD cars in those countries, I got comfortable with it all, and driving there became second nature. In fact, the only nearly disastrous mistake I recall took place in New York City upon moving back in 1986. Exiting Central Park by turning left at 96th Street onto Central Park West, I turned sharply into the left lanes by instinct, thereby facing a barrage of cars coming directly at me. Luckily, they were not close, and I pulled over into the proper right-hand lanes.

But I clearly recall that lost and nearly-out-of-control feeling 50 years ago in Edinburgh.

William D. Turner
Assistant Vice President

CHEMICAL BANK
20 Pine Street, New York, NY 10005
Tel: (212) 770-1142

1968-1973 | New York

WILLIAM D. TURNER

PRINCIPAL
McKinsey & Company, Inc.

55 EAST 52 STREET
NEW YORK, N.Y. 10022
212-909-8727

1973-1988 | New York

WILLIAM D. TURNER

PRINCIPAL
McKinsey & Company, Inc.

74 ST. JAMES'S STREET
LONDON SW1A 1P5
TELEPHONE 01-839 8040

1980-1986 | London

William D. Turner

153 East 53rd Street
New York, NY 10022
Telephone 212 371 2000
Direct Dial 212 527 8590

Price Waterhouse

1988-1995 | New York

William D. Turner
william.turner@atkearney.com

Vice President

1 212 350 3291 Direct
1 917 498 3497 Mobile

A.T. Kearney, Inc.
153 East 53rd Street
New York, New York 10022
1 212 751 7040
1 212 705 1003 Fax

ATKEARNEY

1995-2007 | New York

William D. Turner

A.T. Kearney Limited
Lansdowne House
Berkeley Square
London W1X 5DH
+44 20 7468 8000 Main
+44 20 7468 8494 Direct
+44 20 7339 6747 Fax
william.turner@atkearney.com

ATKEARNEY
an EDS company

1999-2001 | London

William Turner
Vice President

A.T. Kearney, Inc.
Young Poong Building, 12th Floor
33, Seorin-Dong, Chongro-Ku,
Seoul, Korea, 110-752
Main 82 2 399 6000
Direct 82 2 399 6020
Fax 82 2 399 6060
william.turner@atkearney.com

Management Consultants

ATKEARNEY
an EDS company

2001-2003 | Seoul

William Turner
Vice President
Financial Institutions Group
Greater China

A.T. Kearney Co., Ltd.
23/F, 105 Tun Hwa S. Rd. Sec. 2
Taipei, Taiwan 106
Republic of China
Tel   886 2 2755 0000 ext 712
       886 2 2784 1616

A. T. Kearney (Hong Kong) Ltd.
Level 31, One Pacific Place
88 Queensway, Hong Kong
Direct 852 2501 1430
Fax   852 2530 1545
William.Turner@atkearney.com

ATKEARNEY
an EDS company

2003-2004 | Hong Kong

PART TWO

Business & Career— Serendipity by Design

From my early teens onward, working for spending money morphed into working to contribute to college and graduate school, and then, finally, working to 'make a living.'
All along, I was lucky enough to find work that I wanted to learn about, was interesting, was important to do, was something I came to do well, was 'successful,' and was lucrative enough.

This section describes vignettes that portray what I was doing, the family and business environment in which I was working, and where I was.
The sequence of 'write-ups' is meant to provide a taste of my business life and its varied, and at many points amusing, aspects.

The characterization 'serendipity by design' emphasizes that my career and family movements were neither predestined nor designed in advance. I liked what I was doing all along, moving from one project and company and place to another, as seemed appropriate and worthwhile. Luckily, I found almost all of them to be rewarding and the progression reasonable.

Growing into Work

I DON'T RECALL when I first worked for money, but it seems that from age 12 on, I cut a few lawns, and then turned to caddying at a local country club, which also provided an opportunity to play a great golf course on Mondays, when the club was closed to member play.

Then, I served as groundskeeper for a wealthy dentist in a nearby town, using his equipment, coming and going as I pleased, and earning something like 75 cents or $1/hour. (The song

Caddy badge, c. 1960

Barbara Ann by the Regents was a hit that summer, and the dentist couple had an infant daughter of the same name.) These activities served their purpose: keeping me busy, earning some money, playing some golf, and learning how to build fences and keep mowers and other motors running.

Taking a Job

IN THE SUMMER of 1962, next door neighbor Pat Morrissy's father, who worked for Ford, got Pat and me jobs laboring at a Ford subcontractor that outfitted railroad box cars with wooden racks to transport car parts to assembly plants all over the U.S. The work site was a large, former onion barn on U.S. Highway 6 in South Holland, Illinois, about 8 miles from where we lived.

The job consisted of cutting sheets of plywood into a variety of shapes and sizes, and then nailing them together in patterns designed to hold specific parts, like hood and door panels. The finished racks were then fitted into empty box cars and off they went. Tools and machinery included primarily table saws, hammers, and nails, and a single propane-fueled lift truck to move the heavy raw and finished wood stuff around the barn and its large lot.

There were about 15 of us workers, led by foreman Ken, who, together with Pat and me, accounted for the Caucasians and English speakers in the group. All the others were Mexican men, presumably up to work for the summer. I don't recall the pay rate, although $1.50 an hour sounds familiar. It was a good job for us—9 to 5, 5 days a week, inside when it rained, and a convenient commute. Skills required were pretty basic, involving lining up wood pieces and nailing them where they were supposed to be. You could learn everything you had to know in half an hour, although to do it fast and without thinking took a little longer.

I was 16 and had bought my first car—a turquoise and white 1954 Ford sedan—from a neighbor for $50. My dad forbade my having a car during the school year, thinking it a distraction from my 'studies.' (I didn't need a car for that.) In the summer, however, I was allowed to buy one with my own money, and he chipped in to add me to his insurance policy—maybe another $40 or $50 for the summer. So, Pat and I had transportation, and may have split the gas bill, which was not onerous at 30 cents/gallon.

Besides earning spending money, two aspects of the job made it interesting. First was the full-time interaction with the group of Mexicans, who, while friendly and jolly as co-workers, were also older, mostly Spanish speaking, and led lives entirely different from ours. We had great fun with trying out Spanish words, phrases and pronunciations, and heavily accented English pronunciations of Spanish. The second source of fun on the job was our relationship with Ken. Although some years older than we were, we three shared most ethnicities and demographics. We really didn't receive any special treatment. But we were eventually allowed to drive the lift truck, and discovered that one could race with it, spinning its huge knobby tires and spewing up gravel and dirt around the lot.

There was a night crew that we never saw, and their job was to cut down the original sheets of wood into smaller pieces so the day shift could then nail them into the proper finished racks and shelves.

One of the more vivid images from that summer is the morning that Pat and I arrived with the rest of the day shift and found the main table saw closed and covered. It turned out that during the night, the saw operator had fallen asleep while pushing wood through the saw and cut off some number of fingers and/or his hand. He had been taken away in an ambulance before we got there, but the saw was covered with blood and was down for the day.

The other—and somewhat less morbid—highlight of that job and group was the company picnic held on a Saturday in a nearby Illinois Forest Preserve park. All the workers showed up, and we had a festive time. There was plenty of beer, and a lot of food had been informally catered in, with burgers, chicken, and probably ribs cooked in the park's firepit and barbeque grill. But the piece de resistance was the two large galvanized garbage cans full to the brim of cooked goat heads—obviously considered a delicacy by everyone there but three.

Working in Chicago

AFTER PAT MORRISSY'S DAD got the two of us jobs in 1962, my dad returned the nepotismic favor, and we were hired for the summer of 1963 to make contact lenses at Plastic Contact Lens Company in downtown Chicago. On the top two floors (the 11th and 12th) of an office building at the corner of

Wabash Avenue and Monroe Street, PCL had its entire operation, with most of the space devoted to actually manufacturing the lenses, and that's where we worked along with a dozen or more others.

Soft, cornea-sized contact lenses had been invented only a few years before, and two pioneer optometrists, Drs. Newton K. Wesley and George Jessen, had started the company. Previously, the only contacts available had been large glass globes that fit around the entire front half of the eyeball. The breakthrough had been a new process of making rods of plastic that were bubble free and consistently refractive. This enabled extremely thin and light lenses to be much smaller and to ride on the cornea and its tear layer.

Manufacturing consisted of slicing the rods of plastic into fairly thin disks—like checkers—then cutting a concave radius out of one side on a lathe. The disk was then turned around, and a convex radius was carved on the opposite side on a lathe. The refractive power of the lens was determined by the difference between the inside and outside radii, and the lens thickness (measured in thousandths of an inch). Each side of the lens was then polished on a rotating chuck, using wax polishing heads and Silvo silver polish. When the desired thickness and clarity was achieved, the lens was popped out, beveled around the perimeter as required to smoothly rest on the eyeball, and boxed to send to the optometrist who ordered it. (The bevel was called the CN Bevel, developed by Charlie Nakamura, who worked down the hall.)

Pat and my job varied between cutting either or both radiuses and polishing the lenses to their correct power. It was the learning, the people, and the tangential stuff that made it a memorable summer.

The PCL job was my first and only commuter job and took me through three summers. Other than the cost of a monthly train ticked, the commute proved easy, as the Illinois Central train line was dependable and provided newspaper reading and dozing time before and after work. This was the only time I was employed in Chicago.

*　*　*

On the job, a favorite co-worker was Carlos, aged about 40, who's cubicle—with lathe—was at the back of the room, looking out over the other 12 or 15 cubicles. Carlos made the most specialized, often unique lenses. For example, there were lenses that blocked light except for a very small center, for people whose iris had been torn, blinding them with too much light. There were fused bifocals, as well as football-shaped inner radii lenses for astigmatic eyes. And, there were lenses weighted at a certain spot, so that they would not rotate on the eye as normal lenses did. If it was super special or particularly difficult, Carlos did it. Whereas we would turn out a couple dozen lenses a day, Carlos might do four or five. His skills also enabled Carlos to work on his correspondent high school courses every day, and the position of his cubicle protected that diligence.

*　*　*

We quickly found that the key to prescribing contact lenses was a machine then called an Opthalmometer, which measured the curvature of a patient's eyeball, which in turn determined the inside, concave curve for the lens. During a lunch break, we visited the office and used the machine to measure our own eyes. Knowing this, we could then make lenses for ourselves, although it would be only a novelty for fun, since both of us had good eyesight and didn't need corrective lenses.

The lenses (and plastic rods) came in many different colors—18, I believe. For example, there were three shades of blue, green, brown, and gray, hazel, etc. And, there was ruby red. Red lenses were meant for some esoteric eye condition, but most importantly, they were worn by Las Vegas card dealers to foil marked cards. Evidently, cards marked invisibly with lemon juice could be read clearly through red lenses, while invisible to all others.

Deciding what color to make lenses for ourselves was easy: ruby red. Upon purloining the necessary small disks of plastic, it only took 15 or 20 minutes to make the finished lens to our own specs, while simultaneously operating our lathes and polishers with our normal production lenses. We merely added our pair to the day's output.

We didn't wear the lenses many times, as it was not easy for me to properly insert and remove them, and I wasn't motivated to wear them in order to see better. But I do recall once buying something at a Walgreens and having the salesclerk gasp and step backwards as she saw my bright red eyes. I still have those lenses somewhere.

Falling Toward New York & Banking

*A series of short-term decisions—
bordering on accidents—
led me to pursue a career during a period
of fundamental changes in financial markets
and the business of finance.*

AT BROWN UNIVERSITY, when it came time in my senior year to contemplate what to do next—and despite majoring in economics—I realized there wasn't much I could contribute to any business, and I didn't understand what a company would hire me to do. Although I looked forward to going into 'business' in some form, the interviews I generated through the college placement office were not interesting. So, I set my sights on graduate business school, took the business boards, applied to several, and got into Michigan, Northwestern, and Columbia, maybe Wharton, and wait-listed at Stanford.

I selected Columbia for three reasons: First, I didn't know New York City much at all and thought going to school there would be interesting and worthwhile, and after being in school there for two years, I could always leave if I didn't like it. Second, the military draft was hanging over my head, and it was imperative that I become a full-time graduate student as soon as possible. Columbia had a three-semester school year, with a full-fledged semester beginning in June. And, third, Columbia had a top-notch reputation, particularly in finance and related subjects, being in New York City and all. So, Columbia it was, and I started classes only a few weeks after graduating from Brown in June of 1967.

I took the broad assortment of require 'core' courses and then concentrated on finance and accounting, out of interest. I took all the courses necessary for a double major, except 'auditing' (which is ironic in that 20 years later I was a partner in a major auditing firm). To pay my way, I worked from 5 to 9 PM each weekday as a 'clerk' in the market research department of Lever Brothers on Park Avenue, which required a three-train subway commute from my apartment.

I lived on West 120th, between Amsterdam Avenue and Morningside Park, in the only apartment building in the area that Columbia did not own. My apartment, on the top, fourth floor, was a furnished two-bedroom, one-bath, roach-infested place in the back. The roaches were so prevalent, we would pound on the door before opening it, to give them a head start in running back to the drains and other tiny holes where they lived. The rent was $137.50 per month, which I split with my roommate, John Kane, who had lived there for a year or two and posted the vacant bedroom on a bulletin board. John was finishing up a master's degree in economics and left the next year, replaced by a classmate of mine, Steve Canter.

My years at Columbia coincided with the nationwide civil rights and Viet Nam war protests, and foment prevailed on campus, with a group of students and others seizing a central University building, called Low Library, for a few days. Other than a single cancelled final exam, all this activity did not interfere with my classes. Each day for a few weeks, however, several busloads of New York City policemen in riot gear would be parked along Amsterdam Avenue in case they were needed.

After completing three semesters, I was quite out of money and needed a break, so I took the summer term of 1968 off from courses to work in the National Banking Division of Marine Midland Grace Trust Company of New York, a medium-sized bank holding company, with headquarters at 140 Broadway in Manhattan. Marine Midland had been founded and run from Buffalo and had merged several years past with the Grace Trust Company. (As part of that transaction, the family name Grace was to be maintained in the legal name of the bank for at least 10 years.)

After a week's training, I spent the summer as the fourth man in a three-man office responsible for all corporate business in Pennsylvania, Ohio, Michigan, Indiana, and Illinois. My job—really on-the-job-training—was to analyze credit worthiness of borrowers, and to cover communication with and servicing of corporate customers in the mid-west, in place of bank officers as they rotated vacation time during the summer. It was a good job, working with smart, competent bankers, learning a lot.

140 Broadway (3rd Floor Office, above the '140')

Credit Where Credit is Due

LINES OF CREDIT were annually reviewed and renewed during the summer, so much of my analytical focus was on such loans and lines to industrial companies in the region. I would grind through financial statements, tease out information about how the company was performing, and prepare an "Offering Sheet" summarizing whether the bank should or should not renew the line for another year.

The Offering Sheet—plus a big, fat credit file, if needed—was then reviewed by the bank's senior credit committee and either approved or turned down. That committee, formally named the Discount Committee, was chaired by George Schoellkopf, a crusty, large man in his 60s, with a room-filling presence. He was a member of a prominent Buffalo family, members of which had founded and run several large manufacturing businesses. He lived in Buffalo and would travel to 140 Broadway once or twice a month to chair the committee meetings.

The largest and most interesting of my assigned cases was the Erie Forge & Steel Corp., a well-established foundry and forging company, based in Erie, Pennsylvania and a Marine Midland customer for nearly two decades.

In early August, towards the end of my summer stint, I was to attend the credit committee meeting and present and defend the case for Erie Forge. They had had a tough year, with a slight drop in sales and a deterioration in their financial position. But, the majority of their stock had recently been purchased by Roblin Steel, a larger and stronger company, and Roblin had appointed its own executives as new managers at EF&S. With the new backing from Roblin, and a recommendation by me that the new loan be backed by assumption of EF&S accounts receivable, I was recommending approval of the loan to the credit committee—all laid out in the Offering Sheet.

When the agenda got to my customer, I summarized the case that they had in front of them, and there was very little comment around the table—maybe a detailed question or two. Then, George spoke up:

"I don't disagree with the analysis, the company's record, or its good historical relationship with our bank. But I know the Roblins well [Erie is less than 100 miles from Buffalo], and I've become wary, for some reason, of what they are doing. I can't put my finger on it."

His hesitation was pronounced, although seemingly without justification or any ire.

"Maybe Erie Forge, or the Roblins' backing of it, is not as strong as its management and auditors are showing. But the analysis looks right, and I guess we should go ahead and approve the loan."

Which they did, and I left the meeting.

With summer and my 10-week bank stint finished, I was soon back on the Columbia campus for my final semester. Using the business school library each day, I usually looked over the day's *Wall Street Journal* to get a sense of what was happening in the real business world.

One morning during that winter, I read on the front page that Erie Forge & Steel had had a debilitating accident at their main facility in Buffalo. It seems that a huge cauldron of molten steel moving on the sole rail strip between the furnace and the foundry had fallen over, spilling its entire contents all over the tracks. The cold winter weather—and this was Buffalo—hastened its cooling and hardening, with no hope of repair or a 'work around.' About a month later, the company defaulted on its Marine Midland loan and filed for bankruptcy.

* * *

Upon returning for my fourth and final semester at Columbia, I met with a professor to discuss a paper that would be required for his course. During our chat in his office, his phone rang and after a minute or two of listening, he held his hand over the phone and asked if I was looking for a part-time job. I certainly was, and he passed the phone to me. The fellow on the other end knew the professor well, had just graduated from Columbia, and worked in the Financial Studies Group (FSG) of Chemical Bank, at the time the nation's seventh largest bank. This led to fifteen to twenty hours of work a week for me.

FSG was staffed by fifteen or so MBAs who had recently joined the bank, plus a handful of part timers from New York City business schools. The mission was to carry out all kinds of analytical and special projects for the bank's corporate customers. Large corporations—including, or perhaps especially, the large banks—had begun hiring new MBAs en masse, figuring these young folks had dedicated themselves to business lives, had invested in two post-college years to do it, and had acquired new skills that were in short supply.

Chemical Bank was a full participant, and FSG provided a natural corral for these new MBA hires. It was a simpatico group of men and women, and besides interesting analytical work using nascent computers, it provided a chance to meet many experts across the much larger bank, and their customers.

Peak or Nadir of the Wall Street Man-Cave?

ONLY A COUPLE WEEKS into my part-time job, I planned to spend all of Thursday, September 19, at the bank, following an early-morning class. Just after noon, a fellow in FSG beckoned me to go with him around the corner to Wall and Broad Street to watch a girl come out of the BMT subway station

Wall Street crowd anticipating Francine Gottfried, September 19, 1968

on her way to work at a computer center nearby. It seems that a crowd had been gathering each day at that appointed time and place to see Francine Gottfried, a 21-year-old, 5-foot-3-inch full-figured lady from Williamsburg. So we went.

But rounding the corner from Pine Street, we encountered a sea of people—almost all guys—occupying the streets and filling the large 'square' as far as the eye could see. Although the weather was nice, milling around seemed pointless until a huge roar emanated from the square and reverberated across the space for a good five minutes. Francine had ascended the steps and was walking down the street to her office building, escorted by two policemen. She wore a tight yellow sweater and miniskirt.

The crowd was estimated at 5,000, three cars were damaged from men climbing onto their roofs for a better view, and stock trading virtually stopped. The *New York Daily News* headline read, "A Bust Panics Wall Street As the Tape Reads 43."

The crowd the next day was even larger, but her boss had asked her to stay home. She found a different route to work, and commented, "I think they're all crazy...I'm just an ordinary girl."

The On-Ramp & Runway

I graduated with my MBA degree in January 1969, and the last semester was rich in interviews for a full-time job and the decision process for what I wanted to do next.

Because corporate demand for MBAs was booming, I was lucky enough to consider offers from Inland Steel in Chicago, General Motors in New York, Owens Illinois in Toledo, and several others. And Chemical Bank offered me a permanent job in FSD.

Pay turned out not to be a factor, as all the offers were in a narrow salary range, between $10,800 and $13,000 per year to start, and that whole range was a lot to me.

I accepted the Chemical offer and began my first full-time job on February 3, 1969, because:
• I was already working part-time in a place with great people and interesting work.
• It was in New York, where I had come 18 months before but still had not plied much of it, having spent most of my time studying and working.
• It was one of the $13,000 offers.

Riding an Era of Change, 1967-2007

MY WORK and career as a banker—and then as a consultant—coincided with a period of dramatic global growth and change in (a) financial markets, (b) the evolution of many established industries including banking and finance, and (c) the management approaches and effectiveness within those businesses. This half century of change and progress was the backdrop and environment that enabled my serendipitous career opportunities and 'choices.'

From my college years in the mid-1960s, to my retirement from full-time work in 2007, the world economy was transformed from a post-World War II boom in the United States and a period of rebuilding virtually everywhere else, to a largely global and interdependent, more productive and efficient, and technologically supported engine of growth and prosperity.

The sea changes that affected financial markets and banks and other financial institutions presented constant challenges to all those institutions and their leaders.

I was lucky to participate in anticipating and reacting to those challenges. An academy of business management had developed and was growing through business schools in the U.S. and other countries, adding disciplines and new approaches to the theory of the firm. Customer-focused competitive strategy, principled corporate governance, and a focus on building shareholder value became more central to companies' managements and priorities, supported by better financial management, management by objectives, performance-based compensation, and cost management and containment. Increasingly sophisticated theories and approaches to financial markets and financial management became widespread, enabling and requiring greater value added by the banks, brokerages, exchanges, and other pieces of the financial infrastructure.

Management consultants utilized and advanced these approaches and techniques across industries and internationally.

As the changes took place in fits and starts over the decades, my jobs took the form of a series of bobs and weaves, to react to opportunities that popped up and to follow my meandering interests. The opportunities and interests manifested themselves in (a) the types of financial and other client companies with which I worked, (b) the types of management issues and opportunities addressed, and (c) where I worked.

The changes took place in most countries—at different times and speeds—and invariably raised issues of what specific changes banks should make and how to implement them—all of which were different at different banks. The differences were even more pronounced from country to country, each with its unique markets, laws and regulations, and management skills and cultures.

Upon joining Chemical, I had great fun for four years, with a straight-up learning curve. After a few months in the 'credit department' learning how to evaluate corporate loan requests, I moved back to FSG (having become a department—thus FSD) for good, and after two years was asked to manage it. The department grew to a staff of about 30. I became practiced at representing the department and bank, recruiting and hiring, evaluating performance, and other basics of managing people. For the first time I had to learn how to come to grips with firing and counselling out people who deserved it performance-wise. That was wrenching but occasionally necessary.

During this period, some of our projects were for the bank itself, supplementing Chemical's planning department, which

CONTINUED PG. 141

Partial List of Changes Affecting Financial Institutions in the 1960s and Subsequent Decades

- National financial markets grew and became deeper and more efficient in support of growing economies around the world, and the dollar and Eurodollar became the leading currency that facilitated financing of expanding international trade and the linking of national financial markets into a semblance of global integration.

- In the U.S., the Bank Holding Company Act of 1970 became the catalyst for American banking shedding the patchwork of national and state banks, the constraints and inefficiencies of unit banks, and state-by-state regulation of branching. As a result, statewide and nationwide banking took hold, and banks were allowed to invent and provide new products and services.

- The straight jacket on commercial banking activities imposed by the Glass-Steagall Act in 1933, was considerably eased, by allowing commercial bank holding companies to underwrite securities. This represented a considerable broadening of potential service lines for the commercial banks, reduced the historical differences between commercial and investment banking, and lead to the investment banks bulking up their own direct lending.

- American commercial banks began making residential home mortgage loans, which had been the province of savings banks, and the growth of 'securitization' of those (and other) loans transformed housing finance and spurred a continuing increase in home ownership and home-based debt.

- The 15,000 commercial banks in the U.S., and the additional thousands of thrift institutions, began consolidating to achieve economies of scale in marketing, support services and overhead, and in making larger loans and tapping deeper funding sources.

- Credit cards became the payment mechanism of choice, and a multitude of early proprietary cards condensed into a handful of worldwide brands and associations.

- The commercial paper market developed as a major source of short-term funding for the most credit worthy corporations, side-stepping the banks by proving cheaper money for those companies.

- Bank commercial loans evolved from short-term lines of credit to finance seasonal and temporary corporate needs for cash, to longer-term lending, providing cash to be repaid over years instead of months, and from future cash flows instead of from sales of inventories.

- As local economies around the world became stable and grew, constraints on the flows of capital among countries were lifted, and international trade and finance flourished.

- Instruments to finance trade—lead by letters of credit—facilitated world trade as market interdependence became the norm for both goods and money.

- U.S. multinational corporations thrived and expanded around the world, and the banks strived to follow them and meet their needs, initially in liaison with correspondent banks in other countries, and then by establishing their own branches and other operations abroad.

- International banking became a major source of potential business, and competition, for the larger banks. And large foreign banks—especially European and Japanese—made inroads in the American market.

- May Day—May 1, 1975—marked the end of fixed minimum stock brokerage commissions in the U.S., resulting in the advent of 'discount brokers' and a general increase in competition and eventual consolidation among brokerage firms.

- Technological advances changed many aspects of banking and transactions, ranging from the advent of ATMs, to online payments and securities transactions, to how people buy and finance everything from pizzas to airplanes.

- Financial management within corporations became a body of academic and creative interest, with many approaches and techniques enabling companies to finance greater growth more cheaply and efficiently, and also to both incur and mitigate greater financial risks. These included the use of commercial paper, factoring, capital asset leasing, the bond markets, sophisticated cash management systems, and the central concept of the time value of money and present value.

- Banks devoted a new focus on customer profitability, risk management, asset and liability management, retail strategy and branch system management, international and corporate banking and corporate finance strategy, holding company management structure, and achieving the lowest cost sources of funds.

* * *

brought us in close and daily working contact with senior and seasoned managers in important functions and departments in the bank. How the bank should branch across New York State, whether and how the bank might start an REIT, and whether the bank should try to purchase an established network of overseas branches were examples of projects we lead.

House of Four Trees, Jean Dubuffet

* * *

In 1971, I watched out my 13th floor office window as cranes and workers pieced together a several-story-tall Dubuffet black and white sculpture on the adjoining Chase Manhattan plaza. Commissioned by Chase Chairman David Rockefeller, it was an attractive abstract that has stood the test of time. It evidently is named "The House of Four Trees."

Jumbo's New Paradigm

DURING THE LATE 1960S, the big banks were expanding their leveraged leasing businesses, which was dominated by buying new airplanes and leasing them to the airlines. The various banks bid against one another for the airlines' business, based on how low the lease payments would be. That, in turn, was based on the assumed 'residual value,' which was the best guess on what the plane could be sold for at the end of the lease. (The more the plane was worth at the end, the less the annual payments had to be during the lease.)

The proven and accepted history of the aircraft leasing business was that as leases on new planes expired, the planes were resold or re-leased by their bank owners to second and third tier airlines—such as Air Gabon and many others around the world.

The Boeing 747—the largest and most expensive airliner to date—was about to be introduced in 1970, and the banks were salivating and competing aggressively for this new wave of leasing opportunities.

At that time, Chemical Bank had a small group of lending officers who specialized in Aerospace-related loans and were working to determine the appropriate lease rate to bid for a bunch of 747's. Their attention for weeks was on assessing the history of other planes (e.g., DC-8, DC-9, B-707, B-727) in terms of what they sold for when their original leases ran out. These calculations were to provide the basis for assuming what the new 747s would likely be worth at the end—to be sold to other, successor airlines.

After rigorous analysis and many lengthy discussions, the group and the bank's senior credit officers were about ready to decide on the lease prices to be offered to the airlines. At the beginning of one of the final meetings, a junior bank analyst opened the discussion with a new discovery he had made over the weekend. The Boeing 747 required at least 10,700 feet of runway for takeoff, and there were not more than a half dozen runways in the world that were long enough.

Poof! went the analytical results. What airlines would buy the used 747s at the end of their leases, if they can't fly them to most of the world's airports? And, a projected lack of a secondary market meant the banks would need to make much more money on the initial lease, which meant much higher lease rates charged to the airlines.

As it played out over the next two decades, many runways were lengthened. (Today, there are 86 airport runways more than 13,000 feet long.) And a broad secondary market did develop accordingly for the 747 and other jumbo jets.

Dead Letter File

IN THE LATE 1960S Chemical Bank installed a new trust account computer system that automatically created signed letters from the bank to be sent to thousands of trust and estate customers for marketing and other purposes.

The system drew the salutation for the letter from the last word of the name line in the basic account information file, in the same way that mailing salutations were derived for checking account customers. For example: William D. Turner, led to "Dear Mr. Turner."

Being a trust and estates division, the first mailing from their new system went to something like 1,500 dead people, headlined "Dear Mr. Deceased."

The file names were stored as, for example, "William D. Turner, Deceased."

Debuts from Hell

IN 1969, Chemical Bank was at the forefront of developing automated teller machines (ATMs), aiming to provide cash and other teller services 24 hours a day and accessible from outside the bank, even in remote locations.

Working closely with Docutel, a Dallas-based pioneer in ATM manufacturing, Chemical chose the Long Island town of Rockville Center to install and test market the first machines in America. They installed the first machines and publicized them locally, encouraging bank customers in the town to use them to access cash and then later for all their teller needs.

The initial machines were prototypes, and almost everything that could go wrong with them did. Over the first few months of public use, they jammed or locked up, didn't recognize customer sign-in codes, ate cards, ran out of cash, provided the wrong amounts of cash, were broken into, etc., etc. The Rockville Center machines became so known for trouble that the bank removed them entirely.

From the bank's point of view, the test was successful, as the kinks were worked out with the manufacturer, and the levels of service and reliability soon were brought up to target levels and better. With the improved machines and support systems 'shaken down' from the trial period, Chemical proceeded to expand throughout their broad retail banking markets, and along with Citibank was the leading ATM provider in the Northeast. During the 1970s and 1980s, ATMs revolutionized the banking industry, displacing many aspects of branch banking.

However, for a year or two, Chemical delayed installing any ATMs in Rockville Center and did not advertise or otherwise encourage their use in the town, so as not to further rile its customers there—even as the bank aggressively installed the machines all over the rest of the region.

* * *

A few years later as a management consultant, I was doing a series of analyses with the Chase Manhattan Bank, trying to determine the value of installing ATM machines inside bank branches to replace human tellers. Because the majority of teller transactions were either deposits or withdrawals, these were targeted to be migrated from tellers to ATMs.

The analysis boiled down to comparing the cost of the machine and operating it, versus the savings in wages and benefits of a teller—both on a per-transaction basis. We then determined the number of transactions per day that would be required to be switched from the teller to the machine, in order to make the machine worthwhile. I don't recall what that break-even number was, but let's assume it was 90 machine transactions per day.

After installing such a machine in each of a few Chase branches, the bank carefully monitored the number of ATM transactions, and also tracked the number of those types of transactions still done at the teller windows. If 90 or more transactions were being done at the ATM, it was worth installing it.

Over the initial months of the introduction, customers began using the machines and transaction volumes grew. But we found that the number of teller transactions did not decline. Stationing an observer in a couple of the branches, we discovered that customers, untrusting of the machines, would transact as they always had with the teller, and then, especially if they had just made a deposit, would go to the machine to confirm that their account reflected the deposit or withdrawal. As a result, the ATM volume was not *replacing* teller transactions but *adding* to them.

Eventually, customers became confident and trusting, and ATMs proved to be incredibly successful from both the bank and customer points of view. They now blanket the country in branches, vestibules, and remote locations. Chemical's advertisements for the first ATMs boasted "Our bank will open at 9:00 AM and never close again." Long term, they were correct.

Lending Money

AFTER THREE YEARS, in 1972, I was asked to take a job the bank considered to be a traditional 'line' banking job—leading the mid-west region of the National Division, which managed Chemical's relationships with all sorts of customers operating in the 'territory,' which comprised Minnesota, Iowa, Nebraska, the Dakotas, and a slice of Chicago. Chemical had not yet organized by industry groups, so my purview covered companies in all industries, including grain and cereal, toys, flour milling, heavy manufacturing, computers, investment managers, oil exploration, food, fast food, toys, and local banks that did business with Chemical.

Not only was it a stretch on the bank's part to put me in that job with such a lack of knowledge of the many industries I would serve, but it was also a stretch on their part in terms of lending experience, or lack thereof. Although I had spent a few months as a credit analyst, the new job had almost always been staffed by long-term and senior National Division corporate lenders who had spent years making loans and rising up the ranks. With such thin hands-on lending experience and a generally unconventional background, I remain thankful for my mentor at the bank for having the confidence, or ignorance, in hiring me into that role. The job was challenging, but quite doable, and I had an enjoyable and rewarding time building relationships with a few dozen financial executives and expanding the loans and services they took from Chemical.

Accreditation of Threads

During my final semester at Columbia Business School in the fall of 1968, it dawned on me that I needed a new business suit, as I was gearing up my interviewing for a permanent job when I graduated in January. (This would double my wardrobe to two suits.) At my part time job at Chemical Bank, I asked around and was referred by a young colleague to a classic old New York tailor, Gorsart Company, first on Duane Street then on Murray Street, just a few blocks up Broadway from the bank. Gorsart was a suit maker, selling almost exclusively men's wool suits and silk ties. They were located on the second floor of an old warehouse-style building, with a small sign on the brick wall at street level. The steep flight of stairs up led to a large, dingy room full of racks of suits and two or three tailor-type salesmen, with Norman the manager and main greeter. Turns out Norm Gorsart was a Brown graduate and was about 60.

For decades, I wore a size 38 Long suit, and many men's stores didn't even carry that size. Gorsart had full racks of them in different fine wools and cuts. Better yet, they were very affordable—probably a third to a half less than the well-known men's shops like Brooks Brothers, Paul Stuart, Bloomingdales, etc. So, I bought my first suit there that fall and kept going back for all my suits through the 1970s. Although the store seemed to do ok, it was rarely crowded, and none of my evolving group of business colleagues went there. I was content and aggressively loyal, and I was beating the system monetarily.

* * *

In those years, Chemical Bank had several 'advisory boards' in New York City, comprising corporate officers of large and leading companies headquartered there. At quarterly luncheon meetings, top bank executives would lead discussions of current business and finance issues, which, while providing the participants an interesting forum of peers to share points of view, would also burnish the bank's reputation and garner customer loyalty among the attending customers. I was invited to several of them to kick off the discussions of how computer models were being used to greatly improve financial forecasting and the testing of potential future business strategies (or something like that).

***

In 1970 or 71, one such lunch took place in a Chemical Bank conference room in mid-town Manhattan, and it was hosted by that board's Chairman, Hulbert "Huck" Aldrich, the bank's Vice Chairman. To young bankers like myself, Mr. Aldrich was not very visible and a bit of an enigma. He had been a prominent New York banker as long-time President and CEO of the New York Trust Company, which had merged years before with the Chemical Corn Exchange Bank to become the Chemical Bank New York Trust Company. Since that merger, he had been Chemical's Vice Chairman, and would retire in 1972. And he and his ancestors from Rhode Island had become socially prominent in New York, with one marrying John D. Rockefeller Jr.

Huck's position came with a private dining room at the top of the bank, where we and many others in the bank held meetings with customers, because Huck rarely used it. That room had a very large oil painting of a peacock on one wall, rumored to be repossessed collateral for a defaulted loan.

***

Following my luncheon with the advisory board that day, Huck asked me if I wanted a ride back to the bank—no doubt having seen me, the young banker nearly 40 years his junior, for the first time. I accepted and we got into opposite sides of the back seat of a bank-owned Lincoln to be driven downtown.

As the car pulled away down Park Avenue South, there on the seat between us was Huck's folded overcoat, with the label on top: Gorsart Company. I showed him my label and felt even better about my man Norm.

A Banker in the Twin Cities

IN 1971, when Chemical Bank accidentally put me in charge of the bank's corporate and correspondent bank business in the region encompassing Minnesota, Iowa, Nebraska, the Dakotas, and a slice of Chicago, it boiled down to mostly Minneapolis/St. Paul and a slice of Chicago. I spent a week a month in the Twin Cities, calling on customers that included Pillsbury, Honeywell, Cargill, Control Data, 3M, IDS, Dairy Queen, and many other great companies. Such big corporations in that era depended on the New York banks to finance their growth and success, and I was their window to the 7th largest U.S. bank. As a result, although I was younger and less senior than the financial executives that I dealt with, they suffered my visits, and were very engaging. Some reflections:

- The twin cities—and all of Minnesota—was and is a fine place. State license plates say "Land of 10,000 Lakes" but there actually are nearly 12,000 lakes there. A surprising number of folks—especially men—had 'camps' in the far north of the state, where they spent as much of the summer as they could. Some were accessible only by plane and had no electricity or real running water.

- The Chief Financial Officer of the giant agricultural products company Cargill had a large map of the U.S. on his office wall and would have a giant silver pin with the name "Chemical Bank" stuck into New York City whenever I visited, despite Chemical being only a secondary bank in their banking group.

- For the most part, the people in Minneapolis and St. Paul were delightful and interesting, as well as provincial characters. Apache, a major oil exploration company at that time had their headquarters in the landmark Foshay Tower in Minneapolis. The CFO's office looked towards the airport. He lamented the population growth in the area and told me that he wished that every departing flight was full, and every arriving flight was empty. One winter Friday in January or February when I met with him, I asked if he ever took a vacation.

"Yes," he responded. "As a matter of fact, the wife and I are going to St. Croix for a week later this month."

"Aha," I reacted, "After all the grief you give me about the paradise here, it's nice to see that you're going for a warm Caribbean respite."

"No, no," he said. "We go ice fishing on the St. Croix River in northern Wisconsin."

• In that era, there were two large bank holding companies in the Twin Cities—Northwest Bancorp, headquartered in St. Paul, and First Bank System, based in Minneapolis. Both had high-profile CEO's who fiercely competed against one another, for local banking business and also to expand the fastest by buying other banks. Phil Nason was the leader for Northwest, and George Dixon for FBS. The Mississippi River, which split the two cities was sometimes referred to as the 'Nason-Dixon Line.'

• At the New York bank where I worked, a weekly list of newly opened and closed corporate accounts was circulated among the whole corporate banking division. And, although one of my accounts was 3M, one of the most prominent companies in the country, Chemical was a very minor bank to the company. In a period when major corporations were consolidating and reducing the number of their banks, I was worried that they would close their Chemical account and that the closure would be broadcast throughout the bank with my name attached. I discussed this with the 3M CFO, and he agreed to keep it open as long as he could and to give me advance notice of any such intentions. I also offered to keep it open by providing my own cash to the account, but it never came to that.

• I usually stayed in the original Radisson Hotel in Minneapolis, and on each trip would invariably run into a bellboy there with his nameplate: "Isaac Hayes," alas, not the singer.

Minneapolis/St. Paul and its 3 million residents qualify as 'north country' with its 45° north latitude. As a major, modern, commercial center, it is also a jumping-off point for the true north, due north.

Thief River Falls

ONE OF MY corporate customers was Arctic Enterprises, an original and leading manufacturer of snowmobiles (the 'Arctic Cat'), which had grown fast and depended on a big line of credit to support year-around production of vehicles, until the cash came in from sales in the fall and winter. Probably in the spring of 1972, I decided to make my first visit to the company headquarters and plant at Thief River Falls, a town of 8,500 about 300 miles northwest of the Twin Cities—at 48° north latitude.

MSP is the Twin Cities airport that was also home base of Northwest Airlines and remains a major hub in the 'upper Midwest.' But the route to Thief River Falls was via a North Central Airlines Convair 580, twin propeller aircraft. The first stop, about an hour out, was Brainerd, a town of 12,000. It had two runways shaped like an "X." One or two passengers got off, nobody got on. The second leg—about 40 minutes—was on to Bemidji, also with a population of about 12,000, and known as the birthplace of Paul Bunyan (with his blue ox Babe). The

Bemidji runway was a single strip of pavement, with lights surrounding the strip, I believe. Again, one or two got off, nobody boarded. The third and final leg to Thief River Falls took about 30 minutes. That airport consisted of a single, unpaved landing strip with no airport building, but a large chalk board on which someone had written the expected weather conditions, presumably for the pilot's benefit. I was the only passenger left on the plane.

I rented a car from a lot nearby and found my way to the T-59 Motel. There was a wire with a plug sticking out of the car's front grill, that I plugged into a receptacle at the front of the motel's parking space, to prevent the car from freezing up overnight. I had dinner at the small diner/restaurant a short walk down Highway 59.

Even though it was early spring, the plant had a big inventory of finished snowmobiles, stacked high in crates around three sides of the building, reflecting the weak snow conditions in the winter just ended. As a result, production had been shut down earlier than usual. The company had a significant and growing clothing business, staffed by local ladies, evidently including some commuting the 65 miles from across the border in Canada.

The Arctic managers were gracious, welcoming, and happy, clearly relishing their rural environment and their location, three stops from civilization and far from New York bankers.

Humbled

IN THE SUMMER of 1972, my wife and I took a vacation to the lake region of Italy and Yugoslavia. We both had good jobs and no kids, and those were the days when one might actually get away for several consecutive weeks—without cell phones. We originally had planned to visit Spain, but with President Tito celebrating his 80th birthday that year, we figured we should see Yugoslavia before he died and the country went up for grabs.

Our trip was wonderful. We drove from town to town and lake to lake in the north of Italy in a Fiat 500, took the train from Venice to Zagreb and a bald-tired flight toward Dubrovnik, and then made our way up the Adriatic coast to Hvar and Split. The three weeks flew by.

* * *

Getting back to work at Chemical Bank in New York, I felt relaxed and invigorated. As one of the many hotshot MBAs that the bank had hired, I worked in a special division that led the bank's participation in the growing and changing market for lending to large corporations.

In my first week back, I found myself on the elevator with Mirjan Ivanetic—called 'Mike'—on our way up to lunch. (One of the perks was the right to eat in the Officers Dining Room at the top of the building, which I often did.) Mike, in his mid-50s, was the Chief Credit Officer of the division, and was a soft-spoken and congenial man. I knew he was originally from Yugoslavia and had both law and business degrees from American universities. He was an expert at structuring complex loan agreements.

We sat down to lunch, and he asked me all about my trip. As my description of good food, beautiful landscapes, and interesting people waned, he asked what I enjoyed most about the two countries and the three-week stay. I thought for a moment and said that the small Italian town of Bellagio, on the point of land jutting up into Lake Como, was probably the most memorable spot, what with its hillsides of pastel shops, houses, and restaurants; incomparable water views and small marinas; and bustling local people that blunted the effect of the summer tourists. It was delightful.

I asked Mike if he had ever been to Bellagio.

He responded, "Yes, I was there once, as a young man." I was glad to suddenly have this in common with Mike and bayed him to tell me more. In a calm and matter-of-fact voice, he began by saying that, as a 22-year-old, he had decided to flee his home country after the Nazis invaded in April of 1941. Uh-oh, not a circumstance I had anticipated.

He related how he left his home near Ljubljana, with no possessions and little money. Walking and hopping rides, mostly at night, he made his way through Slovenia and into Italy. While becoming in awe of this story, I was feeling smaller and smaller in stature as it unfolded.

Continuing past Venice, Verona, and Lake Garda, he had gone through Bergamo and then, finally, made it to Bellagio—a total trip of some 300 miles. With his remaining pocket change, he bribed the ferryman to take him across the lake to the western shore, where he walked the last few miles into neutral Switzerland. He stayed there, safe, eventually emigrating to the United States.

As he finished his harrowing tale of leaving his home and family, sneaking across three countries at night, with nothing, for weeks, I felt no longer present or relevant to the conversation.

Serving Bankers as Clients

McKinsey & Company, after two successful and high-profile assignments with Citibank and Chase Manhattan, decided to formalize a banking and financial institutions practice, and they commissioned a search to find experienced bankers to help staff and grow it.

After nearly five years at Chemical, a call from a headhunter at search firm Russell Reynolds Associates led me to consider and then move to management consulting.

IN THE RECRUITING PROCESS, I met almost a dozen of the McKinsey people, at all levels, and found them smart, energetic, and driven. I left Chemical and became a McKinsey Associate in April 1973, for basically three reasons. First, I had liked and thrived on my project work at Chemical and realized it had been consulting, and this was a chance to get back into the problem-solving world at the most professional, well-run firm around. Second, I had also come to know banking a bit and the industry was facing constant and major changes, and this would give me the opportunity to work for many banks,

CONTINUED PG. 158

A Consulting Career as Markets and Banking Evolved

1970s (Resident in New York)

• Assisted banks in North America as they restructured their strategies and management organizations, to reflect deregulating markets, and to meet customer needs more directly.

• CLIENTS: United Virginia Bankshares, Chase Manhattan, American Express, Bankers Trust, Wachovia, Royal Bank of Canada, Multibanco Comermex, Rhode Island Hospital Trust, Shawmut Bank, Lincoln First Bank.

1980s (Resident in London '80-'86; then New York)

• Helped shape the strategic, structural, and governance directions of U.S. and European banks and insurers, as the EU market began to take shape, and the internationalization of financial markets accelerated.

• Led policy making and change initiatives at leading Middle Eastern banks, as their local markets and banking systems were maturing rapidly to accommodate growth driven by the surge in oil revenue.

• CLIENTS: CIGNA, Prudential, Barclays, Amsterdam-Rotterdam Bank, Skandinaviska Enskilda Banken, Bergen Bank, Royal Insurance, Midland Bank, Trustee Savings Bank, Bank of Cyprus, National Commercial Bank, Riyadh Bank, Saudi International Bank, Gulf Investment Corporation.

1990s (Resident in New York; then London from 1999)

• Assisted banks active in financial market globalization including inter-regional consolidation with banks in North America, Western and Eastern Europe, and Hong Kong.

• Helped devise early expansion and consolidation roles and strategies for the cross-border clearing and settlement business.

• CLIENTS: Hong Kong & Shanghai Bank, Midland Bank, Euroclear, Cedel, London Clearing House, Bank of Montreal, Visa, Mellon Bank, Commercial Union, CoreStates Financial, Ceska Sporitelna, Bank Zachodni WBK Group.

2000s (Resident in Seoul 2001-3; Hong Kong 2003-4; then New York)

• Focused on Asian institutions, assisting with strategy, governance, and management effectiveness issues, especially in Korea, Greater China (Mainland, Hong Kong, Taiwan), Singapore, and Australia.

• Assisted the Netherlands central bank on bank merger and consolidation issues.

• CLIENTS: Woori Financial Holding Company, Samsung Life, Shenzhen Development Bank, China Minshing Bank, China Development Bank, Taishan International Bank, Wing Hang Bank, Development Bank of Singapore, Westpac, Dutch National Bank.

not just one. And, third, the chemistry seemed excellent, and McKinsey wanted to pay me 30% more than I was making. I can't recall if I thought I was worth it.

* * *

The new and often perplexing industry issues that arose drove a continuing need and desire among bank boards and managements for help from management consultants, who were seen to bring an outside, unbiased point of view, carry out rigorous and fact-based analysis of the issues and alternative solutions, and/or build on experience in resolving similar issues elsewhere.

From the consultant's perspective, the changing environment and new management need brought continuing opportunities to add great value, case after case, without the risk of working on the same issues over and over—especially if clients were located in different markets and countries.

* * *

Prepared to 'hit the ground running' due to my familiarity with banking and banks, and my project work at Chemical, I soon was enmeshed in McKinsey's dedication to client service; extensive programs to train every consultant in every aspect of the job, from identifying key success factors, to data-driven analysis, to effective and persuasive communications and impactful writing; and an impassioned emphasis on ideas, with little regard for hierarchy among consulting team members. The level of thought, energy, and dedication was unmatched and exciting, and all of that seemed to come through to the clients in the way they reacted to our work. The work ethic was palpable—unhealthy for some—and extensive travel was the rule for the many assignments that were outside New York City.

This dedication to the job was illustrated by a hyperbolic

story about a new consultant on his first assignment which required 12-hour days, seven days a week, for the duration. About two weeks in, mid-day on a Sunday, the associate couldn't stand working in his Manhattan office any longer and took a taxi home to take the afternoon off. Entering his apartment, he heard noises in the bedroom and, peeking in the door, saw the partner on the project in bed with his wife. Sneaking quietly back out the door, he took another taxi back to the office. Putting his head on his desk and exhaling deeply, he said to himself, "Whew, I almost got caught!"

With about 350 consultants world-wide, McKinsey was small then relative to today. New York was the largest office with something like 60 consultants, but, overall, more than half the consultants and half the firm's billings were outside the U.S. (By 1986, there were some 450 consultants in the New York office alone, and today the firm is relatively gigantic and everywhere.)

Business was good, I liked the work, and I performed OK, so my pay increased nicely. Enriched by the firm's belief in self-assessments, on-going skills training, a focus on individual development, and an informal but strong mentoring culture, an attentive 'student' could glean a great deal from virtually every person he or she came to work with at the firm.

As I progressed from associate to team leader and engagement manager, and then to partner in 1979, my clients included American money center and regional banks, and a major Mexican bank. Subjects dealt with management structure and corporate governance, corporate and business unit strategy, bank-wide cost reduction, CEO and board reporting, and international and multinational banking strategy. I also spent the good part of a year working on a major project for AT&T, which provided me telecom experience and contributed to the eventual restructuring of the entire Bell System, as it moved from a monopoly to an energetic competitor in its industry.

Headquarters of these companies—and the required 50—100% of my time in those places—included New York City, Basking Ridge, New Jersey, Richmond, Winston-Salem, Providence, Boston, Rochester, and Mexico City. Travel for related visits and interviews added London, Frankfurt, Vienna, Tokyo, Bangkok, and Seoul.

An Alcoholic Career?

WHEN I JOINED the New York office in 1973, and after a bit of orientation and training, my first assignment was to work with a new McKinsey client, United Virginia Bankshares, based in Richmond—as the junior member, of course, on the small McKinsey team. The assignment had been 'sold' and was led by Louis Gerstner, a young McKinsey Senior Partner and finance specialist, and the team leader was a McKinsey senior manager.

To kick off the project, we were all to meet in Richmond on a Monday morning. Gerstner told me to meet him at Newark Airport for the early morning United flight to Richmond and we would go together. I did so, and we had two bulkhead seats, 1A and 1B on the Boeing 737. We settled in, took off, and were reading newspapers when the flight attendant came through and asked for drink and breakfast orders. Lou said yes, he'd like orange juice, two scotches and the scrambled eggs.

I was poker-faced and quiet but flabbergasted. What kind of job was this going to be? I grew up with a father in the advertising industry and can attest to the free-wheeling, raucous Mad Men environment in that industry in the 1950s. But, was consulting going to be like that? Did a top McKinsey consultant always begin his day with whiskey at eight in the morning?

After ordering and wondering what I had gotten myself into,

the food trays came with everything on them. Lou reached forward, took the two bottles of whiskey off his tray, and put them in his suit coat pocket. Turning to me, he said he always did that, because a trove of the small bottles that he built up at home was perfect to take on family vacations.

The trip was redeemed, and Lou, the client, and 15 years at the firm were not disappointing.

'Balance' in the Eye of the Beholder

THE MCKINSEY engagement manager on my first consulting assignment was a PhD in finance from Wharton who had joined the firm in Los Angeles and recently transferred to the New York office. Bob was a smart, cerebral but driven consultant and a congenial, engaging guy —not everyone was. He loved his work and was at it most of the time.

The assignment concerned a bank holding company management structuring problem with United Virginia Bankshares. CEO Kay Randall had asked McKinsey partner Lou Gerstner to do the project, and Bob and I were the team on the ground. And the ground was in Richmond.

On this project, and on two subsequent ones that I saw him lead, Bob worked and traveled constantly—more than most other consultants, and that's saying something. He was efficient and creative and produced superior and polished recommendations and other 'final products.' Still, he was always working. I was there to help, challenge, fill in, and complete the results of our interviewing and analysis, and to help draft the reports. I learned a lot, and the client was pleased with the results.

One of Bob's daughters was found to have a serious disease. Although the relatively radical treatment seemed to be working, Bob's working hours and travel schedule were no longer compatible with the family's needs, and he decided to leave McKinsey and consulting.

He told me that the last straw with the consulting life was on one Friday night, getting into his bed at home and instinctively picking up the phone to leave a wake-up call.

Bob, his wife, and their three daughters moved to Richmond, and he became the head of strategic planning for First & Merchants Bank, a prominent and growing bank holding company headquartered there.

* * *

A couple years later, I was interviewing candidates for summer jobs at McKinsey, and one of them was a fellow between years at Harvard Business School, who had worked several years for First & Merchants in Richmond. During our chat, I asked him if he knew Bob at the bank, and he said, "Of course, everyone there knows Bob, a great guy." I then speculated that, having heard that Bob's daughter had miraculously stabilized, the calmer work environment and better work-family balance must have been a good choice for Bob.

To that, the fellow replied that Bob was known throughout the bank as the hardest worker in the executive ranks. In fact, "he's the only employee with a key to the front door of the bank's office tower, so he can come and go late at night and on weekends."

Homeless at McKinsey

The New York Office of McKinsey in the 1970s served the entire northeastern United States, the closest other offices being located in Washington, D.C., Toronto, Pittsburgh, and Cleveland. As a result, any client assignment in the area was staffed with a rich mix of New York-based consultants, and extensive travel and nights away were assumed. And because the New York office was the largest office and contained experts in many specialized subjects, assignments and travel to more distant clients across the country and overseas prevailed as well. And the office, like the firm, was growing year-to-year.

In 1975 or 1976, one of New York's new MBA hires was Dick Price, who lived in Philadelphia, having just graduated from Wharton. After a few assignments in and around New York, but also at least one large project in Europe, Dick vacated his Philadelphia apartment, put his belongings in storage, and worked out of the New York office. He had no home. His mail came to the office, and life 'services' like clothes cleaning and storage, he arranged with hotels or otherwise when he was in New York.

Being an avid hockey fan, and loyal to the Philadelphia Flyers, Dick did not give up his season tickets or stop going to the games. He took the Amtrack Metroliner from New York to Philadelphia in the late afternoon of game days and returned or stayed in Philadelphia for the night after the game.

Watch or Walk Over You?

MY SECOND or third consulting project as a consultant was a cost-reduction project for the Chairman and CEO of Wachovia Bank in 1974. I spent five days each week for about eight months in Winston-Salem, North Carolina. It was a well-managed bank, the managers and client team were smart, gracious and effective, and the assignment was very successful, thanks to top level support. Although this assignment was longer than average, it serves as an example of the kind of client and team working relationships and all-encompassing focus of a major project with a well-run bank. During that time, some events, observations, and experiences stand out, including the following:

• My favorite restaurant in town was Greek, and I would go for dinner a couple times each week. But they had the odd practice of keeping the bottled red wine in a refrigeration unit, considerably colder than the white wine cabinet.

• In conversation with Reynolds Tobacco managers—at its headquarters there—it was explained that they used a carefully-crafted payment process to pay their huge Federal excise taxes, which amounted to many millions of dollars paid quarterly. To maximize the float (and earnings thereon), they would walk a paper check drawn on the company's account at Wachovia, to the local Post Office, at the last possible moment on the last possible day that the payment was due. Obtaining a date stamp certifying that it was mailed on that date, the mailing envelope was addressed to the Federal Government's lock box for such payments in a west coast city (Seattle, I believe). By the time the check arrived in Seattle, was processed, was deposited through the Federal Reserve clearing house system, and paid by Wachovia, many days would pass, allowing Reynolds to make use of that money all that time.

• The Wachovia team leader and I took a couple hours off one day to take a tour of the Reynolds cigarette factory on the outskirts of Winston-Salem. The building was immense, probably a couple square blocks. But, once inside, about 90% of the floor space was vacant, with a bunch of high-tech cigarette machines placed comfortably in the other 10%. It seems that continuously improving technology over the decades allowed the full output of cigarettes to be produced by a small fraction of the number of machines originally required.

• The deal with McKinsey and client Wachovia was that I went home to New York each weekend, or my wife came to visit in Winston-Salem. On one such visit, we went to a show with the bank's team leader and his wife, in a venue in the basement of the local Holiday Inn. The 'club' may have been named 'The Cave.' In any case, we went to see the Tams, whose 1950s hit was entitled *What Kind of Fool*. The southern group's baritone had an unbelievably deep voice, and that performance was a highlight of my stint there.

• In our cost-reduction mode, we scoured expenses of all kinds, and teed up for management the case for cutting something out or reducing it, versus continuing to spend. One example was the 200 subscriptions to *Golf Magazine* that the bank was buying for employees. Another was the number of company cars the bank bought or leased for managers. One poignant picture we submitted was a photo of a manager's car in Charlotte, showing a boat hitch affixed to the rear bumper. (Yes, we were smart-ass MBAs, and some would say that's redundant.)

• At the time, Wachovia competed with North Carolina National Bank (NCNB), and the Citizens & Southern Bank in Atlanta as the southeast's leading banks. Banks across the country had expanded the new car loan business to the point of saturation with very low credit criteria for granting the loans. NCNB, headquartered in Charlotte, had been particularly aggressive throughout the Carolinas—much more than Wachovia. As they became fraught with car repossessions, NCNB leased a whole parking lot in Winston-Salem to park the cars they took back from delinquent borrowers. To track this, someone at Wachovia would count the repossessed cars from their office window high up in the Wachovia building and report the extent and trend of NCNB's problem.

• Wachovia's Chairman, John Watlington, was nearing retirement and organized the bank among four EVPs of the next generation, from which the Board would pick a successor. Mr. Watlington had hired McKinsey for several projects, partially to encourage and gauge how the EVPs carried out the projects and implemented their results. This positioning was ideal for our cost reduction project, as it implied a competition among the four EVPs and their respective parts of the bank to improve efficiency.

Publish or Perish?

IN ONE OF MY EARLY projects as a consultant, I worked as the Associate on a variety of subjects at Rhode Island Hospital Trust, a regional bank headquartered in Providence. (In case you wonder, it was originally a hospital that long ago spun off its funding entity as a bank.) We helped update and streamline many of the bank's processes, including instituting a new approach and process for managing the bank's overall assets and liabilities. Such asset and liability management (ALM) was still being formalized throughout the industry.

Following that study, and in order to summarize my thoughts on the subject as well as to get my and the firm's name behind it, I wrote an article and submitted it to *Burroughs Clearing House*, a long-standing and high-quality magazine 'for bank and financial officers.' They expressed interest in the subject, agreed to run it in one of their upcoming issues, and sent a photographer to the office to get a picture. Having only a cubicle to myself, I borrowed partner Lou Gerstner's office for the picture —in front of his plexiglass brick of sea horses and seashells.

Weeks later, the next issue of the magazine came. It seems they had made my article the cover story, and there I was with the sea horses on the cover. Mom and dad loved it.

Value Pricing

There is a lot of theory around pricing a product that successful businesses implicitly or explicitly apply, to beat competitors and attract customers. As a banker and then management consultant, I had to learn and deal with a bunch of pricing frameworks.

For example, prices are set to reflect two components of the product: cost and value. The price must exceed the cost of making and selling the product, in order to be profitable at all. But, once the cost is covered, the price can be set at a higher level that reflects the product's *value*, as perceived by the customer. That's part of the reason a BMW may have a higher price than a similar Ford, even if they cost the same to make.

Application of pricing theory can be a nerdy, quantitative practice. But the importance of value pricing was brought home to me in the mid-1970s at McKinsey, not in a classroom, but by a senior partner and his team proposing for a new consulting assignment to the CEO of a major airline. As a lifelong devotee of client confidentiality, let me just say that the particular airline no longer exists, nor does the helipad on the roof of its former headquarters office building in New York.

* * *

The prospective client team—the partner, an engagement manager (eventually to become McKinsey's first woman partner), and another associate or two—had worked for several days creating a detailed proposal for a project to address an important strategic issue at the airline. The partner, call him Charles, had a meeting scheduled on a Friday morning to present and discuss the proposal with the CEO.

On the appointed day, the team met in the office beforehand, to review the proposal and pricing before walking over to the company. The manager had calculated what the project would involve, considering the team size and members, individual billing rates, the length of the project, and the directly related expenses to be reimbursed. It totaled a little more than $600,000 (this was a long time ago), and they debated whether to just go with that number, or to round it down somewhat, for the psychological benefit of being in the 500s, rather than the 600s. The partner and the engagement manager were still considering the nuances of which price to quote, as they rode the elevator down to Park Avenue on their way to the client.

* * *

The client meeting went very well, as they discussed the issues to be resolved, the interviews and analysis to be carried out, the timing and staffing, and what kind of outcomes the client could expect. The CEO asked a variety of questions, which were handled adeptly and evidently to his satisfaction, as he concluded that "this is exactly what we need."

Finally, the client asked Charles how much the project would cost. Charles, without hesitation, said, "Bill, this is going to cost you about a million dollars."

Management Structure

IN THE 1970S, there was a new emphasis on management reporting structures, based not only on the nature and success factors of the business, but also on national and cultural traits.

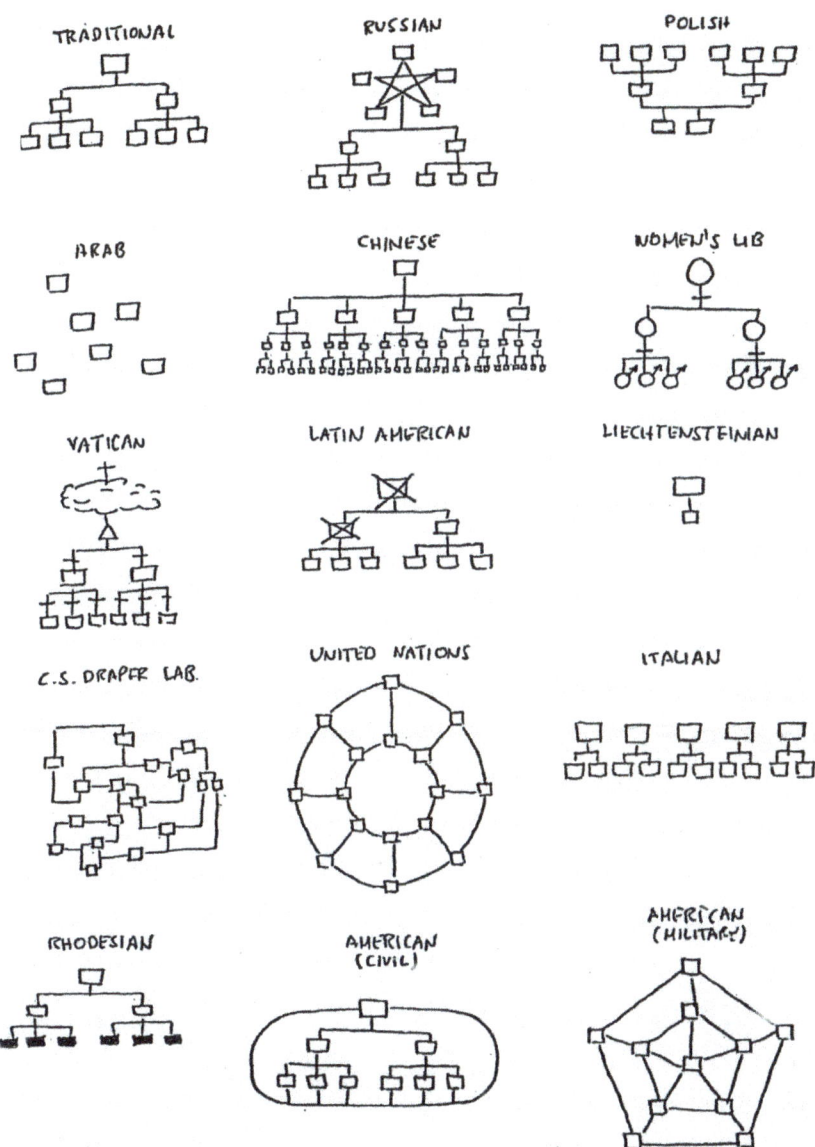

10 Ways to Kill an Idea

1. We've already studied that.
2. That goes against group policy.
3. That's OK for them, but we're different.
4. It won't work at this company.
5. Who's going to pay for it?
6. We're not ready for that yet, but in the fullness of time...
7. It will take 5 years to implement this.
8. The auditors won't like it.
9. That's not how we do it.
10. I agree. What's next on the agenda?

Cubicalism

Consulting in a War Zone?

ONE OF THE EARLY assignments for Bankers Trust, in 1979, required a trip to Asia—my first—to interview bank managers and selected customers in Tokyo, Seoul, and Bangkok. After a few days in Tokyo, I flew to Seoul, arriving at the large old airport near the city and checking into the Hyatt Hotel on the edge of the Itaewon neighborhood, which then was the restaurant, bar, and nightlife center for many of the 40,000 U.S. Army troops stationed in the country at the time.

The large hotel sat high on a hill not far from the Han River and with most of the rooms facing out with long views over a steep slope. (I later learned that the Hyatt was the designated hotel for American presidents and other dignitaries to use, if and when they were to visit Korea.)

It was winter and late at night, so I checked in, took the elevator up a few floors to my room and went to sleep directly.

Just after dawn, I was awakened by blasting machine gun fire outside that was incredibly loud and seemed to reverberate around the room. Leaping out of bed, I went to the window and opened the curtains to peer outside and across the valley to see who was doing the shooting and how much trouble I was in. Edging out from the side of the windowpane, I saw in the midst of a light snow that was falling, two U.S. Army helicopters hovering at room level about 100 feet from the hotel.

The machine gun fire was merely the loud pounding of their jet engines. After a minute or two, they turned and flew slowly away, and I went back to sleep. It turned out to be no special event, and evidently a daily occurrence in some form.

Cambodian Window

ON THAT SAME TRIP for Bankers Trust in the winter of 1978-79, I found myself in Bangkok for three days on the international strategy project. I was there to interview several bank officials, as well as a couple of the bank's corporate customers.

I had been 'ordered' to stay at the Oriental Hotel, a grand old building on the bank of the Chao Phraya River, and it was excellent—slightly out of the way of the crowded and pervasive bustle, but also perfectly located. (At that time, the hotel's driveway wasn't paved.)

When I got to the hotel, however, my schedule of interviews for the next day had been postponed for a day —every one of them, both at the bank and the companies.

It turned out that the Cambodian government had given permission for foreigners to enter that country from Thailand to visit Angkor Wat at the town of Siem Reap for a period of only a few days. The expatriate community in Bangkok considered this a chance of a lifetime, as Cambodia and the monumental temples had been closed to visitors for years by the Khmer Rouge regime and would be again the next week. As a result, whatever business was at hand or brewing would have to wait, as they all made the six-to-eight-hour drive from to Siem Reap and back.

25 years later, I finally made it to the temples: the craving and raving was justified.

DE-BUGGING, REALLY?

FLYING FROM BANGKOK back to London on that trip in 1979 was my first time on Thai Airways (which proved to be excellent in every way). The flight stopped for refueling at Karachi, Pakistan, after the initial nine-hour leg from Bangkok.

The stop was brief and not discomforting, but immediately after the refueling, the plane taxied a bit and a de-icing machine was deployed, moving from nose to tail as is usual in temperate zone airports in winter.

But Karachi temperatures never go below 55 degrees Fahrenheit, so I asked the flight attendant why the de-icing was necessary.

She said they did that most all the time to "sterilize the aircraft before leaving Karachi."

I never found out if that was really the case.

Moving Abroad

*Since joining McKinsey,
a growing number of consultants around the world
who specialized in the banking and financial institutions
industry had become a fairly close-knit global practice,
cemented together by evolving personal relationships,
regular combined practice meetings,
and a great deal of international
cross-staffing of project teams.*

IN 1980, after seven years with the firm, McKinsey asked me to move to Europe, both to replace a departing Dutch partner in Amsterdam who led the firm's relationship at the Amsterdam-Rotterdam Bank, and to support the firm's London-based leader of the European banking practice. So, we moved to London for a couple years and stayed six.

Because each European country had at least three or four major banks facing all the industry changes and challenges, joining the London office plunked me into the center of McKinsey's practice in the U.K. and Europe. Also, the rise of the Gulf states' new wealth from oil production and exports generated a need and desire on their part to establish modern financial and banking infrastructures. Traditionally, this Middle East market was served, or at least coordinated, from London and in English.

I began my six years in London as planned, by working on several large, successive assignments at the Amsterdam-Rotterdam Bank in Amsterdam, which took me to that city nearly every week for almost three years. They were 'transformative' projects, with a close-knit group of executives in a sophisticated, tolerant, and hard-working country. Also upon my arrival in London, we began an assignment at the U.K.'s largest bank—Barclays—structuring the managerial separation of their large and middle-market corporate business and customers from its 3,000 U.K. retail branches. A third major opportunity surfaced when the largest bank in Saudi Arabia inquired for help in broadening its banking focus from Islamic banking in the Kingdom to more international and capital markets services. So, I was busy from the outset, at three major banks in three different countries, all with fascinating issues and people.

In mid-1982, the British head of the European banking practice, and a good friend, died from cancer, and I became head of the London practice for the duration of my stay. There was a group of excellent young consultants in London, so a big part of the job was to mentor and help them to expand the business and their skills.

In England, the Midland Bank became my main client with a series of projects over three years, and I lead projects for the First National Bank of Chicago, the Trustee Savings Bank, the Royal Bank of Canada, and Legal & General Insurance—all in London. In the Netherlands, besides the AMRO Bank work, I also lead assignments at Nuttspaarbank, a savings bank in the Hague, and Royal Insurance's Dutch operation in Rotterdam. And the Middle East produced good assignments at the Riyadh Bank, Saudi International Bank, United Gulf Bank, and the Bank of Cyprus, all on their home turfs. Projects at SEB in Stockholm, the Bergen Bank in Norway, and Aer Lingus and the Bank of

Ireland in Dublin, further extended my air route map.

The specific projects that we worked on were just as diverse as the geography and nationalities. Every assignment was different in dealing with the changing economies, regulatory frameworks, technological advances, and competitive situations—all uniquely combined, country by country and bank by bank. My own client work, participating in the London office partner group, and actively working with the other banking practice partners across Europe consumed the six years in a flash.

A Random Meeting

WHEN WE MOVED to London in the summer of 1980, I went ahead in late June, while Suzanne, two-year-old Nick and one-month-old Andrew sat it out in New York for an extra week or two. Our house in Chelsea wasn't available yet, so we had rented a semi-detached house for two months in Southfields, a neighborhood south of the Thames and adjoining Wimbledon Park. Our place was just up the hill from the Southfields tube stop on the District Line—not too inconvenient for my getting to work at McKinsey's St. James's Street office.

Best of all, it was Wimbledon tennis time, and taxis queued right at the Southfields tube station to run fans from the train to the stadium—the All England Lawn Tennis & Croquet Club. That year pitted John McEnroe against Bjourn Borg in the championship match, with Borg the winner in five sets. The British deemed the match "well regarded;" I deemed it spectacular. But I digress.

On one of my first days in London, about mid-day, I walked down the hill to the taxi rank and was third or fourth in line, heading for the stadium and that day's matches. When the tall, 50-ish, well-dressed man in front of me was next for a cab, he turned to me and asked if I wanted to share one for the short ride. I readily agreed, we got in and had a nice chat, revealing that I was a management consultant and he was a physician. We arrived, exited the taxi, and paid the split bill. As we turned to leave, I introduced myself, as did he—Roger Bannister.

Growing up in Midwestern America in the 1950s and 1960s, even I knew that he was the first runner to break the four-minute mile. That was in 1954: he was 25, I was nine. Nice man.

I don't recall who played the matches that day.

Convergence of Interests

WHEN I ARRIVED in McKinsey's London office in the early 1980s, the financial institutions practice had a British senior partner who had long-standing bank clients in England, Ireland, and Saudi Arabia. I, however, was a young American partner from abroad with no previous work or relationships in the U.K. or Europe.

About the same time, Michael Lafferty, a seasoned financial reporter for the *Financial Times*, left that paper to set up his own group to provide 'knowledge-based' services to the financial community, including a bi-weekly newsletter, banking conferences around Europe, and other creative journalism and media-related activities. His centerpiece from the start was the newsletter, *Retail Banker International,* which reported on consumer financial services, worldwide.

In order to raise my profile in the industry and drawing on developments in the American banking markets and our work there, I began looking to write articles and give talks to audiences that contained potential clients at major banks in Europe. The objective was to get McKinsey's name and my presence in front of a broader group in the industry.

And Michael was voraciously seeking new points of view from new people in the industry as fodder for his potential subscribers and conference attendees. We somehow ran into each other and realized that both our plans could be advanced together.

In the spring of 1982, I had been asked to give a keynote speech at the annual convention of the European Financial Marketing Association (EFMA), held in Monte Carlo. All of Europe's big branch banks—generally three or four per country—attended these conferences, so I exerted myself to create a message of consequence. That message was that the 'free' checking account, or current account, balances were the funds generating most of the banks' profits and that they were going to come under great pressure as the costs of those funds rise.

The presentation—with slides projected on three screens to the 5,000 attendees—went over well, and Michael covered it in the next issue of the *Retail Banker International*. Perhaps the leading retail banker in Europe was Deutsche Bank's Eckart van Hooven, a smart, arrogant, brazen executive. In Michael's cover story about my speech, he made my week by quoting van Hooven characterizing my analysis as "highly theoretical and ridiculous." My references to the retail business as "protected markets," to the free account balances as "a subsidy," and to the big banks as a continent-wide "cartel" didn't go down well. However, some were quite complimentary, and others "thought the matter far too contentious to be quoted."

Over the next few years, I tried to provide fodder that passed Michael's muster for relevance and factual analysis, and he proved a credible and professional outlet for my and McKinsey's ideas and perspectives.

RETAIL BANKER INTERNATIONAL

A bi-weekly bulletin on consumer financial services worldwide

Editor: *Michael Lafferty*

Issue No. 21, 5 April 1982

CONTENTS

Viewpoint	2
Profile: Wolfgang Gruger	2
Belgium's unhappy managers	3
Danish technology dispute	4
Dutch EFTPOS battle	5
EFMA convention	6-9
US savings bank merger	10
Visa in Australia	11
US banks' outlook	12

McKinsey man says 'cartels' will end

European banks have been given a stark warning that the days of easy and high profits, resulting from protected national retail markets, are rapidly coming to an end. They must expect to face challenges in the coming years that are similar to and just as important as those with which American banks are grappling today.

Full report of the EFMA convention, pages 6-9

This was the chilling message delivered to Europe's big branch banks last month by Bill Turner, a principal in the London office of McKinseys, the business consultants. Turner's straight talking provoked great controversy among European bankers and one, Eckart van Hooven, a managing director of Deutsche Bank in Germany, has described Turner's analysis as "highly theoretical and ridiculous". However, others say he is right.

Turner told delegates to last month's annual convention of the European Financial Marketing Association (EFMA), that over the last three years reported net income of banks in France, West Germany, Italy and the United Kingdom had doubled and assets had increased by 70 per cent. "Much of this profitability is attributable to the retail side of the banks, and most banks in Europe could not have sustained their profitable growth without the substantial contribution from retail", he said.

The principal reason for this success, according to Bill Turner, was the fact that protected markets existed in countries like the UK, Germany, the Netherlands, France, Belgium and Scandinavia. "The cartel-like environments that developed in some of the major countries, where a handful of the largest banks virtually control the local market, have helped ensure retail success", he said. It could not be attributed to competitively superior products, low operating costs or technological innovation.

The principal benefit of protection was the implicit "subsidy" that banks have been receiving from their low-cost but high-volume retail deposits. If the British and German banks had paid a market rate for these funds (the interbank rate) their total earnings bases would have been eliminated in the past two or three years, Turner calculated. The subsidy had slowed down competition, technological innovation, and marketing initiatives.

But European banks were already losing a share of personal

Continued on back page

What the bankers had to say . . .

When European bankers at the EFMA convention were asked to comment on Turner's speech (reported above) they produced a variety of responses. Some thought the matter far too contentious to be quoted, but others were less reticent.

Paul de Bellefroid, of Société Générale de Banque in Belgium, said: "I entirely agree with Bill Turner's views. A series of strategic choices were indeed already made by our bigger, and there will be 'winners and losers'," he said. He thought that banks in Continental Europe would try to co-operate more than in the past, "but this does not mean protectionism, and governments may try to create more competition than in the past". He thought, however, that there would be more grounds for co-operation on technical equipment like ATMs.

Wolf-Dieter Schlechthaupt, of deny that European banks are under such a threat. It is a question of sophistication. We have much more to offer private customers than American Banks". In any case, the positions of the UK and German markets were different: "We have five services for the customer and in Britain they have two". McKinseys was partly motivated by a desire for more business, said Dr van Hooven.

Peter Tridvell, head of planning

A Steel Trap

RICHARD SIMMONS was a legendary Wall Street attorney, whose smarts-to-number-of-words-spoken ratio was one of the highest I've ever known—both brilliant and orally concise to an extreme. I first saw Dick about 1970 at Chemical Bank meetings to devise complicated term loan agreements for large international companies. I was a very junior bank officer on the periphery of those discussions, but it was clear that the bank depended heavily on Dick for advice and drafting of key provisions in the agreements.

Simmons was a partner at Cravath, Swaine & Moore, having degrees from Princeton and Yale law school. From 1965 and for 20 years thereafter, he was Chemical Bank's chief outside counsel. He had taken a year's leave from the law firm in 1959 (aged 30) to serve as deputy superintendent of banks for New York State, where he rewrote the regulations governing banks in the State.

He was one of those personalities who, when asked a complicated, difficult question, would remain silent for as long as it took for him to devise the correct answer, then answer in five or fewer words, mumbled at that. He would elaborate if you asked, but, otherwise, was ready for the next question or 'conversation.' One legendary story has Dick and a client team working over a weekend to file an action that required references to New York State regulations, a copy of which was not available due to the files being locked for the weekend. So, Dick dictated the applicable laws from memory to a stenographer, and the team used the resulting text as they continued their work.

As second in the Cravath firm's hierarchy, and beyond his work with Chemical, Dick also played a leading role during the 1980 Iran hostage crisis in resolving claims against the Iran government after the Shah was ousted. After nearly 30 years at

Cravath, Dick joined Chemical in 1985 as a Vice Chairman, but, as a lifelong chain smoker, was forced to retire with lung cancer and died in 1991, at age 62.

* * *

I left Chemical Bank in 1973 to join McKinsey as a management consultant. In 1980, I moved to London for what turned out to be a six-year stint, and I spent about a third of my time with a large bank in the Netherlands, commuting weekly from London to Amsterdam.

The Heathrow-to-Schiphol flight schedule was accommodating, with a very early flight out each morning. And Schiphol Airport was one of the best in the world, in terms of gate locations, efficient customs and immigration, shopping, and transportation into the city.

Upon arriving at Schiphol, we would walk from the gate concourse toward the airport center and curbside taxis, passing through immigration to show our passports. Visas were not required of Americans, and this process was always efficient and quick. Although a few overnight flights from North America arrived early each morning, most incoming visitors that time of day were from Europe, with EC passports, and could walk straight through without stopping. And, those without EC passports stood in a fast-moving line to approach a stereotypical tall, young, blond, serious Dutchman—in security guard uniform—sitting behind a raised desk. You would hand your passport up to him, he'd glance at it quickly, stamp it, give it back, and nod to the next in line to step up. No questions, no delay.

* * *

One morning in 1982 or 1983, on my way to meetings at the Amsterdam-Rotterdam bank, I was approaching the short line to the desk. I noticed that Dick Simmons was in the line a few people ahead of me. He presumably had just arrived from New York.

He handed his passport to the security officer. A few seconds later, I could hear the stamp and then the deep, heavily-accented voice of the young Dutchman as he handed the passport back to Dick: "Be sure to sign your passport, Mr. Simmons."

Yes, the mythical Dick Simmons was human.

A Feisty Mentor

DAVID GRIFFITHS, a British McKinsey partner in London, headed up the firm's European banking practice and helped convince me to move to London to bolster the practice there and help him with a burgeoning client base in the U.K. and the Middle East. I had known David for a few years and was keen to live and do business in London, so we moved there in the fall of 1980.

David had a great wife and five young children. He lived on the edge of Regent's Park, drove a big BMW, and had one of the very few Winnebago motorhomes in England, which the family used for its summer holiday each year, driving as far south in Europe as was required to reach a warm beach. This usually meant southern France, Italy, Greece, or Spain. David acquired the used Winnebago by putting his business card under its windshield wiper in a parking lot, asking the owner to call if and when he wanted to sell it.

Professionally, David had client relationships with several big English banks, a major bank in Ireland, and a big Saudi bank. He made the extra effort for the practice, once convincing officials of the Marylebone Cricket Club to let us have a global banking practice leaders meeting in the 'Long Room' at Lord's, the citadel of world cricket that had never been previously used for an 'outside' meeting. It was a unique venue and a big hit.

David had spent a couple years in Australia in his early years with the firm and had ignored the signs at the beaches there warning of the dangers of unimpeded sunlight. As we know, there is an ozone-layer hole in the atmosphere over Australia, and the signs noted that the warning was especially directed at folks from northern Europe. Less than a year after I arrived in London, David was found to have a large melanoma on his back, which metastasized beyond treatment. He died in 1982. While in the South Pacific, he had come to love Fijian music, and a group of Fiji musicians played at his funeral.

David's sense of humor was strong, subtle at times, and sometimes oddball. Two examples:

- Traffic roundabouts are prevalent all over England, always with the possibility of being cut off by people without the right of way. When that happened, a typical reaction was to give the other driver the finger. David pointed out to me once, that when giving the finger, the recipient seems to be particularly insulted if you don't just flash it but lean your arm out the window and slowly move the fingered hand up and down for as long as it can be seen.

- In taking a suitcase or briefcase out of David's trunk, I noticed a small stack of unused air sick bags with the Saudia Airlines name and logo on them. I asked why he had them. He responded that they are handy to use as trash bags when he drives around England and even on the Continent on the odd road trip there. And, if he can't find a suitable trash bin to throw it into and has to ditch it on the side of the road, whoever picks it up will think "some Arab" threw it there.

Winning Can Be Depressing

Our young family lived for six years at 32 Walpole Street in London's Chelsea neighborhood. Shortly after we moved there, Sir John Nott—our next-door neighbor at #31—was named Secretary of State for Defense. We hardly ever saw him, what with our own busy work schedules, two boys under three, and nannies filling our lives, and a busy cabinet post and a house in the west country filling his.

In April 1982, Argentina declared its ownership of the islands near its coast that had been settled and held by the British since 1765. They were called the Falklands by the British, and the Malvinas by the Argentines. A 10-week undeclared war ensued, with British warships traveling some 8,000 miles from the UK and soldiers deployed on the islands to drive out the invaders.

Perhaps the most consequential single event of the war was the sinking of Argentina's battleship *General Belgrano*. 323 sailors were killed and about 770 rescued, but at the time in London, the authorities and press assumed lives lost had exceeded 1,000. This level of casualties shook even the most conservative Brits, despite the U.K. being drawn into the conflict as defenders of their territory. The order to sink her had been given by Prime Minister Margaret Thatcher at a Friday War Cabinet meeting at Chequers.

The following day, a Saturday I believe, was the only time I recall actually being face to face with John Nott, as he walked from a taxi or car in the street up toward his porch, and I was leaving mine to go somewhere. As we passed, alone and within 10 feet of each other, I said hello, but he only nodded, ashen-faced and as somber as silence could be.

Sinking the enemy ship was a 'win' (the *Sun* newspaper headline that day was, in huge letters, "GOTCHA!"), eliminating any further threat from the Argentine navy, and boosting the image and prospects of the Conservative Party and the Thatcher government. Nevertheless, from the look on the Defense Minister's face and his demeanor, it was clear that the devastation of a large loss of life was deeply felt, at least momentarily, by some in Britain as well.

THE RODNEY

ONE INTERESTING FELLOW and brief colleague I met while working with the client Midland Bank was Rodney Baker-Bates, a former Chase and then Midland banker, who later was Finance Director at the BBC, CEO of Britain's Prudential, and remains Chairman of the Willis insurance group.

He was a classic British banker who enjoyed Americans and financial problem solving, but what I recall the most was his brief description of his father.

We got onto that by my asking him if 'Rodney' was a family name. "Oh no, he said, my father served in the Navy on the H.M.S. *Rodney*, and when I was born in 1944, he memorialized one of us by naming me that." The *Rodney* was a British battleship that participated in sinking the German *Bismark* in 1941.

At another time, after I knocked on his office door to ask him a question, he bade me to come in with "no need to knock." He then told me that his father, a stern man with a strong voice, greeted people at his office door by slamming his palm onto the desk and nearly shouting "Enter, Pray!"

I may recall that Rodney's father was a prominent physician who had lived on Rodney Street in Liverpool. So who can be certain from whence the 'Rodney' really came?

A Difference of Night and Day

IN 1985, we undertook a consulting assignment for the President of the Bank of Cyprus, and the small team made a bunch of trips to the bank's headquarters in Nicosia over the several-month duration of the project.

Since the Turkish invasion in 1974, the island of Cyprus has been divided between the Turkish occupied north and the Greek Cypriot south, reflecting the age-old conflicting claims to the island by the two countries. The line of demarcation runs east and west, cutting straight through the city of Nicosia. United Nations troops—with blue helmets and singular combat uniforms—patrol the 'border' and buffer zone, with fencing, impenetrable clutter, and guard houses strung all the way to the east and west coasts. The island's main airport—at Larnaca—was built after the invasion southeast of Nicosia near the coast to be away from the conflict area.

When we were there, we worked late in the bank's Nicosia offices, then had a taverna fish dinner somewhere (often with a choice of red or white mullet) and returned to the hotel each night.

One evening just at sunset, when all the city lights were coming on for the night, we were still at work and I went to the men's room on the bank's third or fourth floor. Above the urinal there was a long horizontal window facing north over the low blocks of streets and buildings. As I stood there, lights all around were on and bright but only for one block north. Beyond that, there was barely a light as far as you could see to the left, right, and straight ahead, despite the city extending for several miles out.

Figuring there must be a power outage, I asked the President what was happening. He chuckled and said, "that's no power failure, that's the Turkish occupied zone." As subsequent satellite photos have starkly demonstrated—and not unlike the difference between the North and South Koreas—the economic differences between the two 'countries' caused the contrast. The economic growth, standard of living, and infrastructure were far poorer on the Turkish side than on the Greek side.

To a tourist like me and during the day, it was all new and exotic, with markets, restaurants, and shops everywhere, with reasonably easy access across the two or three UN-demarked 'border' crossings. It took the darkness of night to understand the fundamental differences and how consequential the border, called the Green Line, was. Being a bit more observant after that, there were fewer churches and tavernas in the north, and fewer mosques and kebab houses in the south.

Airport Security?

T. JEFFERSON CUNNINGHAM III—Jeff—was a senior international banker at Chase Manhattan Bank, before retiring very early to run his family-owned Fishkill National Bank, about 70 miles north of Manhattan in New York. In the early 1980s, the Chairman and President of England's Midland Bank wanted Cunningham to join their Board, despite Jeff's reluctance to stray from home and recently-increased family responsibilities. Jeff had worked in London before, had many friends and former colleagues there, loved bird shooting in the countryside, and even had a sister living in England. Midland's agreement to allow Jeff to travel to and from London by Concorde helped clinch the deal, and he signed on.

Many times, during bird shooting season, Jeff made sure to arrange an extra day in the country and traveled with his precious Holland & Holland side-by-side shotgun. He was always reluctant to check the shotgun as luggage, and on one return Concorde flight from London, he arranged to take the gun on board. He convinced both terminal and gate security guards to allow him to take the gun through. But, finally, he had to elevate the discussions to the pilot, who agreed only on the condition that the gun stay in the cockpit during the flight. Imagine attempting that now!

Over its 20-year lifetime, the Concorde had persistent problems with its tires, one or more of which occasionally blew out on takeoff—and this occurred on Jeff's flight. Accelerating on the Heathrow runway, a tire blew, and the pilot brought the plane to an abrupt halt.

Out on the runway, the passengers were loaded onto busses and shuttled back to the Concorde lounge in the terminal. Heathrow being British Airways' home base, there was another Concorde aircraft available. So, after a short wait for the new plane to be fueled, stocked, and moved to the gate, the passengers boarded for a second try.

But it suddenly dawned on Jeff—now on the 'new' plane—that his shotgun was in the cockpit of the plane still being towed in from its aborted takeoff.

Although the logic and words of the ensuing explanation and negotiation have been lost, Jeff succeeded in having the shotgun taken off the first plane and placed in the cockpit of the second—without being arrested, and without being lynched by the other passengers.

Amazing.

Trees and Fjords

IN THE 1980'S, consulting assignments took me from London to banks in the capital and other cities of Scandinavia, which provided another version of the 'north country.' Stockholm, Bergen, and Helsinki were my main windows, with bits in Copenhagen and Oslo rounding out that tour over several years while living in London.

They seemed serious, gracious people, many of them hard smokers and hard drinkers, with so many shared traits among the countries. I couldn't understand any of their languages, of course, and some of them couldn't understand the others' either. The bankers were smart and competent, with business impact beyond Scandinavia, in greater proportion than the extent of their overseas presences. And, McKinsey had solid, effective consultants in our offices throughout the region (with one colleague having just gone off to start Viking Lines).

Visiting Helsinki for the first time, in January, was a shock with its two hours of weak sunlight from about noon to 2:00 PM, and with the gas lights in all the squares never turned off. In Stockholm, its unique and fabulous Gamla Stan old town, and the 17th Century warship *Vasa*, which sat then and for 17 years under a liquid spray before being more permanently located in its own museum across the harbor. And, Bergen with its incomparably beautiful setting and restaurant views from up around the fjord. And, Copenhagen's Christmas markets that spring up and add to the year-end festivities.

The trees, climate, and land masses—and nearby seas—define this four-country manifestation of the north country, from 59° to 60° north latitude. I came to appreciate the appeal of the natural beauty and the relatively underpopulated of these climes, located between civilization and the arctic.

The Platters Said It

WELL INTO THE 1980S, smoking was allowed on flights worldwide, and was especially indulged by European fliers on European airlines. Beginning in the 70s, most airlines established nonsmoking sections, although the cigarette lobbies slowed that trend, and the airlines were loath to offend their business and first class patrons who smoked.

Eventually, nonsmoking and antismoking passengers far outnumbered the smokers, and the smoking sections shrunk and disappeared altogether in the mid-90s. (On one overnight flight on a British Airways 747, I recall being able to sleep across several seats in the large Business Class smoking cabin, without a single other passenger in that cabin.)

During these smoking-on-board years of the 1980s, occasional client work in Stockholm, Oslo, and Bergen took me there from London. I usually flew on Scandinavian Airlines—SAS—as they had convenient early morning flights. The DC-9 aircraft had upwards of 85 seats, with rows of two seats on the left side of the aisle and three on the right.

I remember my first such flight after SAS established a non-smoking section. Instead of separating smoking from nonsmoking from front to back—as did every airline I have flown before or since—SAS had banned smoking in the seats on the left side of the aisle and designated the right side as 'smoking.'

As a result, when in my usual, non-smoking aisle seat, my nose was less than three feet from the cigarette across the aisle. And, at least theoretically, there were three of them there, to the two of us 'nons' in every row.

They were short flights, I didn't take them very frequently, increasingly fewer passengers smoked no matter where they were sitting, and SAS finally banned smoking entirely on those routes in 1996.

But, until then, whether you liked it or not, smoke got in your eyes.

Four Downs to a Touchdown

FRANK CAHOUET was a successful banker at First Interstate Bank in Los Angeles, rising to Vice Chairman and CFO in 1984. But he wanted to run his own bank.

Recruited by London's Midland Bank to be Chairman and President of its San Francisco-based subsidiary, Crocker National Bank, Cahouet spent two years there working out Crocker's extensive Latin American bad-loan portfolio. As part of the Crocker 'fix,' Frank created perhaps the first 'good-bank/bad-bank' restructuring, which facilitated Crocker's survival and continued growth, while working out the bad loans.

Frank's participation in Midland Executive Committee meetings in London was always interesting. A stern, serious, and forceful man, he played a good game of snooker, badly beating this author several times. During one Committee meeting, Midland Vice Chairman Brian Goldthorpe quipped about "the lady who was so shy, she ate a banana sideways." As the all-male room collapsed with laughter, strait-laced and rarely-off-color Frank stared at his papers on the table, with a red flush rising up the back of his neck.

On Frank's three-year watch, Crocker moved from losses of $300 million back to profitability. In 1986, Midland sold Crocker to Wells Fargo Bank, and Frank left Crocker, having been recruited to be President and COO of the Federal National Mortgage Corporation (FNMA, or 'Fannie Mae') in Washington.

After only nine months at Fannie, Frank was again recruited, and again moved, this time to join the Mellon Bank in Pittsburg, as Chairman and CEO. Leading Mellon—probably his ideal job and 'platform'—he built the business over a successful 12-year career, retiring in 1998. It was his home run, his touchdown.

So, from 1984 to 1986, Frank moved in top-level positions from First Interstate, to Crocker, to Fannie Mae, to Mellon. In the process, he received three significant signing bonuses, and at least one and possibly three significant separation packages—all in addition to appropriately hefty salaries and stock grants and options.

More power to him.

Mortification

IN 1981, the Midland Bank purchased Crocker National Bank of San Francisco. Midland was one of the largest banks in Britain, and the acquisition significantly expanded its U.S. presence. Crocker was to be managed by its American executives.

Within two years, however, Crocker was in trouble with massive bad loans in Latin America, putting the bank in the cross hairs of the Midland Board and its regulator. The Bank of England insisted that Midland's London management pay more attention and improve its oversight of Crocker.

In response, Midland recruited Frank Cahouet as Crocker's new Chairman, President, and CEO. Cahouet had advanced up the ranks at Los Angeles-based First Interstate Bank to the position of Vice Chairman and Chief Financial Officer, and was known as a serious, hard-working, and driven executive. As a strong and ambitious leader, he instinctively sought and insisted on a high degree of independence.

The opportunity to run his own bank was an important factor in his moving to Crocker. The 5,300 miles separating San Francisco and London—combined with Midland's intent to delegate the running of Crocker to Frank and his American staff—

were paramount to his accepting the job. (As Shakespeare comments about the advantage of distance from God and country authority: "The sky is high and the king far off.")

But the bad loans persisted, leading to continuing pressure by the Bank of England for Midland to get more involved in "Frank's bank." The tension came to a head at a meeting in Midland CEO Geoffrey Taylor's London office.

Midland's landmark headquarters building at 27 Poultry in the City of London, was designed by Sir Edwin Lutyens in the 1920s—when Midland was the world's largest bank. The executive fourth floor had mahogany doors and furnishings, and rich turquoise carpeting, as well as its own elevator from a street entrance. Taylor's office was large and rectangular, with a doorway entrance to a small lobby and the elevator at one end, and an entrance to a waiting area and his secretary at the other end.

Geoffrey had called in Frank to admonish him for resisting and complaining about the increasing Midland incursions into Crocker's day-to-day affairs. Midland Board member Jeff Cunningham joined the two of them.

Following Taylor's comments calling for greater communication and integration, Frank—clearly upset—gave a short rebuttal, to the effect that:

> "I will not allow my bank to be run from London, with people looking over my shoulder who don't know Crocker's market, people, or culture. I was hired to lead Crocker as CEO, and that includes fixing its problems and growing its business. This is a major intrusion on my ability to do that."

With that, and fuming, Frank stood up and turned around, opened the door, and walked sternly into a supply closet.

A World Apart

During and a little beyond our six years living in London in the 1980s, I spent a good bit of time commuting to the Middle East, leading assignments for financial institutions in Saudi Arabia, Bahrain, Kuwait, and Cyprus. Upon arriving in London in 1980, I responded to an international strategy inquiry by the largest bank in Saudi Arabia (the National Commercial Bank (NCB), based in Jeddah), because my senior British colleague was working for the second largest bank in the Kingdom (the Riyadh Bank, based in Jeddah) and was conflicted out. After my project ended, the colleague died of cancer in 1982, and about a year later the Riyadh Bank wanted more help, so I followed that up and worked there for three years. Also, a member of the Kuwaiti royal family was planning to grow the United Gulf Bank internationally (based in Bahrain), and we worked there as well in 1982-83. And in 1983, we completed an organization and management succession project at the Bank of Cyprus in Nicosia.

Although the firm had no office in the Middle East, tradition brought those indigenous companies to London for consulting help, and because McKinsey had a stellar reputation on earlier work, including in Africa, the London office became the hub for that activity. And, they seemed to very much respect American perspectives.

Not only was this exposure new and interesting for me culturally, but it was also at a pivotal time in each of these markets, as oil prices, revenues and national incomes were rising dramatically, requiring the countries' banking systems to be modernized and internationalized. From the work over the course of those years, several recollections stand out:

• As a part of investing in and developing modern infrastructures of all kinds within the Kingdom, Saudi Arabia was establishing a new capital city in Riyadh. It was a central location between the old city of Jeddah on the Red Sea and nearby Mecca to the west, and the oil fields and Arabian Gulf to the east. And it was very near the Saud familial homeland. As a result, major government agencies and institutions—like banks—were required to relocate their headquarters to Riyadh during those years. Most of my work was in Jeddah, where at the time the headquarters of both the National Commercial Bank and the Riyadh Bank were located.

• Many banks and other local organizations in the Kingdom sequestered advisors from western companies to assist in their modernization programs. Such tours of duty were income tax free and allowed the quick accumulation of savings—except for Americans, who are taxed on their world-wide incomes. At NCB, one such advisor was Christopher Arnander, a British banker who had moved to Jeddah for several years. Christopher and his wife Primrose were accomplished musicians who lived at the main expatriate enclave, called The Creek, and they regularly organized concerts and musical 'productions,' one of which was the Mikado when I was there. They also were tennis buffs; due to the intense heat, the courts remained empty most of the day, but were booked at dawn for a few hours and at night. (I recall landing at Jeddah at 1:00 AM; it was 92° F.)

• Saudi Arabia has forbidden drinking alcohol since 1951, when a son of King Abdulaziz killed the British vice consul in an alcohol-fueled incident. The one exception was that expatriates could brew their own beer and wine for their own consumption. (The Arnanders did make their own, with kits brought from Boots in London.) Rumors persisted that 'diplomatic pouches' from abroad occasionally were used to import greater quantities of a wider variety of drinks. At Christmas time one of those years, Christopher was coordinating the importation of a piano from London for the annual holiday concert. He got a call at his desk at the bank from the customs office at Jeddah airport and was told "You need to come now and collect your shipment because your piano is leaking."

• Primrose Arnander compiled a book of Arab sayings and their English equivalents. The title is *The Son of a Duck is a Floater*. Some of my favorites are:

> "If the lion bares his teeth, don't assume he is smiling."
>
> "In the eye of his mother a monkey is a gazelle."
>
> "Go tile the sea."
>
> "A bald woman brags about her niece's hair."

• On my first trip to Bahrain—an island nation 15 miles off Saudi Arabia in the Gulf—I noticed that each evening, small groups of men positioned themselves along the eastern edge of the shore near the major city of Manama. I was told that they were basically lookouts in case the Iranians sent boats across to invade Bahrain. On a roadside in central Manama, there was a huge date palm tree that had a five- or six-foot tall pile of fallen dates around the entire tree. They were evidently so plentiful on the island that nobody bothered to pick or take them—for years, obviously. Not long after my work there, a causeway was completed, connecting Bahrain to the Saudi mainland, enhancing Bahraini security and protection from the Persians.

• On a visit to Riyadh, my consulting colleague Stephen Green and I took an afternoon to travel to Diriyah, a virtually deserted oasis on the western outskirts of Riyadh. The Saud family came from this village in the early 18th century. It was filled with date Palm trees  along a 'river' and was a collection of old mud-brick buildings. There were rusting signs showing 'Kaki-Cola'—evidently a local knock-off of Coca-Cola from previous decades. In the late 1970s, the Saudi government committed to redeveloping the town, and it has grown to become a primary attraction in the Kingdom. It has since been designated a UNESCO World Heritage site.

• On another trip to the new capital city of Riyadh, there was a large hotel nearing completion for one of the international hotel chains. But a Saudi Prince insisted on buying it for his home, and the hotel group had to begin again.

• In August of 1981, the President of NCB was visiting London and my colleague, and we invited him to lunch at the Carlton Club, a 150-year-old Tory bastion on St. James's Street. (At that time, it had its first and only female member— Margaret Thatcher.) The 'Glorious 12th' had occurred the day before, so Grouse was on the menu, and it turned out that our Saudi guest loved game. He was thrilled to hear the story of the opening of the shooting season and ordered his very rare—and in England that means warmish. I tried not to watch, and I don't think my British colleague looked at the bright red meat either. The President reveled.

• In 1982, a new Managing Director (CEO) had taken the reins of the Riyadh Bank, having been the chief investment officer for the Saudi Arabian Monetary Authority (SAMA). It had been his job to invest—globally—the billions piling up from the expanded production and higher prices of oil since the mid-1970s. He was an excellent manager and client, and we had a great relationship. He once related that as a young man, his family and another family had decided on the lady he was to marry—a lingering custom. He was not necessarily averse to it but had not met or even seen the young lady. In order to see what she looked like, he convinced her family's driver to let him substitute and drive the daughter and a group of girlfriends to some event. As a result, he observed her through the rear-view mirror, liked what he saw and heard, and had a good married life.

• The core of the Riyadh Bank work was helping the Managing Director structure and run an 'Implementation Committee' aimed at making sure agreed changes, policies, and initiatives actually got done. The committee included two members of the bank's board, one of whom was a young entrepreneur from Buraydah, a town about 50 miles north of Jeddah. He was sharp and had attended Stanford. He said that when he came home each summer from San Francisco, his mother nearly fainted seeing him in trim and lean physical shape—emaciated in her eyes. She then spent the summer trying to fatten him up.

• Although I cannot recall the reason for the trip, I planned a brief business trip to Abu Dhabi and booked flights through the London office. Before the trip, I asked an American consultant who had done work in Abu Dhabi if there was anything special to see there, and he replied curtly "Tartan on tap"—indicating that British draft beer was available in that country. I asked the travel agent if one needed a visa to visit Abu Dhabi, and she said it was not necessary. When I arrived in Abu Dhabi, however, I found that Brits didn't need a visa, but Americans did. So, unable to enter the country, I took the seven-hour flight back to London two hours later. The same flight crew was surprised to see me.

• The United Gulf Bank, where we worked on international strategy in 1982-83, was founded in 1980 by a member of Kuwait's ruling Al-Sabah family. Sheikh Nasser had also started an Islamic art collection in 1975 and spent years of effort amassing a fine collection of Islamic art and artifacts. It survived the 1990-91 Gulf War and continues to grow as an important and impressive part of the Kuwait National Museum.

Subtle Charisma

I N 1990, I began a three-week stay in Hong Kong, embarking on a consulting project for the chairmen of the Midland Bank of England, and the Hong Kong and Shanghai Bank (HSBC). Midland executives knew me well from years of work in London, but the Chairman of HSBC, Willie Purves, had agreed only after an initial screening meeting—that is, he screened me. His condition for proceeding with the project was that I spend significant time at his bank's headquarters, to get to know the managers there and experience firsthand the bank's history and culture.

On my first day in the office on the executive floor of the bank, Purves called me into his office and asked where I was staying. I told him the Mandarin Oriental. He said he thought so and asked me to move immediately to the three-bedroom suite at the top of the bank's building, in order to save the hotel bill that I would otherwise run up and charge to the bank. I obeyed. The quarters had a high-floor 360-degree view of Hong Kong Harbor and the

Peak, as well as an accomplished cook, Ah Chung. (Paula and I taught her how to make French toast, which Purves thought nice but apparently never ate.)

* * *

Unbeknownst to me, it was the beginning of the horse racing season at the Happy Valley racecourse. Willie, who also served as Chairman of the Hong Kong Jockey Club, traditionally filled his private, finish-line box there with guests invited to watch the races and have dinner.

Willie's secretary came to me one morning and asked if Paula and I would be able to attend opening night at the track. She said Mr. Purves would be driving, and as host would need to be there early to greet the guests. She told me to be at the Des Voeux Road exit of the bank's garage.

We were there at the appointed time and squeezed into the back seat of the BRG Jaguar sedan for the ten-minute drive east into Happy Valley. Willie's wife Becky sat in the front passenger seat, and he asked her to read down the list of who would be coming—a list he hadn't seen. Which she did: the head tax partner of Price Waterhouse in Hong Kong and his wife, Singapore's ambassador to Hong Kong and his wife, and on and on covering 30 names in all. He asked her a few questions—"have I ever met him?", "does he have a wife?", "what's her name?"—which made clear that he did not know many on the list.

We emerged from the track parking garage just in time, as the guests began to arrive. Over the next 20 minutes or so, Willie proceeded to introduce each person as they arrived, to each and every other person who was already there—by name and where they were from. Mind you, that means, for example, that Willie led the last person to each of the 28 others and got the 28 names right.

Very impressive, indeed.

Eerie Éire—To Err is Human

IN ABOUT 1985, we began a series of projects with the airline Aer Lingus in Dublin, to help them sort out their current non-airline businesses (such as servicing other airlines' planes in Ireland, which was to date very successful), and others they might develop. Sigurd, a Swede and senior partner in McKinsey's London office was the lead partner, as he knew the top executive sponsoring the project. That was Jerry Dunphy (if my memory works), who was the company's strategic planner and also was responsible for the non-airline businesses.

Our team manager, Tim, put together the periodic progress review presentations, and we would review them before flying off to Dublin to discuss the results with Dunphy. In the first pre-meeting, Sigurd crossed out the country—Ireland—on the cover page of the presentation, replacing it with "Éire." (Éire is a form of Irish language word based on an ancient Gaelic goddess, and is formally the name for both the island of Ireland and the state. But it has largely passed out of everyday usage, except on coins and stamps.)

The client meetings always went well, because the work was good, and the client and our team enjoyed working together to challenge and refine the emerging conclusions. Closing the presentation document at the end of the second progress review in his Dublin office, Jerry Dunphy turned to Sigurd and said, "You know Sigurd, we don't use and rarely see the word 'Éire' here. In fact, it may be the only four-letter word the Irish never use."

From then on, the client was in Ireland.

New Old Geography & Breadth

In 1986, we decided to head back to New York.

McKinsey's U.K. practice had maintained its preeminent position in terms of client base, consulting staff and reputation.

The Midland relationship was one of the largest, the financial institutions practice represented about 25-30 percent of London office billings, and the local practice had a solid group of young partners.

BY 1986, the New York and U.S. banking practice at McKinsey had grown steadily, and the New York office overall was large and thriving. I began work immediately on a large piece of cost restructuring at Cigna in Philadelphia. I had been out of touch with the New York office manager who had been appointed while I was in London. Rather, I had communicated with and remained very close to the global banking practice leader who was also based in the New York office. With my candidacy for election to senior partner now alive, it would be helped or hurt by the office manager's support. The two of them did not see eye to eye, at least on the matter of my election as a senior partner in New York. The practice leader was a vehement backer, whereas the office manager slammed his fist on his office table and told me, "this is my office, not his."

The manager of McKinsey's Atlanta office approached me to move down there, with the understanding that they needed a senior partner there to grow the surrounding client base. I reasoned, however, that my focus on financial institutions was best served by being in a major financial center, and I preferred to remain in New York. So, after 15 years with McKinsey, I needed to move on.

Price Waterhouse was seeking to add 'strategic' and general management consulting to their growing consulting practice. PW was the smallest of the 'Big 6' accounting firms, but with probably the best reputation for quality work and judgement, as they were the auditors for more Fortune 100 companies than any other audit firm. The PW partner responsible for finding a leader for that initiative was a follower and 'student' of McKinsey. After many interviews with audit, tax, and consulting partners, I agreed to head up their Strategic Consulting Group and joined PW in the spring of 1988.

As partner in charge, my role included all aspects of the practice: generating and completing work with companies across all industries, and across the U.S., recruiting, staff deployment, performance appraisal, etc. An important additional and rewarding dimension was establishing strong working relationships with PW partners in the audit, tax, and specialized consulting practices.

Over seven years at PW, I helped establish and grow the practice, serving major clients across the country in a wide variety of industries, including computer and memory chip manufacturing, book distribution, advertising, motion picture studios, and banking and securities businesses.

Even though most of the clients and work was in the U.S.,

my own client assignments included an important project for the CEO of Euroclear, the largest securities clearing organization in Europe, based in Brussels, and an assignment working with the chairmen of the Hong Kong and Shanghai Bank and the Midland Bank to resolve several remaining issues in their preparation for merging. This latter work required many weeks in Hong Kong and London.

I also was an active member of a variety of firm-wide PW leadership committees and processes. But PW's emphasis and dedication to growing consulting fell increasingly to Information Technology (IT) consulting, rather than strategic consulting. PW and the other audit firms were far behind Arthur Andersen (later Anderson Consulting, and then Accenture) in IT consulting size and reputation, and closing that gap was their first priority.

Duluth

ALTHOUGH NOT QUITE a part of the Mesabi Range, where iron ore was extracted and transported across the Great Lakes, and where Bob Dylan escaped from Hibbing 75 miles north, Duluth (47° north latitude) was the closest I got. In 1992, a friend and business colleague purchased a defunct thrift institution—the St. Louis Bank for Savings—with the intent to fix it up financially and managerially. He and two others of us participated in the purchase and fix up, and two years later sold it to the large regional bank holding company First Bank Systems. During that time, the Board of Directors met every few months at the Duluth headquarters.

The Board consisted primarily of local

businessmen, one of whom founded, owned, and ran a growing chain of grocery stores in northern Minnesota. I never saw Jim without a ski jacket—even in August. He had a summer camp further north, with no electricity or heat. His wife hated it. I recall a conversation during which one of the directors referred in passing to his ex-wife. After a brief pause, Jim the grocery man said, "I wish I could afford an ex-wife." On another occasion, he arrived at a board meeting 10 minutes late, which was unusual. When asked why, he explained that as he had driven past a police car parked on the main street, the cop had opened his door quickly without looking. Jim's car hit the door squarely, shearing it off completely from the squad car. The policeman had been furious, but knew it was his own fault, and Jim parked and came to our meeting.

The city of Duluth, situated at the bottom of Lake Superior, rises up from the lake, providing a cold, desolate view of the water. On one winter trip, I noticed out a bank window that an ore or cargo ship, some ways out in the middle of the visible lake, was not moving. It was explained to me that shipping just continues into the winter, until the lake freezes to the point where ships can't move. This is indicated when one or more ships gets stuck in the ice and has to remain there until the spring thaw.

Manager's Remorse?

WHILE MANAGING the Strategic Consulting Group at Price Waterhouse, I was compelled to let go a consultant in the group, mostly for lack of sufficient market demand for our services at the time. He was a solid guy but came up with one of the short straws for reducing the staff size.

Two years later, I received the following handwritten note - unlike any other in my experience.

Bill,

Thought you'd be interested in what I've been doing—if you haven't heard from others in the group.

After I left PW, I spent a year and a half as a solo consultant doing marketing strategy, new business development and operations consulting in high tech, software, telecom and pharmaceuticals. Had a great time, gave myself a raise and had the opportunity to spend more time with my (2-3 year old) daughter.

I joined Hamilton (a MAC Group spin-off) this winter after a couple of successful joint projects. Great people, interesting client base, and very active ties to business school faculty. Being a solo was fun, but I missed the opportunity to work as part of a consulting team. And the faculty link means a chance to do leading edge work—for example in customer retention and marketing/manufacturing strategy, two current efforts.

Anyway, thanks for the push. I have thoroughly enjoyed the time since leaving PW—especially the opportunity to run my own consulting operation and manage a generally more sane family life—but I clearly would never have done it if you hadn't shown me the door.

Hope all is well.
Regards, Tom

Double Entendre

SEVERAL DECADES AGO, and midway through my career consulting with financial institutions of various sorts, I was discussing a possible new product development project with two executives at a major credit card and travel company—one with its logo encased in a 'blue box.'

The subject was whether to consider leasing travel- and camping-related equipment to vacationers across Western Europe as a new business. Spain was one of several countries that might provide profitable rental business opportunities, what with its rapid growth in young visitors from abroad in need of bicycles, tents, lanterns, cook stoves, and other paraphernalia.

One concern the company raised was the potential liability in leasing cook stoves, if their misuse could cause fires that injured people or burned property.

A scandal in Spain had recently been exposed, with some restaurants having used fuel oil as cooking oil, making many people sick and actually killing a few.

As a result, when the question of whether the rented cook stoves should be accompanied by the required liquid fuel, I pointed out that if the oil were included, the company could become "the lessor of two evils." The project didn't move forward.

A.T. Kearney

SEVERAL FORMER McKinsey colleagues, who had moved to the firm of A.T. Kearney to build a financial industry practice, approached me, and I joined their New York office in 1995.

This not only brought me back to a full-fledged management consulting firm, but also reinforced my financial institution bent. Over four years in New York with Kearney, we continued to build the practice in North America and coordinate with offices in countries around the world. My own client work included large projects at Prudential, the Bank of Montreal, Waterhouse Securities, Visa, and Mellon Bank.

Lucky to Go First

MY FIRST VISIT to Brazil, in 1995, was to give a keynote talk in Sao Paolo at a conference attended by bankers and governmental officials, on the subject of risk assessment and management. I was with A.T. Kearney at the time. A seasoned local Brazilian, Ari Waddington (yes, he was Brazilian), coordinated the introduction of experts around the world to corporate and finance leaders in Brazil.

Brazil was emerging from an extended period of jaw-droppingly high rates of inflation, having stabilized significantly but still trying to figure out how to cope with a more normal economic and financial markets climate. The day-long conference was centered on the subject of risk management, and my task was to set the stage for other speakers and discussions on the subject of emerging requirements for risk management in Brazil's banking and financial system.

Never having worked in, or even been to, Brazil, I had to do some serious study and preparation, and positioned my points mostly about 'learnings' from other countries' experiences in preserving economic stability by managing financial risks through their central banks and local banking institutions. Before going through the specifics, I asserted that "the management of risk is at once the grease and the glue that will enable the Brazilian economy to complete its economic transition, and to prosper and play a leading role in the future world economy."

The room was packed with upwards of 100 attendees, mostly from the large commercial banks, but also representatives of the central bank and the local press. It was an English-speaking group, although there may have been translators for those in need. My 30-minute talk was supported by a few simple slides and seemed to be going well. As I went through my points, I gradually became more confident that I was adding something of interest and perhaps value, in view of the large audience and good eye contact and attention. When I was finished, there were a couple of questions about details, but no requests for elaboration, and no challenges to anything I had said. I took this limited response as a sign that my comments had come across well, and I gathered my notes and sat down.

The next speaker was a man from Moody's, there to announce and discuss the new credit rating being assigned to the country, which would likely be an upgrade to reflect the successful dampening of inflation and generally good outlook for the country's economy and participation in global capital markets. As he rose to speak, the room hushed, and several photographers moved to the front near the stage. He spoke for about 20 minutes and confirmed the hoped-for rating upgrade, creating murmurs across the audience. Several reporters rushed out of the room. When he finished, there were no questions, and three-quarters of the audience left the room, never to return.

It dawned on me that the true purpose and importance of the day's program was the new Moody's rating that would be revealed and help determine Brazil's access to international finance, its trade prospects, and its power in the world as a more even-keeled and well-managed economy. I had misread the packed room and attendant faces during my presentation as interest in my subject. My greatest impact probably was keeping the audience waiting for the announcement that would follow.

It would have been a much more intimate audience for me if the Moody's man had gone first.

It's New York, Already

MY INCESSANT TRAVELING as a Manhattan-based consultant had me flying out of LaGuardia airport regularly, and the American Airlines Admirals Club there provided a calmer, easier, and relatively comfortable setting for anything I had to do pre-flight. In the morning, they provided cereal, fruit, yogurt, juice, coffee—and bagels.

My routine became a quick snack of juice and a bagel, with cream cheese and/or peanut butter and/or jam of some kind. The bagels were already cut and piled up for the taking. And there was a toaster.

One day, without warning and to my shock and dismay, the bagels had been cut in half vertically from the top down, rather than horizontally from side to side. What's up with that? No real surface on which to spread something, too thick and bready, won't fit in the toaster. A few minutes later, another tray of bagels emerges—all cut the same.

I composed a letter of protest on the plane that day and mailed it off to American's most senior customer service official in the Dallas Executive Office. I pointed out that if there were anywhere where folks should know better, it is in New York City. They wrote back, and within a week the reversal was complete.

As a consultant, I became used to clients sometimes deciding not to implement my recommendations. But here was an organization that saw the quality of my analysis and took action. And, it was worth every penny they paid for the advice.

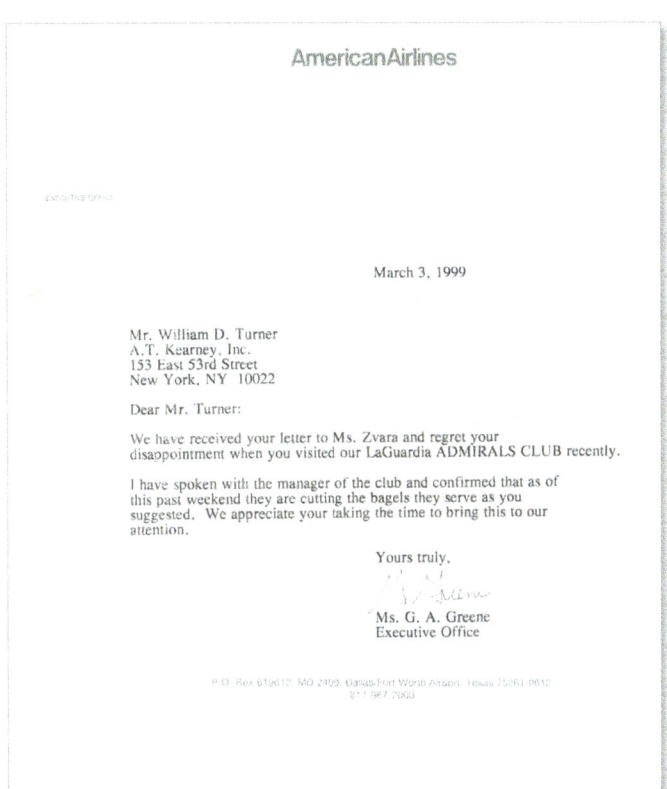

A Crystal Ball?

IN 1987, I led a joint project team at the Cigna insurance company and commuted regularly for several months on the Metroliner between New York's Penn Station and Philadelphia's 30th Street Station. Milling around the 30th Street Station waiting for my train to be announced one evening, I walked towards the men's room through a vast marble hallway and noticed a large sculpture on one wall. On my way back, I took some time to look it over and read the bronze plaque. It was—and is—called the *Spirit of Transportation* and was done by an Austrian-American sculptor, Karl Bitter, in 1895.

Spirit of Transportation
Karl Bitter | 1895

More than 30 feet long, the plaster bas-relief depicts in flamboyant and romanticized style, the advance of modes of transportation over the centuries, starting with covered wagons and farm animals and moving with flourishes through horse carriage travel to a ferryboat. And then at the end—the right-hand tip of the saga—stands a young child holding what is clearly an airship. In his outstretched hands is a basket, with struts leading up to an overhead wing to lift it through the air.

It is a powerful, under-known, and under-appreciated work, quasi-hidden away on the wall of a seatless side hall of a bustling train station.

On my train ride home that night I was struck by the imagery of human flight clearly positioned as the emerging next mode of transportation—a prediction and formulation of the next phase, in its youth as a toddler.

But perhaps more impressive and what has kept this depiction in my mind over these 30 years, is that Bitter portrayed the air travel eight years before Orville Wright took his 12-second trip on the outer banks of North Carolina. How did Bitter know—well before its birth?

Detail from the Spirit of Transportation

212 | THERE'S A PONY IN HERE SOMEWHERE!

Touring Asia

In 1999, with our sons off to college and beyond,
Kearney asked me to move to London
and lead the Europe-wide financial institutions practice,
and we enthusiastically agreed.

Our two years there was hectic but successful and fulfilling,
pulling together the various offices' client
and practice development activities,
and emphasizing recruiting and growth.

Client work took me to major banks in Italy, Poland,
and the Czech Republic.

And work at the European clearing organization CEDEL
in Luxemburg and the London Clearing House
was at a time of marked change in the capital markets,
exchanges, and clearing and settlement industries.

AFTER TWO YEARS heading the European practice, and preparing to return to New York in 2001, a call from Kearney headquarters led us to Seoul, Korea, instead. The office there had the potential opportunity to work for banks and other financial institutions but lacked industry consulting experience. The Koreans respected American expertise in general and appreciated a bit of grey hair, so I was asked to go help out.

After returning from London to New York in 2001, and after a 10-day delay caused by the September 11 attack on the World Trade Center, we moved to Seoul in the fall.

During two years in Seoul, we did substantial work for several clients, including the Woori Bank and Samsung Life, recruited and trained an expanded band of competent financial industry consultants, and raised the firm's profile and reputation. Living and working in a country where I didn't speak the language was a first but soon not uncomfortable. My role changed from being out front with clients and the firm's public face, to one of leading and supporting teams internally, and meeting with clients and the public with a translator always in tow. In Kearney's Seoul office, there were 69 Koreans and me.

The industry executives were effective and appreciative, and the senior Kearney consultants were driven and effective. The most senior associate was soon made a partner, providing local, indigenous leadership.

Appendix 4 ("Surprising Korea") provides descriptions, observations, and comments about many aspects of our experience living and working there.

* * *

In 2003, Kearney's partner leading financial institutions consulting in Hong Kong resigned to join a competitor, and the firm asked me to go there and stabilize that practice.

Over about two years in Hong Kong, we were able to do so and expand the banking practice across Greater China, and my personal client work included a formidable client bank in each of Beijing, Hong Kong, Shenzhen, and Taipei, as well as a bit of work at the Development Bank of Singapore. They were indigenous banks in different markets, and included Taiwan, which could be accessed from Hong Kong but not from Mainland China, because of the decades-old dispute over its 'ownership.'

Appendix 5 ("Whiffs of 'Fragrant Harbor'") contains some special aspects and impressions of our time in Hong Kong.

By the summer of 2004, young Chinese consultants had grown into leadership roles, and it was finally time to return to New York. However, Kearney's Australian team had just been retained by one of that country's largest banks, Westpac, but the partner in line to lead the effort was leaving the firm when the project was supposed to start. So, Paula and I agreed to go to Sydney for four months to help see that through.

The client people were excellent, the work was successful and implemented, the office appreciated the assistance, and we were able to get a first-hand taste of the country's cities, coasts and reefs, and outback.

Appendix 6 ("The Largest Island") reflects on our brief stay in Sydney and beyond in Australia.

Consulting Denouement

FINALLY RETURNING to New York toward the end of 2004, and being nearly 60 years old, I convinced the firm to let me slide down to a half-time commitment but continue to help firm and office management guide and build the practice. This worked well, and I retired from Kearney in the Spring of 2007.

After leaving the firm, I was asked to participate in a Kearney project for the Dutch National Bank, and I used it as a test for continuing to work as an independent consultant. It proved to be a good test case—I knew the issues and the market environment, Amsterdam was worth the commute, and it was lucrative. But I realized that my primary goal was now to be able to travel and work as I wished, not driven by pay.

After some 38 years of banking and consulting, we aggressively sought not to work.

***

The Five Stages of a Consultant's Career

STAGE 1 | Who is Bill Turner?
STAGE 2 | Get me Bill Turner
STAGE 3 | Get me a Bill Turner type
STAGE 4 | Get me a young Bill Turner
STAGE 5 | Who is Bill Turner?

Not Everyone Loves a Consultant

• When asked for the time, a consultant borrows your watch, tells you the time … and then keeps the watch.

• What is black and brown and looks good on a consultant? A Doberman.

• Some clients prefer a one-armed consultant. Otherwise, when you ask them a question, they respond, "On the one hand … but on the other hand …."

"From the violent nature of the multiple stab wounds, I'd say the victim was probably a consultant."

WHITHER THE BRIEFCASE

I WAS IN the generation before backpacks became de rigueur, with a few bookbags popping up in high school and college, but only if carrying a notebook from home or locker to class was not enough. Then, in graduate school, I lived half a block away, rarely carted a book around, but must have had some kind of folder or notebooks to take notes in class. And, my summer jobs as a kid, as well as part-time jobs in college and all the while in business school, were confined to physical and/or on-site work, with minimal need to "take work home" or carry things back and forth.

* * *

With my first real, full-time, 'desk' job came the need for a briefcase. That was in 1969, before cell phones or digital calendars, and there was no internet. Hard copy was the rule then, in the form of books, notes, letters, instructions, menus, phone books, maps, etc. I bought my first briefcase to commute to work, and it carried my small *Manhattan Diary*, HP model 12C calculator, various pens and probably a pencil or two, a short portable umbrella if it was supposed to rain, and, importantly, papers and reports that commuted with me back and forth. I didn't like bulk, so, from the outset, I made do with the smallest—that is, thinnest—size that would accommodate my stuff—about 4" in depth.

Although men had abandoned wearing hats to the office by the late-1960s, and only IBM and a few others still required white shirts, suits and ties remained fundamental and universal. Polished shoes and a suitable briefcase were part of that costume.

The business world at the time was dominated by hard-side, rectangular, black or brown leather cases. One never saw a soft-sided one, and shoulder straps were non-existent. A few distinctive brands, logos, and even design features crept in to differentiate briefcases. But exclusivity never came to mean much, and the basic shape, size, stiff leather shell, and gold or brass lock trim remained universal through the 1980s and 1990s. Metal cases never really took off—something tacky or excessively utilitarian about them—nor did wood ones, probably considered old fashioned or 'un-modern.'

Subtlety and reserve, or conservatism, held out against ostentatiousness. For example, Gucci had their model with the red and green strip tastefully wrapping around the case, but you didn't see many of them. Exotic leathers, such as crocodile, lizard, and ostrich were around but, again, were considered bizarre and the wrong kind of business statement. And, although an occasional burgundy, navy, or green case was available, brown (from tan to dark) and black were dominant.

I only had four successive briefcases from 1969 until I stopped full-time work in 2007. An average of nine-plus years per case is pretty efficient and speaks well for the quality and durability of the cases. Three were tan or light brown, one was dark brown. All had built-in combination locks, and, from the second one on, my combination was 245, the street address of McKinsey's New York office before 1980. The last three cases came from a Madison Avenue shop called Hides in Shape, which had a broad assortment of fine cases, including their own line.

* * *

In the early 1980s, one of the best client executives I worked with at the Amsterdam-Rotterdam Bank was Fop Hoogendijk, who was in his mid-50s and ran the international business. At a meeting in his office in Amsterdam, he said he had just returned from London and had found someone there to make him a new briefcase. He explained that he had inherited a fabulous old English briefcase from his father, but it had finally 'disintegrated' after more than 30 years of use. It seems that the concierge at the Savoy hotel in London, where Fop always stayed, had found someone who agreed to make from scratch an exact replica of the earlier case. Fop had just picked up the new one and was over the moon with it. He refused to tell me how much it had cost.

* * *

My era saw women infiltrating the corporate and financial world, en masse for the first time. My class at Columbia Business School in 1969 had only two women; there were very few in the management training programs at Chemical Bank in the early 1970s; and McKinsey elected their first female partner in 1978, a half century after the firm's founding. In the mid-1980s, I remember returning to New York from London, walking up Park Avenue and noticing a plethora of women carrying business briefcases. I don't recall seeing that before.

* * *

After retiring in 2007, I didn't use my last briefcase at all, and eventually gave it to a thrift shop in Manhattan. Business norms have changed dramatically in the last 20 years, with suits and ties largely disappearing from most jobs in most cities, and hard-side briefcases along with them. Both men and women commute and travel often with nothing but a cell phone or electronic tablet. Informality reigns, with both leather and canvas backpacks and over-the-shoulder bags, and with vibrantly-colored bags appearing even at business meetings.

I have now gravitated to collecting vintage soft-sided cases. There are terrific vintage leather bags out there and available at thrift shops and on the internet. I now have four dozen of them. They are all different, more brown than black by preference, with a few maroon or burgundy. Most have shoulder straps that can unclip.

Yes, I am challenged to invent ways to use them, and using them all would take a lifetime. But, collecting them and having them around is luxurious. Beyond their possible occasional usefulness, they demonstrate excellent craftsmanship, exquisite leathers, and interesting designs. Since I need none and have nearly 50, I call it a 'collection.'

PART THREE
Retreating to the Mountains

---

*In 2007, we began splitting our time
between the Colorado house (in winter and summer)
and the New York apartment (spring and fall).*

*We relish our time in both places, being always sad to leave
and excited to arrive.*

*And, until 2012, we spent two weeks
around Labor Day each year
at Paula's family's shared home on Glen Lake
in northern Michigan,
which was delightful but meant
an early ending to each Colorado summer.*

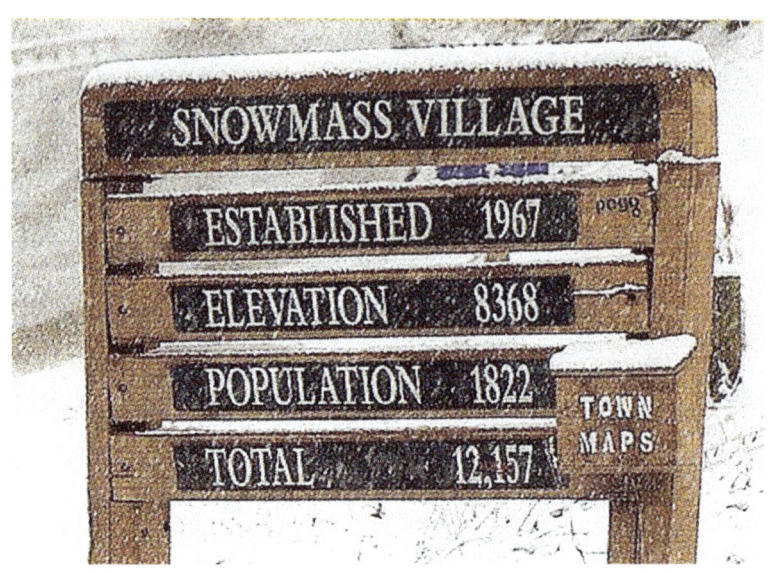

NEW MATH IN SNOWMASS VILLAGE, COLORADO

MOST OF THE WORLD'S attractive destinations are at their best in the spring and fall. As a result, our continuing vacation trips began to seriously reduce our time in New York and shifted the great majority of our 'at home' time to Snowmass Village.

Time at our Dutchess County home had eroded, and we sold it in 2010 for three reasons: We didn't use it, preferring to be either in Manhattan or Colorado; it had a complicated heating system, and we were continually worried that frozen pipes in the winter would destroy the place; and a new owner would enjoy the setting as we had for three decades. We used the occasion to move our legal residence to Snowmass Village, where we had already been spending more time than in New York. And, in 2012, Paula and her siblings—four families living in four different states—decided to sell the Michigan lake house.

A Customer Focus in Aspen

Virtually all airports now closely follow TSA rules, and most post signs that warn travelers to adhere. Aspen's airport has gone the extra mile, aiming warnings and rules at certain travelers. For example, Aspen is a magnet for beautiful people seeking to be seen. The sign below—at the entrance to the TSA line—may be the only one in the country aimed at them.

Global Touches

W E HAVE KEPT UP OUR TRAVEL—without the distraction of business responsibilities—both to places we have seen and liked in the past, and to many new ones. A friend got me interested in Formula 1 auto racing some years ago, and I have been to at least one per year for the past five years, in Austin and Montreal. And the Western states contain dozens of interesting and fun destinations within reasonable driving distance. Especially with our boys on the West Coast, Portland, Seattle, and Hawaii define another triangle we continue to ply. Compiled out of curiosity while contemplating this book, the following list indicates countries we have visited—many for business, all for pleasure.

Veni, Vidi, Exii

'WORKED IN' COUNTRIES	ADDITIONAL, 'VISITED' COUNTRIES	
Austria	Andorra	Philippines
Australia | R (4 mos.)	Argentina*	Portugal
Bahrain	Bahamas*	Russia*
Belgium	Barbados	St. Croix
Brazil	Belize*	St. Lucia
Canada	Bermuda	Society Islands
China	Cambodia	Spain
Cyprus	Cayman Islands	Switzerland
Czech Republic	Costa Rica*	Turkey
Denmark	Croatia	Viet Nam
Finland	Dominican Republic	Yugoslavia

'WORKED IN' COUNTRIES	ADDITIONAL, 'VISITED' COUNTRIES	
Hong Kong R (2 yrs.)	Egypt	Zambia*
Ireland	Estonia*	Zimbabwe*
Italy	Fiji*	
Japan	France	
Kuwait	Germany	
Luxembourg	Gibraltar*	
Mexico	Greece	
Monaco	Hungary	
Netherlands	India	
Norway	Indonesia	
Poland	Jordan	
Saudi Arabia	Laos*	
Singapore	Latvia*	
South Africa	Liechtenstein	
South Korea R (2 yrs.)	Lithuania*	
Spain	Malaysia	
Sweden	Mongolia	
Taiwan	Montenegro	NOTE:
Thailand	Morocco*	R = Resident for more than 3 months.
United Kingdom R (8 yrs.)	Myanmar*	* = First visit post-2007 retirement.
USA R (63 yrs.)	New Zealand*	

* * *

Since retiring, and in the spirit of 'giving back,' I joined the boards of directors of the Brooklyn Navy Yard in Brooklyn, New York, Aspen Public Radio, the local NPR affiliate station near the Colorado house, and the Aspen Science Center, a science education non-profit.

As a board member, and as Chairman for a spell at two of

them, I've been able to help out by drawing on my financial and consulting experience and am enjoying relationships with some very interesting folks.

My skiing makes the winters worth it and fun. I have gotten somewhat more competent over the years and aim for about 60 days of skiing between December and April each season. Both boys like Colorado in general and are excellent skiers, although they don't come enough.

After spending a little time on and off over decades finding out more about a great-grandfather who was a sea captain, I decided to dig more seriously and write up his life as a book. I finished and 'self-published' *The Lucky Captain* in 2016, but only in hard copy form, with the aim of reducing slightly the probability that our sons would throw it away without reading it. I enjoyed that effort enough to start another similar project about my paternal grandfather, who was a Marine 'hero' in the First World War, and whom I knew until he died in 1972. That effort produced *Chuie, the Major* in 2018. And, I'm still on the hunt for the next subject.

I stopped working for money just before the Great Recession in 2008, but I seemed to muddle through those times financially, and have had good fortune in deriving an adequate living so far. Having devoted an inordinate amount of time managing and investing my savings since I retired, I am now dedicated to diminishing my own role and engaging others to do it going forward.

Cash Flows

As a novelist, I tell stories, and people give me money.
Then financial planners tell me stories, and I give them money.

—MARTIN CRUZ SMITH

* * *

October:
This is one of the peculiarly dangerous months
to speculate in stocks in.

The others are:
July, January, September, April, November,
May, March, June, December, August, and February.

—MARK TWAIN
evidently an unsuccessful investor

* * *

Markets in the Mountains

Epitaphs

A selection from a 1984 *New York Magazine* competition for potential epitaphs of well-known persons

WALTER WRISTON, CITICORPSE

IVAN LENDL, CANCELED CZECH

HERE LIES CYRANO DE BERGERAC, ON HIS SIDE

MOHAMMED REZA PAHLAVI, SHAH LOAM

EDWARD G. ROBINSON, THIS IS THE END OF RICO

HERE LIES ROSENKRANTZ. OR GUILDENSTERN.

RONALD REAGAN, DEADTIME FOR BONZO

JAMES CAAN, GAAN

THE RODNEY DANGERFIELD MEMORIAL URINAL

HERE LIZA MINNELLI

HERE LIES ULYSSES S. GRANT, STUPID

DON RICKLES, WISH YOU WERE HERE

JACQUES COUSTEAU, SLEEPS WITH THE FISHES

DAVID COPPERFIELD, I AM DEAD

ST. FRANCIS OF ASSISI,
WAS HE ANY GOOD OR WHAT?

F. LEE BAILEY, THE DEFENSE RESTS

WELCOME TO MR. ROGER'S NEW NEIGHBORHOOD

RICHARD M. NIXON, I AM NOT A CORPSE

HERE LIE THE SEVEN SANTINI BROTHERS,
PACKING OUR SPECIALTY

HELLO, MY NAME IS VICTOR KIAM
I LIKED THIS COFFIN SO MUCH
I BOUGHT THE COMPANY

APPENDIX 1

Religion

(BLIND FAITH IS REDUNDANT)

MY PARENTS were church regulars, Sunday school was interesting, and I have marveled at some fabulous religious edifices and sanctuaries around the world, but I've never gone for the faith part.

With religion such a visible and prevalent part of human history and today's world, but with it not playing a central role in my life, I feel guilty that I don't feel guilty about it. As Ron Reagan declares in a TV ad for an atheist society, "I'm not afraid of burning in hell"—but maybe I should be.

I'm not anti-church, anti-god, or anti-faith. In fact, 'some of my best friends are religious,' which I respect and, in a way, admire. And, I see great value for individuals able to rely on and be guided by faith in a god, the Bible, Torah, or Quran, and church preachings. They can be a source of hope, a perceptibly impartial or divine authority, and a source of perspective and guidance. I just do not understand how folks attain faith in a divine creator, supreme being, redeemer, an afterlife, and the like.

Why write about it? This note is merely an attempt to lay out some of the notions and rationale for my inability to believe in or live according to strictures attributed to supernatural powers. In doing so, I cover Religion in My Life, Religion in Society, Is there a God?, and Faith is at the Core.

Religion In My Life

MY PARENTS—both with protestant upbringings—were adult members of a new, multi-denominational protestant church, which in its early years in the 1950s held Sunday services in a movie theatre in a new suburb in Chicagoland. It was led by a smart, charismatic, young minister, and the congregation soon built a large modern church building. I often went along with my parents to the services—when Sunday school didn't conflict—and was impressed by the 'content' of the sermons and the hymns, the wonderful organ and choir music, even the flowers and fancy Sunday dress.

I attended Sunday school for several years through sixth grade, without resistance, and found the bible stories and other teachings interesting, in the manner of a history course. The church services, Sunday school, and constant comments and nagging from my mother created in my mind the notion that there was right and wrong, and one should do what was right. Aspects of accountability and consequences were there somewhere, but it was unclear who would invoke them, beyond my parents and law enforcement.

In high school, I was an active member of a youth group of a different protestant church, where many of my school mates attended the activities. This group was more an extension of school and social life than religious. (To qualify for a protestant 'confirmation' service, I was baptized, never having been as a baby—an omission, not a statement, by my parents.) Notable trips included my first-time skiing at an area in northern Michigan, reached by a long bus ride. Panty raids were explicitly forbidden; the remote outhouse was a 100-foot walk away from the male bunkhouse; and the temperature reached a record -38 degrees during our second night. It was a terrific and memorable weekend, purely social and athletic. The other noteworthy trip was a visit to a similar church youth group in Columbus, Ohio, basically just to get to know another set of similar teenagers. It was marked by several of us lifting a VW beetle and turning it sideways in a crowded parking lot, so that it was wedged between the adjoining parked cars and impossible to move.

In college, I chose a religious studies course as an elective—basically a good comparative religion and religious history course. My girlfriend (an estranged Roman Catholic) and I went to a few Easter or other services, including once to a local Roman Catholic church, a couple times to a long-established Episcopal church on campus (Saint Stevens, referred to as 'Smokey Steve's,' due to the use of High-Church incense), and also to the Unitarian Church down the block that housed bells cast by Paul Revere. These services were not uninteresting, but you can infer the little I took away.

Since then—more than 50 years—I have participated in church services mostly brought on by weddings, funerals, and an occasional baptism or bar mitzvah. In the 1980s, Christmas services in London's Westminster Abbey were wonderful and mostly music oriented. (One year, my son Nick and I sat in a pew above Isaac Newton's floor 'plaque.' By the end of the service, eight-year-old Nick knew Newton's three laws.) As a tourist, I have visited, and often been enthralled by, many religious venues—churches, temples, mosques, shrines, and the like—in many countries. But, religiously visiting these wonderful places, has not been religious for me.

The above recaps all that I have done and been exposed to. What I have come to think and believe is described below.

Religion In Society

OVER PREHISTORIC and more recent centuries, religion emerged from interpretations of natural events, and evolved to totems, to gods of many things, and to single gods but with differences among them—which is where we are today.

• An early lack of understanding of the physical world sowed the seeds for many super-human or religious myths and beliefs—events including meteor showers, shooting stars, eclipses, earthquakes, volcanic eruptions, tsunamis, changes of seasons, diseases, weather extremes, and even physical differences among people.

• Populations grew and tribes and communities expanded, and defining and harnessing the myths became a way to acquire and use power to control and exploit other people, in the name of improving everyone's lot.

• Different communities in different locations produced very different and sometimes unique totems, religions, and sacraments, which then grew and radiated, when one religious community tried to invade, dominate, or replace others.

As a result, today's major religions rest on different historical and ideological foundations. One person's "an eye for an eye" is not the same as another's "do unto others," yet these two almost opposing concepts are central tenets of two of our 'leading' religions.

AUTHORITY, POWER AND CONTROL | Emerging from mankind's search for the source of inexplicable natural events was a vacuum of understanding that begged explanation, and philosophers and others moved to fill the void. Those observant and creative leaders and authors asserting and documenting poignant events, stories, lessons, and parables, invoked the existence of super-natural and divine powers. The 'authors' and others were then relatively quick and effective in imbuing themselves with those powers. ("Author" is contained in "authority.") And, the people were quick to grant-by-accepting such power and authority, either within feudal governing structures or more broadly.

Religion and its hierarchy and control grew and perpetuated as an organizing and leadership structure. The church became a venue for assembling and herding human 'sheep,' as well as a source of leading and managing communities as they grew and spread, and as they dealt with the problems of the day. The church became an important sponsor and provider of schools and education, both to improve lives through learning and to control what they learned.

Most places have both governments (local and far off) and the local church or churches, as co-existing authorities for governing the population. When the church is aligned (or one and the same) with the manor or other form of government or 'state', they reinforced each other in terms of delineated authority, power, and influence on the society. But when they were not in line, and in some ways competed, depending on the strength of the religious force, 'separation of church and state' has required an agreed set of relative regime activities divided between them.

Architecturally and decoratively magnificent—and expensive—church edifices were built to impress the populace and convey the church's power and strength, stability, security, and trusteeship. Such buildings dominated many towns and cities for centuries.

GOOD FOR INDIVIDUALS? | One observation about religion's role and influence on members of society is: "I feel that religion, adopted purely, is ultimately representative of blindly making someone else's beliefs your own." This rings true for me, and I must make the generalization that the religious views and commitments of many or most people were introduced, exposed, taught, dictated, force-fed, etc. to them by others, often parents and their tribal contemporaries. (Keeping in mind, however, Voltaire's comment that "All generalizations are false, including this one.") Religious beliefs are not inherent or genetic; they are taught and learned. They may be true or false, but they exist merely because they are believed. And without observability or fact-based proof, they are believed on faith.

Religious beliefs—and the religions themselves—have provided valuable meaning, respite, and balance to millions of people—however force-fed or rote-learned. This value continues today, despite the decline of observant followers among many faiths.

The adage "There are no atheists in the trenches of war" probably is essentially true, and 'praying' is undoubtedly practiced by otherwise less- or non-religious individuals at times of need, as an expression of hope. Prayer itself can create or reassure oneself of hope, whether or not linked to a belief or faith in a god. As Gandhi defined: "Prayer is not asking. It is a longing of the soul. It is daily admission of one's weaknesses. It is better in prayer to have a heart without words than words without a heart." Prayer without faith is valuable in itself and is in no way contradictory. It does not require a recipient or respondent.

Beyond prayer, faith-based religion can help an individual cope with life's uncertainties, pressures, disappointments and losses, and fears. However, as we reflect on the sociological progression from individuals to families, tribes, nations, and broad geographies around the world, mankind's self-governance has come to be built around mainly legal and political frameworks. These frameworks, and the behavioral structures and strictures within them, are invented by 'man,' with religion as one of them—with the authorities, powers, and controls cited earlier. Widespread "faith" in the frameworks and structures is required to make all of them work, but only religions require the faith in a central, superhuman presence of god. The other, non-divine frameworks and structures require belief only in the structures themselves. They are all man made.

For individuals without true religious faith, religion can still play an insurance role, from a risk management point of view. That is, in case there really is a god, and if my life and any afterlife is determined by that god, and if god treats me according to how I conduct my life, including praising or paying tribute to Him—if all that's the case, then during my life I'm damn well going to try to act in a way that god will find appropriate. There is no empirical evidence that any of those conditions exist, so without faith, adopting such behavior is the only way to protect oneself . . . just in case. Church strictures on how to act are inventions of other humans, historically formalized and imposed by churches and their leaders.

For those who need faith, and live happier and more productive lives as a result, more power to them. Whether acquired by means of revelations or acceptance of unproven assertions, faith in a supreme being and an afterlife can be a rare and valued source of hope and optimism beyond this life. The more a person is suffering calamities or is in a bad situation with little hope of doing better, the more valuable may be a belief and trust in a God and a better life after death. It is more or less the antithesis of "eat, drink and be merry, for tomorrow we may die." With faith, "it is God's will," "God will take care of me," and "there's always tomorrow," meaning the afterlife.

But for some with faith, a belief and trust in a watchful,

omnipotent, and stern God may actually add a degree of disappointment, dejection, fear, and hopelessness, resulting in the individual carrying a burden of their own construct. In that situation, faith makes it a bigger bet on an afterlife and redemption.

GOOD FOR MANKIND? | With religious notions and practices being potentially of great value to individuals, a separate issue is whether, collectively, religion has been a net positive or net destructive force in human history. The issue is complex and beyond my scope. But it certainly is a valid issue, in view of the multitude of conflicts, wars, millions of deaths, and changes in the course of history that have been caused and suffered in the name of god and religious imperative.

WHITHER THE BIBLE? | The Bible—and the equivalent gospel, scriptures, or 'Word' in non-Christian sects—conveys powerful teachings, lessons, parables, and recommended behavior, that no doubt has had great and mostly constructive impact over the centuries. As a publication, the Bible trumps Shakespeare in its poignant writings. Even the events that can be criticized as exaggerations or fiction by doubters (e.g., perhaps parting of the seas, one-touch healings) do not detract from the messages and behavioral norms espoused. In fact, they add positive effect. Whether or not the reader considers the Bible 'holy,' literary license is welcome and enriches the messages.

Is There A God?

GOD is at the center of most religions, and is invoked throughout our daily lives, even where a separation of church and state is proudly declared and mostly honored: "We are God's children;" "God willing;" "In God we Trust;" "God fearing;" "God only Knows;" etc. But, is there a god?

"I have the whole universe to look after, so I'm putting you in charge of this planet."

Although we cannot answer that, or prove it one way or the other, we can make some observations and explore how 'yes' or 'no' answers might be relevant to our lives.

PREDESTINATION VERSUS FREE WILL | If there is a god, and human behavior and events are predestined, then the extreme diversity of that behavior and events shows that god does not practice evenhandedness. That is, goodness, mercy, beneficence, or rewards on earth do not universally prevail over evil, brutality, maleficence, or penalties, beyond any average or general improvement in the human condition overall. Or, at least history does not offer patterns or empirical progress that we can decipher, that god ensures positive outcomes in all events at his command. From what we know, intelligent design and predestination either does not exist or has built a very mixed history of mankind.

If there is a god, but no predestination—with free will in control—then the plight of mankind is wholly determined by the sum of individual human choices and behavior. That would be largely indistinguishable from human history and a world without a god.

THE BULKING-UP OF MANKIND | As we look for hints about the existence and nature of god, it is instructive to examine the increase in human population, and how that growth might imply—and be influenced by—the existence or absence of god.

- **IF THERE IS A GOD...** | With 7.6 billion human beings on earth, it's difficult to fathom how or why god could watch over and navigate for each of his 7.6 billion children, as many religions hold or imply. This is a case for free will. But some would argue that god's capacity and 'scalability' is infinite. It would have to be, when you add in every living thing, the lives of which god would have to know and determine, let alone the rest of the universe.

Assuming god is the maker, architect, and/or implementer, why would he or she create or allow so much 'bad' or non-social, self-destructive actions of individuals, tribes, and higher-level communities? The same question arises for 'natural disasters', including sickness, plagues, harmful accidents, earthquakes, volcanoes, meteor showers, assassins, wars, competing religious beliefs, etc.? The notion that the 10 commandments are his word, and that god tolerates rampant and continuing violations occurring within mankind, is another hint at free will.

- **WE ARE ANIMALS** | There is plenty of evidence that humankind is subject to the same evolutionary forces as are other living organisms—both flora and fauna.

Humans are unique (read 'superior') vis-à-vis other species in important respects. These include, for example: Highlyfunctional brains; an ability to impact the environment and ecosystems; producing and managing food and nourishment; creating and wearing clothing; developing machines and harnessing animals and other humans to do work and produce things conducive and valuable to human life; inventing and running mechanisms, organizations, and processes to govern themselves; and on and on.

However, over time, human well-being is not assured in the face of population growth, the near certainty of continued natural disasters, myriad bad actors, technological advancement used to the detriment of human life, and a globalized world without an agreed global political, economic, or cultural framework—let alone one that has proved successful and durable.

Meanwhile, there is ample reason to assume and believe that the eons-old evolution of mankind will likely follow the same forces of change and vagaries determining the destinies of other animals and plants in the face of natural disasters and self-inflicted changes and devastation. Such forces at work include impacts of genetic mutation; climate change; overpopulation; shortages of life-enabling oxygen, food, and shelter; subjugation of some peoples over others; nuclear or other devastating accidents; etc.

In fact, there is no proof or conviction that we are different from other species, as victims of these same forces whether they are 'man-made' or 'natural.' Even if there is a god, our future is unclear (at least to us) and, in the long run, unpredictable—perhaps subject to most of the same forces that affect other living things. Just as there is no proof god exists, there is none that Darwin was wrong in concept. Human population growth doesn't bode well.

• **IF THERE IS NO GOD...** | The same forces at work would seem to apply to and be perceived and experienced by all of us—even without a god—determining the outcomes that have occurred and will continue to occur.

Particularly concerning, yet rarely dealt with, for example, is the tripling of the world's population since the 1950s, posing what could turn out to be existential challenges to mankind. It is unclear, for example, if our global economic system, with its ever-advancing technology, Artificial Intelligence potential, and global integration of all kinds, will be able to sustain high employment and the creation and distribution of wealth and improved lifestyles, as we know them, for all people. The role of religion and faith in acknowledging, grappling with, and overcoming this challenge to global human society is elusive, invisible, or absent to me. And, to the extent that advances in medicine and the avoidance of epidemics, wars, and famines can be achieved, the population will grow even faster and demands on all systems will accelerate.

We cannot accept the risk that a god can show us the way to find the right choices or best solutions for these basic problems. God may not do that, and god might not exist. We need to find—and will be accountable for finding—a way to overcome these challenges. To the extent that religion and faith is or becomes a crutch, it will hardly address or fix the root causes. We will be better to assume there is no god in addressing the challenges and needs.

WHAT ABOUT AN AFTERLIFE? | I see no clear evidence of an afterlife and am not confident there is one. An afterlife, inclusive of reincarnation or not, could be a figment of religious leaders and sages who were in need of devising a payoff or comeuppance for living and acting appropriately during this life. And, the notion of heaven and hell are obvious manifestations of a carrot and a stick—for later, and 'afterwards.'

The possibility that "next time I would or will do things differently, make different decisions, or live a different life altogether," provides psychological comfort and, again, hope in the face of one's own perceived mistakes, shortcomings, regrets, or unfulfilled desires. The notion of an afterlife—as well as heaven or hell as potential destinations—provides that possibility.

A risk management frame of mind again makes sense in the face of the uncertainty of an afterlife. If we rely on an afterlife and compromise how we live or what we do or might do in this life, and low and behold there is none, we have foregone something for naught. So, that exaggerated phrase of "eat, drink and be merry" comes to mind as a reasonable way to live, in case there turns out to be no afterlife. The serious implication is that one should do what is right and righteous and desired during this life. Then, if in the event there is indeed an afterlife, it will be an unanticipated bonus.

Faith Is At The Core

Whether there is a God as creator and as divine architect, judge, and meter of positive and negative sanctions by virtue of how one lives one's life and adheres to gods perceived teachings, boils down to one's *faith* in all that. The heart of it is whether an individual acquires or attains such faith by osmosis or otherwise.

Each individual soul and spirit is susceptible and eligible to come to have faith in god and god's powers and actions, despite that faith neither being implanted in DNA, nor being a conviction supported by empirical evidence.

Since the cave men, the absence of empirical or physical proof of a god as a basis for faith in a divine being has provided a vacuum when it comes to gestating and instilling god and religious beliefs. This vacuum has been filled over the ages by making non-scientific and physically-unprovable leaps to beliefs in unseen powers. By circular argument, these leaps are attributed to acquired 'faith' on the part of those making them.

With faith in hand early on, the myriad forms of religious gospel, teachings, dogma, and requirements have heavily influenced social norms. And, generations and eras of social norms have influenced the evolution and interpretations of the church and its teachings. With faith on the part of the converted, all that has been possible; without faith, few religions have legitimacy.

FAITH VERSUS SCIENCE | Over the centuries of human history, scientific logic and discoveries have increasingly explained and proved how and why our world works, answering many basic questions of the physical world, humanity, and our individual mental and physical processes.

I admit that when arguing about the origins of nature, space, matter, the universe, etc.—even accepting a big-bang start and evolutionary history of our existence and the cosmos—the question of "what or who caused the Big Bang, and what was there prior to that?" cannot be answered. Over the centuries, the vacuum of proof of original determination has been filled—or defaulted to—by the invention or assumptions of gods, with their powers and their dictums. Many scientists invoke a god or supernatural power, which is as good a guess or proposition as any.

I thought it a paradox that faith is accepted, and can dominate important aspects of human life, while being ignored or rejected in other aspects. For example, all through the COVID-19 pandemic, many ignore, reject, or dismiss the clear scientific basis of the virus and its manner of spreading and threat to life. This reaction is furthered, no doubt, by the fact that the virus itself is invisible, passed through normal everyday contact, and delayed in its presentation and debilitating effects. As a result—and seemingly irrational—some people take few if any precautions and refuse to act differently, to prevent their acquiring or passing on the virus. Meanwhile, millions of these same people believe and live major aspects of their lives according to faith in a perceived god and religious teachings, standards, and requirements that are equally invisible, but also unprovable or non-existent. The implication is that many believe that the unidentifiable god will protect them from the identifiable virus.

FAITH VERSUS HOPE AND LUCK | When there is no hope, try faith. And, the less hope, the more needed and valuable faith becomes. Hope is a desire to match or beat the odds, where the odds are often or usually known or estimable. Beating the odds is almost always possible, even when heavily stacked against—it is a matter of probability. The other side of hope is risk that the outcome will go against what you hope.

Faith is hope with no physical or provable basis. It is confi-

dence in the certainty of an outcome—whether or not the outcome is subject to probability. That is, it denies probability and assumes certainty—probability of 100%. If someone has faith in an outcome that is actually subject to probability, the faith is misplaced or a deception.

Faith and hope are not mutually exclusive. I have faith that the sun will rise tomorrow, and I also hope that it will. But certainty replaces both hope and faith, because it is predictable and can be anticipated and dealt with—either exploited or protected against.

Similar to hope, luck is either beating the odds of an outcome, or experiencing a serendipitous outcome—an unexpected, positive event. I hope that I am lucky enough to beat the odds, but I have no basis for having faith that I will. The odds are predictable, but a single outcome is not.

The notion of divine intervention contains a mix of these. Such intervention is usually ascribed to something good happening that was not expected to happen or to be as good or desirable. We do not hear much of divine neglect or divine disappointment.

SPIRIT WITHOUT A SPIRIT | Although the notion and manifestations of a Holy Spirit requires faith in a god and divine forces, which may not exist, the notion of spirit at an individual and even collective level is an important trait. Spirit, defined simply as the non-physical aspects of human life, can come to characterize or define a person's behavior, psychology, personality, and social interaction with great impact. And that impact can range from very positive, constructive, and uplifting, to very negative, destructive and depressing. We all know some people who are 'mean spirited,' which can be attributed to what we consider a negative, destructive, or evil objective and outlook, and which manifests itself in behavior that goes against the individual and common good. On the other hand, there are those folks who are even-keeled or positive and exude constructive attitudes and behaviors that can be infectious.

'Holy spirit,' in contrast, shifts the central meaning to one of faith in, and the power of, a supreme being based on faith. As a result, spiritual has generally come to denote a characteristic based on holiness and the forces of such a supreme being—virtually always as a positive trait. One rarely hears reference to negative or destructive spirituality.

But this inference or underpinning of faith-based religion is unnecessary in accepting and defining the meaning and potential importance and impact of spirit. We all have and deploy spirit of some kind, without the requirement of a (divine) spirit.

SUMMARY

I'M NOT ANTI-RELIGION, or anti-faith, or anti-church, although I don't understand how folks attain faith in a supreme being and divine creator and redeemer, in our lives on earth. It's just not for me, because I cannot come to believe in those very basic aspects. In fact, I respect and see the great value for individuals able to rely on and be guided by a faith in a god and church teachings, which can be a source of hope, a perceptibly impartial authority, and a source of perspective and guidance.

Although I—and everyone—cannot factually answer the question "Who or what created the universe?" or "Who created Nature?", I believe there is not a god as many religions define it. However, I fully subscribe to many of the teachings and norms of behavior held by many religions and their scriptures, and I try to live by them. I am unhappy and feel guilty when I don't abide by or follow through on those tenets and am dedicated to doing better. More specifically:

- The adoption of faith and practice of religion have proven valuable to society to assuage individual insecurities, fears, and other psychological needs that affect most of the world's population in one way or another.

- The advent and development of faith-based religion— "the church"—has emanated partially as a means and institution for building and exerting power and governance over peoples and their societies.

- Perhaps the cumulative value of faith at the individual level over the centuries, is greater than the wars, suffering, and lives lost in the name of god; perhaps not.

- To the extent that church teachings have reinforced constructive and non-selfish morals, ethics, and behavior, religion has been positive and helpful in that way too.

- Non-scientific and physically unprovable faith is required to believe in god and his/her divine powers, in predestination, or in an afterlife or reincarnation. It is an interesting issue as to whether such faith can be taught, and how it is otherwise acquired.

• From a risk management perspective, I try to act non-selfishly, morally, and ethically, but with a presumption that there is no god or, if there is, that the outcomes of my life are not in god's hands, but my own. After all, it's not the "fear of god," but actually the fear of bad outcomes.

APPENDIX 2

Collections

I Remained Calm, Cool...and Collected

T HIS ALPHABETICAL LIST of my main collections indicates the target and limiting characteristics of the various items, their vintage and 'nationality,' the period when I acquired them, approximate number of items in the collection, and in a few cases, particularly useful reference books.

- **Banks:** still (i.e., not mechanical) and in the shape of bank buildings; vintage, 19th/20th Century American, British, French, Nordic countries, Hong Kong; acquired 1970s—late 1980s; 15 of them; excellent book—*The Penny Bank Book.*

- **Beer steins:** ¼ - 0.3 liter; lidded; mostly ceramic, but also glass, wood and metal; vintage 19th—20th Century German, Austrian, American, Belgian; acquired 1980s onward; 73 of them.

- **Bottle openers:** nude figurines, metal; vintage early 20th Century French, British, American; acquired 2000s onward; 6 of them.

- **Briefcases:** vintage leather; handle and shoulder strap type; soft-sided; brown and black; early 20th Century onward; acquired 2005s onward; 50 of them.

- **Buddhas:** wood, porcelain/ceramic, metal; standing, sitting, multi-faced; vintage 19th—21st Century China, Cambodia, Viet Nam, Myanmar, Thailand, Laos; acquired late 1990s—early 2000s; 12 of them.

- **Cocktail shakers:** small; vintage 19th—21st Centuries American and British; silver, pewter, stainless, glass, plastic; acquired 1990s—2010s; 25 of them.

- **Coffee pots:** porcelain, electric percolators; vintage early-mid 20th Century American; acquired 1980s; 11 of them; excellent book—*Collector's Guide to Porcelier China.*

- **Coins:** U.S. cents (large, Flying Eagle, Indian Head, Lincoln), two- and three-cent pieces, nickels (Liberty, buffalo, Jefferson), ½ dimes and dimes, Quarters (Liberty and Washington), half-dollars; acquired 1950s—1980s; hundreds in many albums.

- **Decanters:** crystal, mostly British, 19th/20th Century, acquired 1980s, 8 of them.

- **Guns:** rifles, shotguns, pistols; vintage late 19th Century—1970s; acquired 1970s onward; 8 of them.

- **Ice cream scoops** (or 'dippers'): vintage pewter covered brass, aluminum, other metal, plastic; lever, squeeze handle, and non-mechanical types; various scoop sizes; vintage late 19th Century—1940 American; acquired 2010s onward; 55 of them; excellent book—*Ice Cream Dippers.*

APPENDICES | 251

*A single example from most of the collections.
Missing are coffee pots and oil lamps.*

• **Oil lamps:** 'Aladdin shape', single flame; silver, stone, other metal; vintage 19th-20th Century Middle Eastern, English, American; acquired 1990s—2010s; 18 of them.

• **Opera glasses:** Brass, metal, mother of pearl, plastic; vintage 19th and 20th Century French and British; acquired 2000s onward; 6 of them.

• **Pickle forks:** silver; vintage 19th Century British; acquired 1980s onward; 3 of them.

• **Paint/calligraphy brush stands**: vintage 20th Century Korean; wood, stone, ceramic; acquired late 1990s; 7 of them.

• **St. Francis statuettes:** wooden, one cast metal; height 8" to 15"; vintage 20th Century American, Latin American, Italian; acquired 2000 onwards; 9 of them.

- **Semaphores, model railroad:** single- and multi-arm type; free-standing and bridge type; wood, metal, plastic; electrified and not; height 2"–18"; various gauges; vintage 19th–20th Century American, British, German, Japanese; acquired 2010 onward; 115 of them.

- **Snuff bottles** (Paula's collection): vintage 19th—20th Century Chinese; acquired late 1990s—early 2000s; 12 of them.

- **Stamps**: U.S. and world-wide postage; some canceled on envelopes/postcards; more unused; many sheets, first-day covers; acquired from father; hundreds in many albums.

- **Thomas W. Lawson artifacts:** ship models, ships in bottles, photos, books, porthole glass, brass barrel tap, captain's personal items; rescue boat half-hull model; vintage early 20th Century onward British and American; acquired 1970s onward; many excellent books.

- **Toast racks:** vintage 19th Century British; porcelain, silver; acquired 1980s onward; 3 of them.

- **Wine bottle stoppers:** metal, plastic, rubber; various shapes, figures; vintage 20th—21st Century French, American; acquired 1990s onward; 6 of them.

APPENDIX 3

Cars

27 Keys to Transport and Freedom

GROWING UP in the Midwest, cars represented transportation, but more importantly, independence.

Due to cheap used cars and motorcycles in the 1960's, and employers providing cars when stationed overseas, my first 13 vehicles cost me a total of $6,940, over the 25 years from 1961 to 1986! Of the 10 new cars I've owned, I bought six, employers bought four. Four of the cars were right-hand drive. Prices have risen since, as have the quality and performance. A gallon of gasoline in the 1960s averaged 31 cents.

Cushman/homemade motor scooter. Black. (1959, ~$40)
No driver's or vehicle license required; town streets only; single cylinder; centrifugal clutch; kept 2-3 years.

1954 Ford 4-door Sedan. Turquoise and white. (1961, $75)
Bought from neighbor; new driver's license; one summer only; sold for $75 to junk yard.

1952 Chevrolet Valet Sedan. Matt black primer. (1962, $50)
No hood fastener; one summer only; sold to junk yard for $50; POS car; 1 can oil for every gas tank fill.

1949 Oldsmobile Sedan. Dark green/gray. (1963, $75)
Straight 8; 3-speed on column; heel hole in floor under clutch pedal; one summer only; sold to junk yard.

Yamaha 250cc Motorcycle. Red and cream. (1964, $250)
2-cycle road bike; 5-speed; side turn signals; sewing machine sound; bought at Brown; trained in parking lot; sold in Chicago via newspaper.

Yamaha 250cc Motorcycle. Silver. (1965, $400)
Newer, higher-tech but same set up; bought from newspaper; kept at Brown; sold in Chicago in 1966.

1958 Ford Convertible. Turquoise and white. (1966, $0)
Classmate gift; another classmate borrowed and shot at it; drove to Chicago with motorcycle 'in' trunk; then sold it for ~$0.

1961 Pontiac Tempest Compact. Fernando Beige. (1966, $650)
First 'real' car; automatic (lever), low gear stopped working on GW Bridge; parked on NY street; kept till 1970.

1965 Ford Mustang Sedan. Robin's egg blue. (1970, $0)
Suzanne's college car; drove into ground in NYC; traded in in Rhode Island 1973.

1972 Volkswagen Super Beetle. Elm Green. (1973, $1,200)
Almost new; commuted NYC-Providence; totaled by Chrysler on ice in Wingdale with 4 adults/1 child in VW; maybe first beetle with A/C.

1974 Toyota Corolla Wagon.* Red. (1974, $4,200)
First new car; NYC garage; NYC-Wingdale; sold when went to London, 1980.

1977 BMW 730. Blue metallic. (1980, $0)
RHD; used; Ex-pat benefit; drove all over UK/Scotland/French coast; parked on street; water pump and cam shaft broke; broke new car leasing policy.

1984 Honda Accord.* Burgundy. (1983, $0)
RHD; Ex-pat benefit; replaced BMW; picked up in Rotterdam, ran out of gas at dock lot, raced for day's last ferry to UK.

1986 Volvo 240DL, Wagon.* Red. (1986, $14,000)
Bought in London; export deal to NYC; delivered to NJ docks; NYC garage; sold in Wingdale 1990. London dealer became an upscale restaurant.

1987 Jeep Wrangler Convertible.* Red. (1987, $10,000)
Special black fabric roof; kept in Wingdale; removable doors; crashed NYC toll gate; sold to Wingdale housekeeper ~1993.

1991 Toyota Previa.* Garnet Red. (1990, $14,000)
Whale van; NYC garage; sold in Wingdale ~1998.

1982 Porsche 911 Targa. Pale yellow (Bombus Beige) (1993, $12,500) 97,000 miles at purchase; speedometer only to 80 mph due to U.S. gas crisis; kept in Wingdale; sold for $12,500 to Texan 2010.

1997 Porsche 911S. Arena Red. (1998, $72,000)
One year old/7,000 miles; last air cooled/hips; keep in Colorado.

1998 Mercedes ML320.* Green. (1998, $36,000)
Princess Di influence; shipped to CO in 1999; AMENDS plate; bit of a tin can; kept until 2004.

1998 BMW 530si.* Glacier Green. (1999, $0)
RHD; manual; Ex-pat benefit; parked in street; fabulous; kept until left London 2001.

2001 Hundai Sonata.* White. (2001, 0)
Ex-pat benefit; one year with driver; kept until left Seoul in 2003.

1990 Porsche 911 Roadster. Peach. (2003, ~$10,000)
RHD; 10th owner/30K miles; ticketed for non-conforming plate (LA5 893); sold in 2004 for same $; Chinese only buy new, thus a large used supply; investigated export business.

~2001 Lexus 300xl. Light blue. (2004, ?)
Used/off lease in NYC; totaled in CT.

~2006 Lexus 350xl. Gold. (~2016, $?)
Used/off lease in NYC; 2008; hybrid; battery recharge conflict; sold 2011.

2005 Audi S4 Avant (wagon)* Moro blue. (2004, $46,100)
Bought/keep in CO; Quatro; buying criteria-overpowered, quiet, AWD; excellent/decline after 10 years/50,000 miles.

2003 Audi A4. Black. (2013, $5,700)
Bought in CT; blew up in Omaha en route to CO; sold for $1K ten days after the purchase; pristine but for needing new engine.

2015 Audi A7 TDI*. Garnet Red. (2014, $73,000)
Bought/keep in CO; diesel; excellent car but too large.

NOTE:* = Bought new. RHD = Right-hand drive.

First Motorcycle—Yamaha 250cc

1961 Pontiac Tempest

1991 Toyota Previa

1982 Porsche SC Targa

1990 Porsche 911 C2 Roadster

1997 Porsche 911S

APPENDIX 4

Surprising Korea

The following descriptions, observations and comments are drawn from our two years living and working in Seoul, 2001 to 2003.

BIG AND MODERN | Seoul was a city of just under ten million Koreans, growing and sprawling with new glass and steel buildings. (New York City's population was about eight million.) Korea's total population is about 47 million, which is about double that of North Korea. Unlike images of other parts of Asia, there were virtually no bicycles in sight, with cars everywhere—mostly Hyundai's and Kia's built by the local companies. There were taxis, trains, and buses that were dependable and on time, and shuttled everyone around.

As a pedestrian, one must be careful and wary of the buses running throughout Seoul. The drivers receive bonus money for completing their routes on or ahead of schedule. This incentive is obvious from the aggressiveness and lack of hesitation as the busses pull in and out of the bus stops, speed through yellow lights, and generally race along their routes.

MONOLITHICALLY KOREAN | It was eerie—not uncomfortable, but stark—that virtually everyone we saw was Korean, with exceedingly few 'round eyes' anywhere. For example, we would go to a modern shopping mall (one included a 20-screen cinema) on a Saturday, spend several hours in the crowded stores and restaurants, and never see a Westerner. In fact, we were the strangers. Little children would often approach Paula as a curiosity, with the older ones trying out their budding English, and with some wanting to be photographed with us.

WORK ETHIC | Although generalizations are dangerous, the Koreans are industrious and hard-working, striving to get ahead. There was a vacant lot in our neighborhood that went from barren overgrown grass to a completed modern house in about six weeks. Around the clock and every day, trucks and workers would arrive with the next load of concrete, lumber, and supplies and finishes of all kinds to be used immediately to complete whatever was next.

We needed a couch, drove out of town to a custom leather furniture showroom and found a couch/loveseat arrangement that we wanted but in a different color from their current inventory. No problem. Three days later, a small flatbed truck arrived at the house with the couch and loveseat in the color we wanted, covered with a layer of bubble wrap—custom made and delivered in three days, with no extra charge, no hassle.

FINANCIAL RECOVERY | The government and business community showed the same can-do work ethic. The financial crisis of 1997/98 hit Korea and other Asian countries hard, with the IMF making large loans to keep Korea afloat as it restructured and streamlined its over-leveraged family-owned 'chaebol' conglomerates and grew its way back to financial health. When we arrived in 2001, Korea was well on its way to paying back its IMF loans years ahead of schedule. A broad consolidation and strengthening of the banking sector was well underway, resulting in an increased appetite for consulting advice.

One result of the economic upheaval was the merger of the two leading Korean automobile manufacturers, Hyundai and Kia, which have now become the fifth largest car manufacturer in the world, nearly half again as large as Ford. Samsung, Hyundai, and LG continue to lead the large Korean industrial groups.

ECONOMIC DEVELOPMENT AND GROWTH | The Korean's (like the Japanese decades before) had become superb at reverse engineering, copying, and improving manufactured products, ranging from ocean-going ships, to cars, to consumer electronics, and all at relatively lower cost and with rapidly ramped-up product quality. Combined with their concentration and hard work, this underpinned the country's economic growth before and after our stint there.

Shortly after we arrived, we noticed card tables set up on main street corners in downtown Seoul, selling and loaning cellphones to passersby with picture-phone capabilities. This was new and not yet available in the U.S., but the Korean networks and phone technology was already testing it all out and making it available to consumers in the Korean home market.

The Korean movie industry was booming and making a name for itself in the world. Global exporting was followed by establishing manufacturing plants in many countries. And the two major Korean airlines expanded globally.

JAPANESE INFLUENCE | Japan ruled Korea from 1910 to 1945, and the influence is subtle but everywhere still. As the Japanese insisted on managing and changing territories and their inhabitants in their own cultural image, even the Seoul city hall was architecturally Japanese, as were some other buildings scattered throughout the country.

Seoul is a walkable city downtown, with sidewalks and pedestrian underpasses designed to speed and ease the flow. Often when I whisked along and dodged people walking in the opposite direction, I would move to the right to avoid them, as I had done all my life in the U.S. But I would invariably run into folks as they moved to my right (their left). I was baffled, since cars drive on the right in Korea. So, I asked a young consultant in the office how he would avoid an oncoming pedestrian on a sidewalk. He thought for a moment and said he would move to his left. I asked him, "Why, when you would do the opposite in a car?" and he had no answer, other than to point out that everyone would always walk to the left, and since virtually everyone was Korean, there was no problem. I am convinced that it is a left-over habit from the days of Japanese occupation. They and Korea drove on the left until the end of World War II, when American and Russian influence shifted everything to the right—on the road but evidently not on the sidewalk.

Our consulting office had close working relationships with a couple of retired Korean businessmen, who would assist us on projects, drawing on their specialized expertise. They were in their late 60s or 70s. It turned out that they spoke fluent Japanese, learned in school and university. During the Japanese occupation, the Japanese language had been a requirement in all Korean schools. Since 1945, it was dropped as a requirement, and relatively few learned Japanese.

We were told that the best examples of antique Korean furniture from past eras are not in Korean museums, but in upscale homes in Japan.

LOVE-HATE JAPANESE RELATIONSHIP | Despite the half-a-century occupation, Koreans—both businesses and consumers—have active and mutually-beneficial business relationships with the Japanese. There were duty-free shopping stores and malls near airports and in downtown Seoul, purpose-built for visiting Japanese tourists. Packaged shopping tours, including flights and hotels in Seoul were sold in Japan.

The two countries shared hosting the World Cup championships in 2002, building many stadiums in both countries for the event.

Even the advent of the Hyundai auto name must have been influenced by the Japanese "Honda." The logos are so similar, too.

For years, many people in the U.S. thought Samsung was a Japanese company.

My company's Seoul office had been managed by a Japanese fellow who admitted to me that he would avoid meeting with some Korean executives because he recognized the "cultural sensitivities involved." A sharp young Korean had just taken over the office as manager which was obviously a step forward.

WESTERN AND U.S. INFLUENCE | As their wealth and well-being has grown rapidly over the decades, and their economy became dependent on exports and foreign markets, Koreans have become avid followers of and travelers to countries across the globe, especially the U.S.

- Families customarily send their young children to English lessons after and outside school.

- Many go abroad to American and other Western universities and graduate schools and hope to have their children do the same. The young consultant manager I worked with most had an MBA from the University of Chicago, where his wife had learned English from scratch in the two years they lived in the U.S.

- Those who can afford it travel internationally incessantly for pleasure and adventure—family excursions to Antarctica, jeep tours in the Sahara, driving vacations across the U.S.

- Three traits were important for me to gain credibility with Korean business clients: I was an American, had experience assisting Western banks, and had increasingly gray hair (in what order, I don't know).

- The Koreans valued and pointedly displayed Western brand names and logos in fashions, autos, sports equipment, restaurant chains, you name it.

The Korean Peninsula at night

HISTORY AT A GLANCE | The National Museum of History—near the Itaewon neighborhood, but old then and since no doubt enlarged and reconstructed—was a special place.

Of the two main floors devoted to national and cultural history, one focused on history prior to the Korean War and partitioning of the peninsula (1952), and the other on the decades since. The maps and exhibits demonstrate that up until that war, the north of the country (north of Seoul) was the industrial base, with the south consisting primarily of farmland. Since then, it has been dramatically reversed, with South Korea and its manufacturing and high-tech development representing the 12th largest economy in the world, and the north struggling to get along. We are familiar with recent satellite photos of the peninsula at night showing the south and its cities well-lighted throughout, and the north dark except for a dot of light at Pyongyang.

FOOD AND KIMCHI | Although I quite liked the Korean barbecue and some of the unique other local dishes (e.g., Bibimbap), I wasn't enamored by kimchi. But, no problem, as traditional Korean meals usually consisted of up to two dozen separate dishes, often on a lazy Susan, from which you chose what you want. As a result, even if half the dishes were of varying kimchi, I could feast by selecting around them.

Kimchi was so strong that opening a taxi door would signal whether the driver had had kimchi the night before. Even the Koreans had separate kitchens for the kimchi, separating it and its containers from everything else.

There were plenty of non-Korean restaurants, representing virtually all Asian cuisines, as well as Western chains, such as TGIF, and Tony Roma, a Place for Ribs, in Seoul. In fact, these chains were the passion of young Koreans and often had long lines at all hours to get in. The restaurant at the Weston Chosun hotel was called "O'Kim's." The only German restaurant we found was a good one on the second floor in Itaewon, run by a German cook and his Korean wife. It was called Memories and was excellent. But some ethnic cuisines were missing altogether. Searching for a Greek restaurant, we asked the driver for the Greek ambassador who lived across the street from us, where they went in Seoul for a decent or better Greek meal. "We don't, there are none," was the response.

RELIGION | At night, Seoul was dotted by lighted Christian crosses high up on churches and other buildings. Due to the hills, these white or neon-colored crosses could be seen dozens at a time. Although more than 50% of Koreans are not religious, Christianity is the largest faith in the country, accounting for about 60% of those who declare a religion.

UNDER DAILY THREAT | Seoul—with 10 million residents, nearly 20% of the country's total—is only about 30 miles from the North Korean border—about the same distance as from Seoul south to its airport at Incheon. The threat of invasion, artillery attack, and general interference has prevailed since 1953, when the Demilitarized Zone (DMZ) was established.

Massive concrete 'fake bridges' are positioned on the roads leading north from Seoul to the DMZ. They are poised with explosives to be detonated should the North Korean military try to invade the south with tanks. When triggered, the massive piles of concrete would make the roads impassable. The objective is to delay by at least a day, the tanks' ability to reach Seoul. (With more modern, airborne weapons aimed at Seoul now, these defenses are less important.)

YELLOW DUST | At least a dozen or so mornings each winter, we would find a layer of yellow dust had fallen on Seoul overnight. The fine, dry grains covered everything, being most noticeable on cars, especially dark ones. At first glance, a black car would appear pale yellow, and the windshield would need to be wiped off. Although we never found out exactly what the dust was, it was imported from China via the prevailing westerly winds, curiously only occasionally and only at night.

EXPAT COMMUNITY | It was a pleasure to be a part of a small expatriate community that was quite diverse and not composed primarily of Americans. Rather, the informal 'group' consisted of Australians, Germans, French, Irish, and others. As demonstrated by the common fact of agreeing to live in Korea, it was a curious and inquisitive bunch, taking every opportunity to see the country and also to travel anywhere and everywhere of interest in the region beyond the peninsula.

Korean travel agents were many and creative, arranging tours to just about everywhere outside the country, primarily for Koreans, but with every trip having a good complement of non-Koreans. Perhaps our most noteworthy was a week in outer Mongolia—only a three-hour flight from Seoul—visiting the holiday festivities in Ulaanbaatar, the nearby mountains, the vast open Steppes with no fences and herds of wild camels and horses, and staying in gers (or yurts) used by the nomads constantly moving around the country. Annual festival horse races, with five-year-old jockeys on bareback are something to behold.

WORLD CUP | The 2002 FIFA World Cup was co-hosted by Korea and Japan and captivated the population over the summer months. Both countries built stadiums expressly for the matches, and the matches were held alternately between the countries and among the stadiums. Coincidentally, Korea had a great team, managed by experienced Dutch player Guus Hiddink, who had managed several European teams previously, and who quickly became a Korean national hero as the team won matches. The excitement was infectious. Reflecting the American and English-speaking influence, the team's motto was "Be the Reds," which was on everything from t-shirts and hats, to billboards, to posters across the country.

In June, we travelled to the city of Daegu (population 2.5 million) to watch the Koreans tie the United States team, 1—1, and were careful not to be the only two people out of the 66,000 attending to cheer for the Americans. Following the match, more than 200,000 fans celebrated in the central square near the Seoul city hall. Korea beat Poland, Portugal, and Italy before being beaten by Germany, 1—0, in the semi-finals, and then by Turkey in the battle for third place. The Korean team became the first and only team outside Europe and the Americas to reach a World Cup semi-final.

SPORTS | Despite the world cup stage for soccer, baseball is the leading sport in Korea, with a professional league and teams—sponsored by the major corporations—and stadiums in most major cities. With Seoul's main ballpark a short drive across downtown Seoul, we went to some games. Well-practiced and perfectly choreographed women cheerleaders manage the fans for both teams. The level of play is usually excellent, and there are many experienced Western players, along with the majority of Koreans.

Korean businessmen and women were generally avid golfers, diligent at the game, dependent on skilled lady caddies, and with a disposition that lets them laugh heartily if and when they blow a shot. There are many challenging and well-kept courses. Several buildings in downtown Seoul have netted driving ranges on their roofs, and they are almost always busy, with as many Korean women as men golfers.

DIVING | The summer Olympics were held in Seoul in 1988, and Korea used the event to build many facilities and actually spur the expansion of Seoul across the Han River to the south. One such facility was the Olympic diving pool, which served as the main training pool for Scuba diving. We went at it and got our open water certification following our ocean 'test dive' off Jeju, an island 50 miles off the south coast in the Korean Strait. Thanks to the hand signals common to Scuba, learning how to stay alive under water from Koreans speaking Korean turned out not to be a problem, and the licenses turned out to be issued in English.

KNOCK, KNOCK-OFFS | This news article appeared in the *JoongAng Ilbo* (*The Central Times* in English), one of the three large Seoul newspapers, around 2002. It laments the counterfeit clothes being imported into Korea, disrupting the traditionally robust market for locally-produced counterfeits.

Pirate Burberry imports replace local fakes

By Kwon Hyeok-ju
JoongAng Ilbo

Imported counterfeit clothes are driving homegrown fakes off the market.

Counterfeit Burberry goods valued at hundreds of thousands of dollars are being traded domestically. Recently, fake Burberry goods imported in bulk have been discovered; previously, most such counterfeits were locally produced.

Euro Co., which imports and distributes Burberry products in Korea under contract with the British clothes maker, said Thursday that it has, over two years, exposed fake goods worth 1.2 billion won ($923,000), including 2,500 shirts, 500 mufflers and 300 handbags. About 60 people have been penalized for making or selling the fakes.

Recently, imported fake Burberry mufflers have been found on sale on a well-known Internet auction site. A trading firm reportedly imported the goods from an Italian middleman believing they were genuine, and 10,000 pieces, worth 500 million won, were sold, including about 6,000 through the Web site. After the counterfeits were discovered, Burberry Ltd. asked customs in Seoul, Busan and Incheon to check Burberry imports carefully.

woongju@joongang.co.kr

APPENDIX 5

Hong Kong

Whiffs of 'Fragrant Harbor'

OUR STAY of less than two years in Hong Kong gave us the sense that we were in the commercial and cultural center of North Asia, in the window or doorway to China, and in a mix of cultures unlike any others in the world. A few experiences and impressions are as follows.

DENSITY | Hong Kong's population is approximately 7.5 million, and Hong Kong Island's density is about 42,000 people per square mile. (New York City's density is 26,000 per square mile.) Yet, it 'works' in terms of transportation, vigorous business and work ethics, and an ability to move around and get in places, ranging from restaurants and movies, to sporting events and concerts.

TRANSPORTATION | Relatively few residents have private cars, and buses, taxis, subways, and ferries are everywhere, reliable, and inexpensive. Although many taxi drivers don't speak English, they recognize streets, buildings, and locations enough in English. For example, we lived in Tregunter Path, which they all knew, even though only a couple blocks long and way up toward the peak.

LANGUAGE | The Hong Kong Chinese, and those in the far south of the mainland speak Cantonese, which is quite different from Mandarin, the primary language in Beijing and most of the north. Folks from Hong Kong and from the north sometimes cannot communicate well orally with each other.

SCHENZHEN | Just across the border on the Chinese mainland is the city of Schenzhen, with a population of some eight million and a density of 44,000 people per square mile. It grew as a manufacturing center in past decades as part of the experiment of capitalism and free enterprise within China. Although only a 20-mile drive from Hong Kong Central, the immigrations and customs delays at the border can take hours. Trucks and other traffic crossing the border into China are required to have native Chinese drivers, often requiring a change of driver at the border for drivers of other nationalities. Despite all this, some employees commute daily from Hong Kong to Schenzhen.

MACAU | This former Portuguese colony—now encompassed by the Chinese state—is an island about 60 minutes west of Hong Kong by hydrofoil or catamaran. It had charming neighborhoods and parks when we were there. It has always been a gambling city, with a few old established casinos. Over the last two decades, the large global gambling companies have built a raft of large casinos. Macau remains the main center of gambling for the Chinese people, with gambling on the mainland severely constrained. On one of our visits to Macau just prior to leaving Hong Kong, we saw a wood and glass coffee table that we wanted to take back to the U.S., but it was the wrong size and shape. No problem: the small shop made up another to our specifications and had it delivered to our apartment in Hong Kong three days later.

RESTAURANTS | Food of every nationality and ethnicity can be found in Hong Kong, and most of them are authentic and excellent—no matter how cheap or expensive. One of our favorite Italian restaurants was Nicolini's in the Conrad Hotel. It could have been in Milan. Each year, they had a truffle 'festival' when every item on the menu contained fresh truffles. Another favorite experience was to take the 30-minute ferry ride to Lamma Island and have dinner at one of the five or six excellent restaurants clustered around the ferry dock. And even Macau was in striking distance for dinner.

DURIAN | A tree fruit found in several southeast Asian countries, and served in not many places even there, Durian was totally unknown to us, but is considered a specialty by some Hong Kong Chinese. It certainly is special—with so awful a smell and taste that you can smell it a block away and consider that too close. It is banned on public transportation in some places but can be found in some restaurants scattered around Hong Kong. It is less obnoxious when well cooked, although the aficionados would consider that ruining it.

CHINESE APPRECIATION OF HONG KONG | It seemed that when we were there—only six years after the handover—retired Central Chinese Military brass and political leaders had 'discovered' the attractiveness of living in Hong Kong with its freedoms and western culture, administration, and activities. Upon retirement, they were buying Hong Kong apartments.

OPTIMIZING LAND USE | With so little land, and none undeveloped, any cleared building was quickly replaced, often with a skyscraper—expanding footprints vertically. An old landmark hotel on the Island right at the harbor—the Furama—had recently been raised. In the years waiting for its replacement, the cite became an outdoor concert park. We attended two to see the Rolling Stones in their first performance in China, and also Santana. Quite a venue, with fans standing in the warm evening, with the Peak rising behind the stage, and Hong Kong Harbor immediately behind you.

SIZE AND 'DISTRICTS' | Although the island is only eight miles long, and public transportation is excellent, it was nice to have a little car to meander from the Central, Admiralty and Peak areas where we worked and lived, to the other towns on the island. These included Stanley, Aberdeen, Repulse Bay, and Pok Fu Lam to the west where our dog stayed in quarantine for four months. One of our favorites was Shek O, a low-key village at the eastern tip (a 10-mile, 25 minute drive from Central), with a small beach and a favorite restaurant: The Black Sheep.

ASIAN TRAVEL | Hong Kong's location is an ideal hub for easily visiting different and new-to-us sites and cultures across the continent. Destinations within a three-hour flight from Hong Kong's Chek Lap Kok airport include: most of mainland China's provinces, Viet Nam, Cambodia, Laos, Myanmar, Thailand, Taiwan, Korea, Japan, Philippines, and even Brunei. On our brief stay, we only got to a few of these, but did fly a bit farther west for a first visit to India.

APPENDIX 6

Australia

The Largest Island

D URING OUR BRIEF and hectic stay in Sydney, we got only a taste of the vast Australian island continent. (The distance from Sydney on the east coast to Perth on the west coast is the equivalent of from New York to Salt Lake City, but with close to nothing but desert outback in between.) A few impressions are listed below—mostly revelations to us.

TRUCK TRAINS | Outside the cities on seemingly endless highways across the interior of the country—the outback—semi-trailers were hitched together to form 'trains' with a single cab and driver up front. The longest we saw had six or seven semis. The record is 113, although it only drove about 1,500 feet.

ULURU | Referenced also by the western name of Ayers Rock, this huge monolith is visible for miles, and is stark and majestic as it appears to change colors, depending on the angle of the sun and the makeup of clouds above. Its greatest source of erosion is from lightning.

Uluru, or Ayers Rock, Northern Territory

HARBOUR BRIDGE | The daring tourist attraction is to climb all along the top of the bridge rising to a height of 440 feet above the water. The views and experience climbing and walking across are breathtaking. The man who first suggested it as a permanent attraction was turned down by city authorities, with more than four dozen objections. Over nearly a decade of research, he satisfied them all, and the bridge climb opened in 1998.

DROUGHT | The Australian climate occasionally leads to years-long droughts so severe that important rivers cease to reach the sea. At those times, people rig up barrels and reservoirs to catch and store rainwater, but even that requires a license and has limitations, as rainwater is deemed a public resource.

RARE AND ODDBALL ANIMALS | Some of the most poisonous snakes in the world are found in Australia. Kangaroos, while often portrayed as cute cartoon characters, are wild and

Sydney Harbour Bridge, with people on the climb/walk

powerful, able to rip out a person's stomach if made angry. Rabbits and sheep were imported in past centuries and are now everywhere, devouring vegetation that is scarce across the country. On the north coast, there are saltwater alligators on the ocean side, as well as freshwater ones on nearby lakes and rivers inland.

DONUTS | We discovered the only Crispy Cream donut outlet in Sydney when we came upon a long line of suited businessmen on their way home, well after rush hour, waiting to get into the store to take home at least one big box of donuts. The queue was like that every night.

ILLUSTRATION SOURCES
(BY PAGE NUMBER)

TITLE PAGE. Turner family collection.

xii. (Cartoon) W. B. Park, The *New Yorker*, July 29, 1985.

6. (Dietrich/Turner) Turner family collection.

12. (Turner/Morrissy) Turner family collection.

17. (C. Tuepker) Turner family collection.

20. (Drake Oak Brook logo) Hotel logo, found at dhbusinessledger.com.

28. (Don/Mary) Turner family collection.

46. (Draft card) Turner family collection.

52. (Cartoon) David Coverly, *Speedbump*, 2010, at gocomics.com.

63. (Cartoon) Eric Lewis, The *New Yorker*, November 18, 2002.

64. (Cartoon) Victoria Roberts, The *New Yorker*, November 20, 1995.

71. (Cartoon) Doug Reina, 1996, King Features Syndicate.

73. (Thompson) Turner family collection.

76. (Wingdale house) Turner family collection.

82. (Rosetta Stone) *Created by Today I Learned Something New,* August 25, 2013; accessed at britainusatranslations.tumblr.com.

84. (TV license) Turner family collection.

87. (Petra) *The Adventurous Flashpacker'* accessed at theadventurousflashpacker.com.

90. (St. Lucia) Turner family collection.

92. (Ennismore Mews) Turner family collection.

95. (HK harbour) Jean Beaufort, public domain.

97. (Sydney bridge) Jonny Melon, February 14, 2020; accessed at jonnymelon.com.

98. (Sand Gnat logo hat) Turner family collection.

100. (Elephants and ultra-lite) Turner family collection.

103. (Sea Cloud) *Late Cruisenews,* November 20, 2018; accessed at latecruisenews.com.

120. (Business cards) Turner family collection.

122. (Caddy badge) Turner family collection.

130. (140 Broadway) Augustine Pasquet, Untapped Cities; accessed at untappedcities.com, January 11, 2017.

134. (Broad street and Francine) Left image: *Tampa Bay Times*, 1968. Right image: Accessed at sigforum.com.

141. (Dubuffet) Turner family collection.

147. (Gorsart label) Turner family collection.

166. (*Clearing House* cover) Turner family collection.

169. (Management structures) Turner family collection.

170. (Cartoon) Tom Cheney, The *New Yorker*, October 20, 1997.

179. (*Retail Banker International* cover) Turner family collection.

197. (Kaki-Cola) Legoking; accessed at i.imgur.com/zBvEiPD, 2018.

204. (St. Louis Bank logo) Turner family collection.

211. (American Airlines letter) Turner family collection.

212. (Bitter sculpture) Upper image: Wickimedia Commons; accessed at commons.wikimedia.org. Lower image: justacarguy.blogspot.com, March 26, 2001.

217. (Cartoon) Mathew Diffee, The *New Yorker*, 2001.

222. (Snowmass Village sign) Turner family collection.

223. (TSA sign) Turner family collection.

227. (Cartoon) James Stevenson, The *New Yorker*, June 21, 1958.

239. (Cartoon) Sam Gross, The *New Yorker*, 1999.

245. (2 statues) Turner family collection.

246. (Cartoon) Claude Smith, The *New Yorker*, 1948.

252. (Collections photo) Turner family collection.

258-9. (Six vehicles) Turner family collection.

265. (Korea Peninsula) Anton Balazh; accessed at antonbalazh/shutter stock.com.

270. (Korea newspaper article) JoongAng Ilbo, Seoul, Korea, c. 2002.

276. (Uluru) Turner family collection.

277. (Sydney bridge) Phillip Minnis; accessed at Britannica.com

INDEX

3M 149, 150
24 Heures du Mans (Le Mans) 77, 78
30th Street Station, Philadelphia 211

A

Abu Dhabi 198, 199
Admirals Club, American Airlines 210
Aer Lingus 175, 201
afterlife 50, 51, 231, 237, 238, 242, 243, 249
Air Force 4, 21, 23, 25, 30, 31, 45, 47
Air Force ROTC 47
airports 65, 83, 106, 142, 173, 223, 264
Alaska 104-106
Aldrich, Hulbert "Huck" 148
Ali, Muhammad 42-44
Allingham, Paul and Winney 77
Al-Sabah family 199
Alzano Lombardo, Italy 71
Amarillo, Texas 73
American Express 156
Amsterdam 107, 129, 130, 156, 174, 175, 181, 216, 219
Amsterdam-Rotterdam Bank 156, 174, 175, 219
Anchorage, Alaska 65, 104, 105
Angkor Wat, Cambodia 172
Ann Arbor, Michigan 32
Apache 149
Arctic Enterprises 151
Arnander, Christopher 195
Arnander, Primrose 196
Aspen, Colorado ix, 223, 225
Aspen Public Radio 225

Aspen Science Center 225
Atchison, Kansas 77
A.T. Kearney viii, 89, 92, 97, 98, 207, 208, 213-215
ATM (automated teller machines) 143-145
AT&T 159
Australia ix, 19, 96, 157, 183, 215, 224, 275-277
Ayers Rock (Uluru) 97, 275, 276

B

bagels 210
Bahrain 85, 194, 196, 224
Baker-Bates, Rodney 185
Bangkok, Thailand 108, 160, 171, 172, 173
Bankers Trust 156, 171, 172
Bank Holding Company Act of 1970 138
Bank of Cyprus 156, 175, 186, 194
Bank of England 192, 193, 199
Bank of Ireland 175
Bank of Montreal 157
Bank Zachodni WBK Group 157
Bannister, Roger 177
Barclays Bank 92, 156, 175
baseball 2, 12, 18, 53, 98, 269
basketball 2, 16, 19, 20
Beatles 55
Beijing 215, 272
Bellagio, Italy 153, 154
Bemidji, Minnesota 151, 152
Bergamo, Italy 71, 72, 154
Bergen Bank 156, 175
Bible 50, 231, 238
Bitter, Karl 211, 212
blackout 40
Boeing 747 142

bowling 2, 19
Brainerd, Minnesota 151
Brazil 208, 209, 224
briefcases 43, 58, 183, 217-220, 251
British/English Rosetta Stone vi, 82
Brooklyn Navy Yard 225
Brown University 4, 9, 13, 17, 34, 39, 128
Buraydah, Saudi Arabia 198
Burroughs Clearing House 167
business school 9, 128, 132, 206, 217

C

caddying 24, 122
Cahouet, Frank 191, 192
caiman 66
Campbell, Jean 14
Canter, Steve 129
Cape Cod, Massachusetts 4, 20, 66
Cape Town, South Africa 99
Cargill 149
Carlton Club 197
cars 4, 13, 16, 24, 36, 62, 78, 109-111, 114-117, 119, 122, 134, 165, 166, 233, 254-260, 262, 263, 267, 271
CEDEL 157, 213
Ceska Sporitelna 157
Challoner, Kit (Dietrich), Mike 6, 8-11
Charleston, South Carolina 98
Chase Manhattan Bank 144, 187, 156
Chemical Bank 10, 13, 48, 49, 73, 74, 118, 133, 135, 142, 143, 146-149, 153, 180, 181, 219

INDEX | 281

Chesapeake Bay Bridge
    Tunnel 115
Chicago, Illinois vii, 3, 4, 8,
    11-13, 15, 17, 20, 21, 26,
    29, 33, 34, 41, 46, 53, 68,
    72, 76, 77, 110, 112, 113, 124,
    126, 135, 145, 149, 175, 255,
    264
Chicago Heights 11, 12, 15,
    16, 33, 34
China 95, 96, 157, 215, 224,
    251, 268, 271, 272, 274
China Development Bank 157
China Minshing Bank 157
Chuie, the Major 226
church, the 51, 235, 244, 248
CIGNA 156, 202
cigars, Cuban 107
Citicorp Center 93
civil rights 7, 34-36, 49,
    129
civil rights movement 34, 35
Clearwater, Florida 9, 11
cocktail shakers 57, 251
coffee pots, porcelain
    electric 61, 251
coins 2, 12, 58-60, 201,
    251
collecting 23, 56, 57, 59-62,
    220
collections 2, 57-59, 61,
    63, 250-253
Collegiate School 88
Colorado iv, ix, 10, 11, 15, 19,
    58, 89, 90, 98, 104, 110,
    221, 222, 225, 226, 256
Columbia Business School
    34, 47, 69, 70, 73, 128, 129,
    132, 133, 146, 219
Columbia County 15
Columbia, Missouri 9
Concorde 52, 187, 188
Commercial Union 157

consulting, management
    2, 155-173, 174-201, 202-211,
    213-217
contact lenses 17, 24, 124-126
CoreStates Financial 157
Cravath, Swaine & Moore 180
Crocker National Bank 191,
    192
Cubicalism viii, 170
Cunningham, T. Jefferson
    III 187
consulting, management 2
    13, 26, 155, 203, 208
Cyprus 85, 156, 175, 186, 194,
    224

D

Dan Dan Noodles 107
dark chocolate truffles 106
Darwin, Charles 241
Daytona Beach, Florida 117
Dayton, Ohio 66, 69
Deer Isle, Maine 81
Demilitarized Zone
    (DMZ) 267
depression 25, 29
Development Bank of
    Singapore 157, 215
Diriyah 65, 197
Dover Cliffs 70
Dow, George W. 32
Drake Oak Brook 20, 278
drinking 24, 26, 27, 195
Dublin, Ireland 65, 176, 201
Dubuffet, Jean 141
Duluth, Minnesota viii, 204,
    205
Durian 273
Dutchess County, New
    York 15, 21, 75, 76, 83, 222
Dylan, Bob 55, 204

E

Eagles 54
Earhart, Amelia vi, 76
Edinburgh, Scotland 118, 119
eel, smoked 107
Elvis 55
Ennismore Mews,
    Knightsbridge 92, 278
era of change, 1967-2007 vii,
    136
Erie Forge & Steel Corp. 131
Euroclear 157
European Community (EC) 83

F

faith 28, 50, 51, 231, 236-238,
    242-249, 267
Falkland Islands 184
falling asleep 113-115
Federal National Mortgage
    Corporation (FNMA, or
    'Fannie Mae') 191
FIFA World Cup 268
'Fight of the Century' 42
financial aid 40
Financial Studies Group and
    Department (FSG,
    FSD) 133, 135, 137, 141
First & Merchants Bank 162
FNMA, or 'Fannie Mae' Federal
    National Mortgage
    Corporation 191
fragrant harbor 215, 271
free will 239
Freshman Class President 34

G

Gandhi, Mahatma 236
General Belgrano 184
Gerstner, Louis 160, 161, 167
Glass-Steagall Act in 1933 138
Glen Arbor, Michigan 67
Glen Lake, Michigan 67, 68,
    221

Glorious 12th 197
Goldthorpe, Brian 191
golf 2, 19, 30, 54, 89, 122
Gorsart Company 146, 148
Gorsart, Norm 147
Gottfried, Francine 134
Grant Advertising 26
Great Barrier Reef, Australia 19, 97
Green, Stephen 197
Greenwich Village 40, 73
Griffiths, David 182
Gulf Investment Bank 156
guns 21-23, 58, 59, 251
Gutman, Jeremiah 49

H
Hamburg, New York 31
Hancock, Maine 81
Happy Valley, Hong Kong 200
Harbor Bridge, Sydney 97
Hayes, Isaac 151
Hiddink, Guus 268
hitchhike 9, 36, 69
Homewood-Flossmoor 13, 17
Hong Kong ix, 10, 54, 81, 95-97, 107, 110, 120, 157, 199, 200, 204, 214, 215, 225, 250, 271-274
Hong Kong and Shanghai Bank (HSBC) 157, 199
Hong Kong Jockey Club 200
Hoogendijk, Fop 219
hope 206, 245
Hunt, E. Howard 33
Hutton, E.F. 103

I
ice cream scoops 57, 58, 251
Icelandic Airlines 79
iguana 39
Intrepid 52, 53

Ireland 70, 176, 177, 182, 201, 225
Irish Sea 70
Istanbul, feast 108
Italy 70, 72, 74, 79, 80, 152-154, 182, 213, 225, 269
Ivanetic, Mirjan 153

J
JB, Dalmatian 90
Jeddah, Saudi Arabia 85, 86, 194-196, 198

K
Kaki-Cola 197, 279
Kane, John 129
kangaroos 276
Karachi, Pakistan 173
kimchi 266
knock-offs 270
Kodiak Island, Alaska 104
Korea 6, 9, 14, 19, 45, 46, 92, 95, 157, 171, 187, 214, 260-270
Korean Peninsula 265
Kuwait 85, 194, 199, 225

L
Lafferty, Michael 177
Lake Superior 205
Lamma Island 273
Larnaca, Cyprus 186
Le Mans 77, 78
Lending Money vii, 145
Les Ambassadeurs Club 43
Lester B. Knight & Associates 26
leveraged leasing 141
Lever Brothers 10, 129
Lincoln First Bank 156
Livingstone 99, 101
lobsters, live Boston 107
Lola, Havanese 90

London Clearing House 157, 213
London, England 6, 81, 92, 118, 174-179, 182-185, 187-193, 213
Lou Gerstner 160, 161, 167
Luang Prabang, Laos 65
luck 99, 245
Lucky Captain, The 226

M
Macau 272, 273
Maine 80, 81
Maltesers, Bangkok 108
management structure viii, 169
Manama, Bahrain 196
Marine Midland 130-132
markets and banking, evolution of vii, 156
Marsh, Fred (roommate) v, 9, 11, 37-39
Martin, Glenn L. 25
Marylebone Cricket Club 182
May Day—May 1, 1975 140
MBA 34, 47, 48, 50, 73, 133, 135, 163, 264
McKinsey & Company vii, 13, 74, 88, 89, 155, 158-162, 165-168, 174, 176-179, 181, 182, 189, 194, 201-203, 207, 219
Mellon Bank 157, 191, 208
Meribel, France 83
Merrill, Dina 104
Midland Bank 156, 157, 175, 185, 187, 191, 192, 199, 204
Milan, Italy vi, 70-72, 79, 80, 273
Minneapolis-St. Paul 107
Mobil Oil 14, 74
Mongolia 3, 95, 225, 268
Moody's 209, 210

INDEX | 283

Morrissy, Patrick 12-15
motorcycle 41, 101, 111, 112, 255
Mount Desert Island, Maine 81
Multibanco Comermex 156
Munich 107
music 2, 23, 29, 37-39, 54-56, 183, 232, 233
music, performed 56
Mutual Insurance Company of New York 74

N
National Commercial Bank (NCB) 156, 194, 197
National Museum of History, Seoul 265
Newport News, Virginia 11
New York City 13, 19, 29, 47, 52, 81, 83, 88, 89, 98, 114, 119, 128-130, 133, 147, 149, 158, 160, 210, 260, 271
New York Magazine 228
Nicosia, Cyprus 186, 194
nonsmoking section 190
north country 81, 104, 106, 151, 189
northern latitudes 68
Nott, Sir John 184
NPR (National Public Radio) 225
Nuttspaarbank 175

O
oil lamps 57, 58, 252
opera glass 58, 252

P
Palm Beach, Floria 9, 36, 66, 115-117
Paris, France 14, 29, 78
Park Forest 8, 33
pay 111, 135

Petra, Jordan vi, 85-88, 278
pickle fork 58, 62, 252
Pitzer College 90
Plastic Contact Lens Company 124
Post, Marjorie Merriweather 103
Portland, Oregon 90
predestination 51, 239, 249
Price, Richard (Dick) 163
Price Waterhouse 89, 200, 203, 205
Providence, Rhode Island 4, 9, 13, 17, 36, 39, 41, 54, 66, 112, 113, 115, 116, 160, 166, 255
Prudential Insurance 156
Purves, Willie 199
Pyongyang, North Korea 266

Q
QE II Cunard Line's 93
Quaker Hill Country Club 19

R
Reagan, Ron 50, 231
reincarnation 51, 56, 242, 249
religion 7, 35, 50, 51, 231-249, 267
Rensselaer Polytechnic Institute 31
Retail Banker International 177, 178, 279
RHD, right-hand-drive 119, 256, 257
Rhode Island 4, 9, 17, 54, 66, 81, 111, 113, 148, 156, 166, 255
Rhode Island Hospital Trust 156, 166
right-hand-drive (RHD) 119, 256, 257

Riyadh Bank 156, 175, 194, 195, 198
Rockefeller, David 141
Rockville Center, New York 143, 144
Rolling Stones 54, 96, 274
Royal Bank of Canada 156
Royal Insurance 156
Russell Sage College 31

S
Samsung Life 157, 214
Sand Gnats, Savanah 98, 99
San Francisco 13, 60, 107, 191, 192, 198
Sao Paolo, Brazil 208
Sargent & Lundy 27
SARS 95
Saudi Arabia 85, 175, 177, 194-196, 225
Saudi Arabian Monetary Authority (SAMA) 198
Saudi International Bank 156
Scandinavia 189
Scandinavian Airlines (SAS) 190
Schenzhen, China 272
Schiphol Airport 107, 181
Schoellkopf, George 131
science 225, 244
Scilly, Isles of 92
Scruffy, terrier mix 90, 92, 93
SCUBA 19
Sea Cloud 102, 103, 278
Seattle, Washington 90, 164, 224
SEB, Skandinaviska Enskilda Banken 156, 175
Selective Service, the 'draft' 46
semaphores, model 253
Seoul, South Korea 10, 92-96, 120, 157, 160, 171, 214, 257, 260, 262-264, 266-270, 279

Shanghai Development Bank 157
Shawmut Bank 156
Shek O 274
Shenzhen 157, 215
Shenzhen Development Bank 157
Simmons, Richard 180
skiing 2, 19, 75, 83, 113, 226, 232
Sleeping Bear Dunes National Park 68
Snowmass Village, Colorado iv, ix, 10, 15, 98, 222, 279
snuff bottles 57, 253
Social Security Administration 90
sourdough bread 107
South Africa 99, 225
spirit 211, 212, 247
Spirit of Transportation 211, 212
sports 2, 4, 13, 16, 18, 24, 33, 43, 47, 62, 88, 89, 105, 265
stamps 29, 30, 58-60, 201, 253
Stevens College 9
stingray 67
St. Francis statuettes 252
St. Louis Bank for Savings 204
St. Lucia 19, 89, 90, 224, 278
Stockholm 175, 189, 190
student loan 40
Sydney, Australia 96, 97, 215, 275, 277-279

T

T-59 Motel 152
Taishan International Bank 157
Taipei 215
Tams, the 165
Taylor, Geoffrey 193
Thief River Falls, Minnesota vii, 151, 152
Thompson, Suzanne Keys (Turner) 10, 14, 40, 73, 74, 79, 83, 88, 89, 176, 255
ties, in Rome 107
truck trains 275
truffles, champagne 108
Trustee Savings Bank 156
TSA 223, 279
Tuepker, Cindi (Turner) 16-18
Tuepker, Tracy 18
Turner, Andrew 80, 81, 88, 90, 176
Turner, Donald 24
Turner, Mary Dow 28
Turner, Nicholas (Nick) 76, 88, 90, 176, 233
Turner, Paula (Alllemang) 10, 11, 15, 66-72, 89-91, 93, 102, 114, 116, 117, 200, 215, 221, 222, 253, 261

U

Ubi Tempus Quietus 21
Ulaanbaatar, Mongolia 268
ultra-lite plane 100
Uluru, Ayers Rock 97, 275, 276
United Faith Protestant Church 33
United Gulf Bank 175, 194, 199
United Virginia Bankshares 156, 160, 161
Uphouse, Gary 115
USC 90

V

value pricing vii, 167
van Hooven, Eckart 178

Victoria Falls 99, 100, 101
Viet Nam 20, 44, 95, 129, 224, 251
Viet Nam war protests 129
VISA 157

W

Wachovia Bank 156, 163, 156
Waddington, Ari 208
Wall Street vii, 74, 94, 132-134, 180
Watlington, John 166
Weiss Wurst 107
Westminster Abbey 233
Westpac 97, 157, 215
Whitehall Street 48
wild rice 107
Wimbledon 83, 176
Winston-Salem, North Carolina 163
Wing Hang Bank 157
Woori Bank 157, 214
World Trade Center 93, 214

Y

Yamaha motorcycle 111, 255
Yugoslavia 74, 152, 153, 224

Z

Zambia 99, 225
Zimbabwe 99, 102, 225
Zurich 108

www.ingramcontent.com/pod-product-compliance
Lightning Source LLC
Chambersburg PA
CBHW051543010526
44118CB00022B/2563